Facets of the Great Revolt

1857

T0327197

Facets of the Great Revolt

1857

edited by

Shireen Moosvi

 Tulika Books

Published by **Tulika Books**
35 A/1 (third floor), Shahpur Jat, New Delhi 110 049, India

© SAHMAT

First published in India, December 2008
First reprint 2010

ISBN: 978-81-89487-44-7

The financial assistance of the Indian Council of Historical
Research (ICHR) is gratefully acknowledged.

Typeset at Tulika Print Communication Services, New Delhi;
printed at Chaman Enterprises, 1603 Pataudi House,
Daryaganj, Delhi 110 002

In memory of the
Rebel Bengal Army Sepoys
who died for their country

मैं वु कुश्ता हूँ कि मेरी लाश पर, ऐ दोस्तों,
एक ज़माना दीदये हस्त्रत से तक्ता जायगा।
ऐ ज़फ़र क़ायम रहेगी जब तलक इक़्लीमे हिन्द,
अख्तरे इक़बाल इस गुल का चमक्ता जायगा।

I am that murdered man, whose corpse, O friends,
A whole age will go on looking at with grief and envy.
O Zafar, for as long as this country of India endures,
the star of glory of this flower will continue to shine.

Contents

Preface

The Revolt of 1857 is being increasingly recognized as one of the major events of the nineteenth century, a turning point in the history of imperialism, an early anticipation of the saga of anti-colonial resistance of the twentieth century. No apology should therefore be necessary to add to the literature on 1857, which has naturally grown in volume as the country observed its 150th anniversary.

Some of the essays collected in this volume are revised versions of those which had previously been printed in *Social Scientist*, and some have been written especially for this volume. I am grateful to the contributors, and have tried in the Introduction to set their themes in the context of a general understanding of the Revolt.

Thanks are due to the Indian Council of Historical Research for a generous grant for the publication of this volume. Dr Prabhat Shukla, the then Member Secretary of the ICHR, took great interest in making it see the light of day. I am indebted to both Dr Rajendra Prasad of SAHMAT and Mrs Indira Chandrasekhar of Tulika Books for agreeing to publish the volume.

Mr Muniruddin Khan has processed the entire manuscript at the office of the Aligarh Historians Society. Ms Samira Junaid of Tulika Books has copy-edited the text. Many thanks are due to both of them.

SHIREEN MOOSVI

Elegy: 1857

(Gayi yakbayak jo hawa palat . . .)

How suddenly has the wind changed, how restless has my heart become!

How can I describe this tyranny, so grievously wounded is my breast from sorrow,

The people of India are utterly ruined; what cruelties have they not suffered!

Whomever the present ruler sees, he says: 'He is fit for the gallows!'

Has anyone heard of such oppression, that people are hanged for no fault at all?

Still, the rulers continue to be bitter in their hearts about those who recite the formula of the faith.

Delhi was not simply a city – a garden it was. What shall I say of the peace it had!

They have erased all its repute; now it is simply a place laid waste.

This straitened condition that all are in: this comes from how the Lord's will works.

The spring turns into autumn, autumn into spring.

Those who were weighed in flowers day and night, how can they bear the thorns of sorrow?

When chains were put on them in prison, they were told: 'This is your garland, in lieu of flowers'.

No one buried them in any garden, no one gave them a funeral shroud.

They never could get to their native land; nor even leave a trace of their grave behind.

BAHADUR SHAH 'ZAFAR'

Introduction

Shireen Moosvi

The Revolt of 1857 is one of those events which have been interpreted on several occasions – by nationalist leaders, historians and officials. For one, here we have an uprising which for its sheer scale alone demands explanation, whatever view of history we may adopt. Then there is its unique place in the narrative of anti-colonial resistance. Irfan Habib, in his opening essay to the present volume, underlines also the fact of its international significance, in being 'the greatest armed challenge to imperialism the world over during the entire course of the nineteenth century'.

The designation 'Mutiny', given by the rulers and accepted by the ruled (who traditionally referred to it as the 'Ghadar'), loses its pejorative and restrictive colour when applied to so great an event. Indeed it was a mutiny not of a small group, but one involving the vast bulk of soldiers of the largest modern army in all of Asia at the time. The Bengal Army comprised 132,000 native sepoys, out of whom barely 8,000 remained loyal to the English. The Mutiny involved troops stationed in the east, from Barrackpore near Calcutta, all the way to Peshawar on the north-west frontier of the subcontinent. The Revolt was nevertheless much more than a mutiny. In a large geographic region, whose population today amounts to nearly a quarter of the population of this country, the Revolt took on the complexion of what Disraeli and Marx pronounced to be a 'national revolt'. In this extensive space, large masses of the civilian population also joined the soldiers' rebellion. Whether the Revolt was 'national' simply in this sense, or 'nationalist' in inspiration and design as well, can always be debated, and, similarly, the absence of ideas of social equality among the rebel leaders can also be legitimately stressed. But what surprised even the English opponents of the Rebellion was the stress laid by the Rebels on the unity between Hindus and Muslims, which has surely been an important, perhaps even the crucial, building block for the modern Indian nation, despite the Partition. There was, also, a fairly strong notion of India ('Hindustan') and the need to free it of foreign rule, which went beyond the immediate local or parochial grievances of the Mutineers, and was given expression to in virtually all the important Rebel proclamations.

From these generalities, one must pass to the specific problem of reconstructing the story of the Revolt on the basis of the mass of information that exists, much of it still waiting to be explored. J.W. Kaye's *History of the Sepoy War* and G.B. Malleson's *History of the Indian Mutiny, 1857–58*, written in the immediate aftermath of the Mutiny, deserve credit for extracting information from materials of this kind for a reconstruction of events, even when full allowance is made for their obvious bias. The authors would have been the last to claim that they had exhausted all the possible sources, or that they had been called upon to see the events from the Rebel point of view as well, though, to be fair, sometimes Kaye does attempt even this. Much new information has since been published, and the series of collections of documents on the History of the Freedom Movement, commissioned after Independence by the various state governments, especially the set of five volumes edited by S.A.A. Rizvi, issued by the Government of Uttar Pradesh, deserve special mention. The National Archives of India as well as the State Archives contain much material, still unpublished, that needs to be utilized. In particular, attention must be given to the large amount of material in Urdu, then the language universally used in the lower levels of administration and in the newspapers of upper India, and so also in the Rebel orders and papers. The unfortunate decline in the study of that language in India, and still more in the decipherment of the cursive (*shikasta*) script, has greatly handicapped a thorough exploration of this rich set of sources. If the inner history of the Rebellion, with an emphasis on what the Rebels thought, did or aimed for, is to be reconstructed (a task in which S.N. Sen's *Eighteen Fifty-Seven*, the officially sponsored account in Independent India, unfortunately fails us so very lamentably), then this obstacle needs first to be overcome.

The first essay in this collection, by Irfan Habib, gives an overview of the factors that led to the Rebellion of 1857, as well as the ideas that motivated the Rebels. Here, it is important to understand both the goals the Rebels set for themselves, including unexpected elements of modernity seen among the Sepoys and the educated, and the limitations from which their outlook and strategy suffered. Irfan Habib's essay seeks to bring to life this complex picture and helps us understand what moved so many people to sacrifice their all for the cause, as they saw it, of their faith and their country.

Delhi was the city from where the flames of the Revolt spread the most powerfully and for which the first bitter battles were fought. But it was Awadh where the true strength of the Rebellion was ultimately displayed and resistance to the British proved to be the most stubborn. For this there were certain specific local reasons. The historical setting of the Rebellion in Awadh was framed by the British annexation of the kingdom in 1856. Lucknow, the capital of Awadh, was the largest city in India at the time, with over 650,000 inhabitants. Its court and revenues sustained numerous traditional arts and crafts and a rich culture, aided by the printing press. The annexation destroyed the basis of this prosperity. Moreover, the *taluqdars* and peasants were threatened with a heavy increase in revenue demands. There was, therefore, a surge of popular sympathy for the fall-en regime. One could see the glimmerings of resentment against the English based on these grounds much before the actual outbreak of the Rebellion. Of the extant Urdu news weeklies, the *Tilism* of Lucknow began publication on 25 July 1856 and continued till 8 May 1857. Another contemporary Lucknow weekly, *Sahar Samri,* started five months after the *Tilism,* on 17 November 1856, and the last issue came out on 18 May 1857. Faruqi Anjum Taban, in her paper in this volume, uses mainly *Tilism* and two Delhi-based news weeklies, *Dehli Urdu Akhbar* and *Sadiqul Akhbar,* to establish how civilian unrest was preparing the ground for the Revolt in Awadh.

The two Delhi-based weeklies mentioned above are of extraordinary importance since they continued to be issued right through the period of the Rebels' control over Delhi. My own paper is based on a study of their files and I hope to bring out the fact that these rebel Urdu journalists are entitled to a special niche in the history of Indian journalism, which has so far been inadvertently denied to them.

In the next essay, Iqbal Husain uses the *Dehli Urdu Akhbar* as well as other archival material to reconstruct a picture of the Rebel administration at Delhi. It is remarkable how the Sepoys took to the British methods of holding consultations and constituting committees and councils. The constitution (*dastur-ul amal*) of the Court of Administration in Delhi (its original text in cursive hand is preserved in the National Archives of India) was reproduced by S.N. Sen in his *Eighteen Fifty-Seven,* but still needs to be closely studied. It was established not by an order of the Mughal king, but by a decision taken by the Sepoys themselves in July 1857. There is a hint here of Sepoy 'republicanism', which Percival Spear had also noted in his very fair-minded account of Delhi, *Twilight of the Mughals.* Both the Delhi newspapers and the archives strongly bring out the Sepoy General Bakht Khan's no-nonsense attitude towards any attempt to provoke Hindu–Muslim differences.

S.Z.H. Jafri reconstructs the biography of Ahmadullah Shah, a saintly (though not a Wahabi) rebel who was already in prison at Faizabad on the charge of sedition when the Revolt broke out. It is debatable how far his own querulous attitude, bringing about a duality of leadership (the court's and Ahmadullah Shah's own), at Lucknow proved to be detrimental to the Rebel cause.

Iqtidar Alam Khan traces the history of the Gwalior Contingent, which, although betrayed by the Scindia, nevertheless marched on and occupied Kanpur on 28 November 1857, inflicting on General Windham one of the few defeats in an open engagement ever suffered by the British in India. The resistance offered by the men of the Gwalior Contingent remained stout-hearted to the very end. As late as 27 February, exactly two months before the capture of Tatya Tope, a telegraphic report (of 3 March 1859) reads: '. . . during the night 6 hundred of the rebel Gwalior Contingent went in the Bhilsa camp [near Agra] announcing themselves as a British force. They poured in several vollies captured and killed about two hundred and burnt the camp so the enemy now have four guns.'[1] This adherence to the cause and persistence makes the memory of the Gwalior Contingent particularly sacred for us.

The late K. Suresh Singh describes the role of the tribals of Jharkhand in

1857 – an oft-forgotten chapter of its history. We may remember that K. Suresh Singh, the distinguished Director General of the Anthropological Survey of India and the editor of the *People of India* volumes, was especially dedicated to reconstructing tribal history.

Four other essays deal with the impact of 1857 in different ways: Badri Narayan explores local folklore for its perception of Kunwar Singh and his brother Amar Singh, the famous Rebel *zamindars* of Jagdishpur who conducted a march of epic proportions from the neighbourhood of Arrah to Rewa, Kanpur, Lucknow, Azamgarh and then back to their home territory, challenging the British all along and combining with the rebelling Sepoy regiments with remarkable success. Amar Singh, it should be noted, gets a special word of praise from Engels for his readiness to move and conduct mobile warfare.

Pankaj Rag, advocating an approach 'from below', explores the Revolt of 1857 as it survives in folk memory. How folk memory is influenced by later events makes for an interesting theme on its own. S.P. Verma studies the work of British artists, usually done in conformity with the textual accounts of events of 1857, but also drawing on the imagination and perception of artists themselves. While many of these drawings depict the brutalities alleged to have been committed by the Sepoys, at least a few of them also portray the English acts of terror, such as the blowing away of rebellious Sepoys from the mouths of guns, a practice already perfected by the English in Afghanistan, as a reader of the works of the famous traveller Masson would find. Ramesh Rawat takes issue with the alleged connection between 1857 and the 'Hindi Renaissance', a view widely held amongst today's Hindi litterateurs. The debate on the role of religion in 1857 in the historiography of the Rebellion has been analysed by Farhat Hasan.

It is hoped that all those who are interested in the role of imperialism in India and the history of the nation's resistance will find these studies of some use and interest.

Note
[1] S.N. Sinha (ed.), *Mutiny Telegrams*, Lucknow, 1988, p. 90.

Contributors

IRFAN HABIB, Professor Emeritus in History, Aligarh Muslim University.

FARHAT HASAN, Professor of History, Delhi University.

IQBAL HUSAIN, Professor of History (retd.), Aligarh Muslim University.

S. ZAHEER HUSAIN JAFRI, Professor of History, Delhi University.

IQTIDAR ALAM KHAN, Professor of History (retd.), Aligarh Muslim University.

SHIREEN MOOSVI, Professor of History, Aligarh Muslim University.

BADRI NARAYAN, Senior Lecturer, G.B. Pant Social Science Institute, Allahabad.

PANKAJ RAG, Director, Film and Television Institute of India, Pune.

RAMESH RAWAT, Reader in Hindi, Aligarh Muslim University.

Late KR. SURESH SINGH, former Director General, Anthropological Survey of India.

FARUQUI ANJUM TABAN, former Research Scholar, Department of History, Aligarh Muslim University.

S.P. VERMA, Professor of History (retd.), Aligarh Muslim University.

The Coming of 1857

Irfan Habib

The Revolt of 1857 began as a Mutiny of the Bengal Army sepoys, who, throughout the course of the Revolt, proved themselves to be the most steadfast in its cause. The Bengal Army was much larger than the other two of the East India Company's Presidency armies (Madras and Bombay) combined; it was in fact the largest modern army operating east of Suez. By the time it broke into revolt, it had 1,39,807 'natives' as sepoys, officered and watched over by 26,089 'Europeans'.[1] For the previous eighteen years or more, the Bengal Army sepoy had been continuously employed in pursuing the frenzied territorial ambitions of Free-Trade Britain. He bore the brunt of the First Afghan War (1839–42), the sanguinary clash with the Scindia's troops (1843), the war in Sind (1844), the two closely contested Punjab Wars (1845–46 and 1848–49) and the Second Burma War (1852). He was shipped across the seas to fight in the Opium Wars against China (1840–42 and 1856–60) and the Crimean War against Russia (1854). An expedition was sent against Iran in 1856. There were few armies in the world after the fall of Napoleon in 1815 that had been called upon to risk the lives of their soldiers so constantly for such a long period. At the first signs of unrest within the Nineteenth Infantry at Berhampore in late February 1857, its Colonel (Mitchell) immediately threatened it with being 'sent to Burma or to China, where the men would die'.[2] The gallantry with which the sepoy had served his masters now seemed to be his undoing as the calls upon him to do battle became endless, while the fatalities mounted.

If his role as the cannon-fodder of imperialism was at last telling on the sepoy's morale, there was the constant reminder too of his absolutely servile position within the army that further inflamed an inner resentment. He could rise after long service (for seniority was the only consideration) to be a 'Jamadar', and then 'Soubahdar', there being ten of each rank to a regiment, and, finally, to the rank of 'Soubahdar Major', only one for the whole regiment. With these ranks, obtainable only by a few after long years of service, the chain ended. In these promoted capacities the sepoys were merely expected to act as informants and errand-boys. Authority lay only with the Europeans, who monopolized all ranks from subalterns upwards.

The Bengal Army was formally the army of the Governor-General's own

Presidency of Bengal that extended over the whole of northern India. But, in fact, the Army's recruitment zone was largely confined to the limits of the present-day Uttar Pradesh, minus the Himalayan districts, but plus Haryana and western Bihar. This may partly have been because the English found it convenient that the sepoys should share a common language ('Hindustanee'). The enlisted men came overwhelmingly from the class of small landowners. In the infantry, comprising the bulk of the Bengal Army (some 1,12,000 men), the Brahmans formed the largest segment, followed by Rajputs and other Hindus and Muslims. In the cavalry (over 19,000 men), Muslims ('Syeds and Pathans') appear to have predominated. The much smaller arm of artillery (less than 5,000 men) had a more mixed composition.[3] A surprisingly large number of the sepoys (about 40,000) were recruited from Oudh, comprising the present-day Lucknow and Faizabad divisions. It is important to consider this territorial affiliation of the sepoys, because it coincided with the area where the 1857 Rebellion flared up most strongly. Moreover, it helps us to find yet another explanation of the sepoys' growing alienation from the colonial regime.

The enlistment area of the Bengal Army, if one excludes Oudh, lay under the *mahalwari* system. Unlike the Permanent Settlement of Bengal and Bihar, this involved a constantly increasing revenue demand. After 1833 the '*mafi*' lands, of which the Brahmans and upper strata of Muslims had been the major beneficiaries, began to be extensively resumed. The increase in revenue and the *mafi* resumptions pressed hard on the landholdings of the families from which the sepoys came. Only in Oudh things had been different. Before the Annexation of 1856, the sepoy as a landholder there had been protected by the British Resident whenever he preferred complaints against the Nawabi government and its officials. But after the Annexation, the sepoy's favoured position vanished. Indeed, the *mahalwari* system was now to be extended to Oudh; and, if it came to pass, this would soon deprive the sepoy of much of his former income and possibly his land as well.

As the grievances of the sepoy against the military authorities and the civil administration mounted, he began to see his own identity cast more and more in a religious colour. For the sake of his morale, the army authorities had encouraged giving to the Bengal Army the reputation of an upper-caste army. The enlistment of lower castes was specifically discouraged by the Regulations of 1855. The Army authorities also took much care to encourage respect for caste taboos, by letting the sepoys cook privately. Not surprisingly, the sepoys became particularly sensitive about their caste and religious status. At the same time, the regiments were made up of a diverse composition to thwart the growth of any common feeling among the sepoys. But the result of such mixture, as Syed Ahmad Khan noted, was the opposite: by coming together in the same companies, bonds grew between Hindu and Muslim sepoys, and both came to consider each other as brothers.[4] So when the issue of greased cartridges arose, with fear of pollution from beef and pork, they found it natural to unite as one on the single cry of the defence of their faith, or '*Deen*' and '*Dharam*'. The greased cartridges for the new Enfield rifles were designed to make the Bengal Army more effective. Biting the cartridge made reloading far quicker than breaking it by hand; for the sepoy too, the time gained might make all the difference between life and death in the battlefield. There were good reasons, therefore, for the Army authorities to press on with both the new weapon and the fast method of using the cartridge, even when the alarm and indignation of the sepoys became manifest as the year 1857 began. Concessions came too late and were not believed: enough combustible material had otherwise gathered in the breast of the sepoy, to make the greased cartridge just the torch that could set the whole Army aflame.

When, on 29 March 1857, Mangal Pandey, the Revolt's first martyr, called upon his comrades at Barrackpore to rise, the immediate summons proved abortive. The 19th and the 34th Infantry allowed themselves to be disarmed and disbanded. But the call spread from cantonment to cantonment until, on 11 May, the Meerut mutineers occupied Delhi and sent out the signal for a general uprising of the entire Bengal Army.

That signal, with some passage of time, was almost universally obeyed. In September 1858, the India House could report only seven regiments with just 7,796 sepoys surviving in service from the Bengal Army of two years earlier, when it had a 'native' strength of some 1,39,000 men.[5] There can therefore be little doubt that the sepoys who mutinied and went into armed rebellion must have numbered well over 1,00,000. They constituted not only the bulk of the armed strength of the rebels, but also the most modern force within their ranks. Their anxiety to copy the organization of the Bengal Army as they perceived it is manifest in the 'councils' created for governance of regiments and other military formations, and the ranks of 'Generals', 'Colonels' and 'Captains' they gave to their leaders. This was a visible departure from the traditional Indian military organization; and the sepoys otherwise also quite often showed their indifference to, or even scorn for, the conventions and hierarchies of the traditional Indian regimes.

And yet, if the Sepoy Mutiny formed the backbone of the 1857 Revolt, it is equally certain that it would not have acquired the dimensions it did, had the Revolt not immediately touched a sympathetic chord in the hearts of large sections of the civil population of the large tract from Haryana to Bihar from whose villages the sepoys came. The Mutiny took on the complexion, over large areas, of an agrarian revolt.

We have already seen that the sepoys as landholders felt troubled about the oppressiveness of the *mahalwari* system that prevailed in the larger part of their enlistment zone. It was a real irony of history that the very territory from which the British authorities decided to recruit the bulk of their mercenaries was also the area on which, by a kind of gradual elimination, the burden of Britain's tribute from India fell the heaviest. The Permanent Settlement in Bengal and Bihar, and the fixed tax-rates in the *ryotwari* areas of Madras Presidency checked the extent to which revenue could be increased in these early-acquired parts of the Company's dominions. The *ryotwari* system of the Bombay Presidency was so framed as to enable the revenues to be enhanced in a more flexible fashion. But it was the *mahalwari* system of northern India where an almost unbridled urge for revenue maximization was given full play. In the first part of the nineteenth century the revenue increased in real terms (i.e. adjusted to prices) by nearly as much as 70 per cent, reaching the level of Rs 5.60 crore by 1844–45 in the Agra province (present Uttar Pradesh plains minus Oudh). The further insistence on collective responsibility for revenue payment under this system forced unprecedented alienations of lands, affecting both zamindars and peasants. In the district of Aligarh, 50 per cent of the land changed hands between 1839 and 1858, while 'the moneylending and trading classes' increased their share of landholding from 3.4 to 12.3 per cent. In Muzaffarnagar district, between 1841 and 1861, a quarter of the land changed hands; and the share of 'non-agricultural classes' in the land increased from 11 to 19.5 per cent.[6] These statistics show why the anxieties of the rural classes had become acute at the very time the sepoys were receiving their greased cartridges. The aftermath of the Annexation of Oudh (1856) engendered similar anxieties among the *taluqdars* and peasants of Oudh, since it was proclaimed that the *mahalwari* system would be extended to the annexed kingdom. Indeed, as a preliminary, taxation was so much enhanced that many *taluqdars* and other proprietors lost large parts of their land within the very first year of the Annexation. As a result, those who had just recently treated the last 'king' of Oudh, Wajid Ali Shah's departure with such marked indifference began soon to bitterly rue the end of the Nawabi regime.

To one local English official, Mark Thornhill (reporting on 15 November 1858), it appeared that the ordinary peasants were the most to blame for the agrarian uprisings accompanying the Mutiny:

> However paradoxical it may appear, it is a matter of fact that the agricultural labouring class – the class who above all others have derived the most benefit from our rule (!) – were the most hostile to its continuance, while the large proprietors, who have suffered under our rule, almost to a man stood by us.[7]

Thornhill was speaking of the old *mahalwari* areas of western Uttar Pradesh. Speaking of Oudh, the Secretary of State for India, Sir Charles Wood, said in the House of Commons in 1861:

> In consequence of that opinion [of the perfect nature of the *mahalwari* system] it was introduced into the newly acquired province of Oudh. We fancied that we were benefiting the population, and relieving them from the oppression of their chiefs [the *taluqdars*], but in the rebellion the ryots of Oudh took part against us and joined their chiefs in the rebellion.[8]

As in every revolt or revolution, the class configuration on the ground in 1857 was not exact. There were bodies of zamindars and *taluqdars* who remained aloof from the Rebellion, and, at the opportune moment, even went over to the English; and many peasants defied the British as well as the rebel authorities, since, as Eric Stokes puts it, the 'basic peasant impulse remained liberation from the tax gatherer of whatever hue'.[9] But the general situation was that over practically the entire Uttar Pradesh plains, British rule collapsed in the villages and authority passed over to rebelling zamindars and peasants, whose mutual contradictions of interest now took for them a second place.

The disaffection against the English was not purely rural. There was the devastation to which urban handicrafts, especially textiles, had been subjected owing to the intrusion of English competition and the disappearance of demand created by the deposed local courts and ruling classes. In his proclamation of August 1857, the rebel prince Feroz Shah underlined the fact that 'the Europeans by the introduction of English articles into India, have thrown the weavers, the cotton dressers, the carpenters, the blacksmiths, and the shoe-makers, etc., out of employ and have engrossed their occupations, so that every description of native artisan has been reduced to beggary'.[10]

Why the townspeople joined the Revolt so rapidly is explained also by the following eyewitness Englishman's description of Lucknow – the largest city in India at the time with a population probably exceeding 6,00,000 – on the eve of the Mutiny:

> That the Lucknow people should rise against us [the English] was a very probable event, notwithstanding the false reports which we received of their universal contentment. We had done very little to deserve their love and much to merit their detestation. Thousands of nobles, gentlemen, and officials, who during the king's time [before the Annexation, 1856] had lucrative appointments, and who were too idle to work, were now in penury and want, and their myriads of retainers and servants thrown out of employ of course. Then the innumerable vagabonds, bravos and beggars, who under the native rule infested the city and found bread in it. The native merchants, shopkeepers and bankers, who, while Wajid Ali was on the throne, made large profits from supplying the luxurious wants of the king, his courtiers and the wealthy ladies of the thronged harems, found no sale for their goods, and the people in general, and especially the poor, were dissatisfied because they were taxed directly and indirectly in every way.[11]

The participation of the city's poor as auxiliaries in the Revolt was quite a noticeable feature at many places. At Delhi, 'weavers, artisans and other wage-earners' joined the sepoys under the rebel commander Bakht Khan.[12] In the detailed memoir that Syed Ahmad Khan wrote on the events of the Revolt in the district of Bijnor, he noted scornfully that the professional sepoys and soldiers under the local rebel leader Mahmud Khan, were reinforced by 'cotton-carders and weavers who had never held any sword, except yarn'.[13]

Undoubtedly, ideological factors also played their part. The fact that the East India Company's government, partly under pressure from the missionaries, officially patronized church activities created a situation where its aims became more and more suspect in the eyes of both Hindus and Muslims. On 28 January 1857, General Hearsey at Barrackpore was complaining of 'some agents of the religious Hindoo party in Calcutta (I believe it is called the "Dharma Sobha") spreading rumours about the Government being intent on converting the sepoys'. And he attributed this to Hindu indignation in Calcutta over the recent legislation permitting the remarriage of Hindu widows.[14] In northern India, the 'Wahabis' had been spreading the net of propaganda about *jihad* or holy war, though much of this had been actually directed against not the English but the Sikhs on the Afghan frontier.[15] It is likely, however, that their rhetoric of *jihad* could now be put to a totally different use by persons who were least concerned with the Wahabis' version of theology or their sect. The term *mujahid* or *jihadi* in 1857–58 usually meant no more than a Muslim civilian who volunteered to take arms against the British. Like the sepoys in the first four months of the Revolt, such volunteers formed bands in different places and made their way to Delhi to join in its defence.[16]

While it was natural that the cry of religion should be employed by the rebels so often, it is also important to remember that they did their best not to let such sentiments create divisions in their own ranks. When, on 22 July, the Muslim Iduz Zuha festival, with its customary animal sacrifices, was to be celebrated in Delhi, the rebel regime took care to forbid the slaughter of cows, oxen and buffaloes, and even undertook the impounding of cows owned by Muslims in order to prevent the outbreak of any Hindu–Muslim dispute.[17] In the fiery pamphlet *Fath-i Islam* (*Victory to Islam*), issued from Lucknow in July 1857 apparently under the aegis of the sufic rebel leader Ahmadullah Shah, the appeal is repeatedly made to both the Hindus and Muslims to fight together to drive out the English and so unitedly protect their own respective faiths.[18] The insistence on the religious cause can perhaps be interpreted as an evidence of the weakness of national consciousness. But the sense of 'Hindustan' as the country whose destiny was in question is often prominently present in rebel statements. Feroz Shah's proclamation of August 1857 begins with the following words: 'It is well known to all that in this age, the people of Hindoostan, both Hindoos and Mohammedans, are being ruined under the tyranny and oppression of the infidel and treacherous English.'[19]

The weekly *Dehli Urdu Akhbar*, which continued to appear during the four-month rebel regime in Delhi (May–September 1857), makes use of several kinds of arguments, often invoking a shared monotheism, a shared fate as victims of English cruelty and, most importantly for us, a shared love for the country, to enjoin a firm unity of Hindus and Muslims in opposing the English. Its editor Muhammad Baqir explicitly condemned Wahabi-type arguments (Hindus to be shunned as 'infidels'; *jihad* not possible without legitimate *imam* or leader) as the work of English agents.[20]

In a spirited reply to Queen Victoria's Proclamation of November 1858, the Oudh prince Birjis Qadr asked the people not to believe Queen Victoria's words for 'the wise cannot approve of [the English] punishing the whole army and people of Hindustan'. The counter-proclamation's list of villainies committed by the English records those committed against the ruler of Bharatpur, Maharaja Dulip Singh of Lahore, the Peshwa, Sultan Tipu, the Raja of Banaras, Scindia and the Nazim of Bengal, besides the Oudh rulers themselves.[21] In other words, again, not simply the princely house of Oudh or its subjects but all the people and princes of Hindustan were seen as the victims of English oppression, and were summoned to join the rebels' cause.

That, in practice, much parochialism and factionalism prevailed in the rebel camp, there can be little doubt about. Much of it was due to the rebels' failure to establish or accept a centralized authority. The Revolt had broken out without any large political design, and this had its effect on the ad-hoc nature of the arrangements the rebels made to establish systems of command and control.

The natural thing for the rebel sepoys to do was to look immediately for the rulers whom the British had dispossessed or downgraded. Until 1835 the East India Company's rupees had continued to be struck in the name of the Mughal emperor or Badshah; and there was a widespread feeling that all legitimate political authority could be derived only from his grant. It was, therefore, inevitable that the 1857 rebels should first use the name of that phantom ruler and declare their cause to be one of restoration of his authority. For this, the possession of Delhi and the person of that emperor became crucial; and so long as the rebels held Delhi from 11 May to 21 September, Delhi remained a magnet for all sepoys, wherever there were no other local or regional princely claimants to authority beckoning, like the house of Oudh at Lucknow, the Nana Sahib (as the proclaimed Peshwa) at Kanpur and Rani Lakshmi Bai representing the deposed dynasty at Jhansi. It was inevitable that between such representatives of the old order, on the one hand, and the products of a modern army, like the sepoys, there would arise some difficulties. In Delhi the 'republican' tendencies of sepoy leaders like Bakht Khan rendered them unpopular at the fort, the seat of the court and residence of the titular emperor. The famous constitution of the 'Court [of] Administration' (so termed in Urdu) at Delhi, with its twelve articles, was an obvious attempt to establish a kind of elective military rule: Of the ten members of the court, six were to be chosen (*muntakhib*) from the three arms (i.e. two each from infantry, cavalry and artillery).[22] A similar court or council was also established by the sepoy leaders at Lucknow.

At the same time, it will not be valid to overlook the cases where successful collaboration occurred between the old-order leaders and the sepoys. The epic campaign of the two zamindar brothers, Kunwar Singh and Amar Singh, which involved passage from the vicinity of Arrah to Rewa, Kalpi, Kanpur, Lucknow, Azamgarh and Ghazipur, was necessarily built on such collaboration. Amar Singh won praise for his tactics from even the distant and discerning Engels.[23] Similarly, Tantia Topi, the lieutenant of Nana Sahib and, later on, of Rani Lakshmibai of Jhansi, worked well with the famous Gwalior contingent that had defeated General Windham near Kanpur in late November 1857. Moreover, the fact that as late as 1856 Oudh had possessed an administrative apparatus of its own under its 'king' enabled the administration, demolished by the Annexation, to be resurrected, its old troops re-established and its officials re-installed, so that the revival of the old kingdom provided the Revolt with a very large administered area that proved to be an especially stubborn zone for the English to subjugate.[24]

The rebel regime made considerable effort to establish popularity for its cause by printing proclamations. In Delhi three weekly newspapers (two in Urdu, one in Persian) carried rebel pronouncements and proclamations throughout the duration of the rebel regime. In Oudh the Persian language of the old court was replaced by Hindustani, with Hindi and Urdu texts given side by side, as illustrated by the proclamation ('*Ishtihar Nama*') addressed to 'the Zamindars and People of this Country Generally', issued in the name of Birjis Qadr, on 6 July 1857. The simple language used (practically all of it is common to both the Hindi and Urdu columns) is admirable.[25] A very detailed programme drafted to appeal to various sections of the population with specific details of administrative, fiscal and financial measures to be taken, was issued by Prince Firoz Shah, dated 25 August. Here, on behalf of a contingent 'Badshahi Government', the zamindars were assured of a reduced, reasonable 'Jumas' (*jama*, revenue assessments) and of 'absolute authority' within their zamindari (over their *ryots* presumably!); all trade was to be reserved for Indian merchants only, with free use of government 'steam vessels and steam carriages'; all public offices were to be given to Indians only, and reasonable daily pay decreed for the sepoys; employment to be given to artisans by 'the kings, the rajahs and the rich'; and rent-free lands granted to the 'Pundits, Fakirs and other learned persons'.[26] This programme is important for its modern identification of classes, though its obvious effort to placate the zamindars (and to practically disenfranchise the peasantry) is disconcerting. However, whatever their limitations, documents such as these show that there was some talent and vision on the side of the rebels; and the rebel regimes were not mere royal or princely old-order restorations.

The Rebellion, when it broke out, was accompanied by atrocities, much exaggerated naturally by the English and for which terrible vengeance on the innocent was wrought immediately thereafter. But one needs to remember that there were rebel leaders themselves who condemned these atrocities. Feroz Shah, in a second proclamation after the fall of Delhi, denounced the killing of women and children as wicked acts violative of 'the commands of God'.[27] No such compassion for the victims of her country's 'white terror' in India appears in Queen Victoria's Proclamation of 1858; and it is not to be forgotten that the English at single places butchered more ordinary people, often with bestial torture, than all the European civilians killed during the entire course of the Rebellion. One also forgets that the rebels' violence too was fed by reports of what the English were doing. Kaye, in his classic *History of the Sepoy War*, poses what appeared to him a haunting dilemma:

> An Englishman is almost suffocated when he reads that Mrs Chambers or Miss Jennings was hacked to death by a dusky ruffian; but in Native historians, or, history being wanting, in Native legends and traditions, it may be recorded against our people, that mothers and wives and children, with less familiar names, fell miserable victims to the first swoop of English vengeance; and these stories may have as deep a pathos that rend our own hearts.[28]

They also hardened the hearts of the mutineers.

At the present moment, we can visualize many sentiments and grievances that motivated those who had raised, and those who would soon join, the Rebellion. The diverse motives explain, but in no way detract from, the immensity of the enterprise the rebels had begun – one that proved to be the greatest armed challenge to imperialism the world over during the entire course of the nineteenth century. In these days when globalization and Hindutva and Muslim fundamentalism seem so much to flourish, it may look odd to some that the 1857 rebels showed such consuming bitterness against foreign rule, or that Hindus and Muslims so unquestioningly shed their blood together. Perhaps, for that very reason alone, we need to recall 1857 as frequently as we can.

Notes and References

1 Figures derived from Parliamentary Papers in Haraprasad Chattopadhyaya, *The Sepoy Mutiny, 1857*, Calcutta, 1957, p. 64.

2 J.W. Kaye, *A History of the Sepoy War*, Vol. I, 9th edn, London, 1880, p. 502 fn.

3 Cf. Chattopadhyaya, *The Sepoy Mutiny, 1857*, pp. 71–76.

4 Syed Ahmad Khan, 'Asbab-i Baghawat-i Hindostan' ('Causes of the Indian Revolt'), Appendix to Hali's *Hayat-i Jawed*, Lahore, 1957, pp. 926–27.

5 Kaye, *History of the Sepoy War*, p. 621.

6 These data are from Irfan Habib, *Essays in Indian History: Towards a Marxist Perception*, New Delhi, 1995, pp. 308–19. On the connection between the Revolt and the harshness of the Settlements, see also Syed Ahmad Khan, *Asbab-i Baghawat-i Hindostan*, pp. 906–09.

7 Quoted by Eric Stokes, *The Peasant and the Raj*, Cambridge, 1978, pp. 195–96.

8 A.C. Banerjee, *Indian Constitutional Documents*, Vol. II, Calcutta, 1946, p. 24.

9 In *Cambridge Economic History of India*, Vol. II, edited by Dharma Kumar, Cambridge, 1983, p. 56.

10 S.A.A. Rizvi (ed.), *Freedom Struggle in Uttar Pradesh*, Vol. I, Lucknow, 1957, p. 458.

11 L.E.S. Rees, *A Personal Narrative of the Siege of Lucknow*, London, 1858, pp. 33–34.

12 Iqbal Husain's biography of Bakht Khan in *We Fought Together for Freedom*, edited by Ravi Dayal, Delhi, 1995, p. 18.

13 Sayyid Ahmad (Syed Ahmad Khan), *Sarkashi-i Zila'-i Bijnor*, edited by Sharafat Husain Mirza, Delhi, 1964, p. 178, Sayyid Ahmad's heavy humour is rather off the mark, since there is no way in which yarn can be compared with a sword.

14 Kaye, *History of the Sepoy War*, Vol. I, p. 496.

15 In 1847 Syed Ahmad Khan, in the first edition of his book *Āṣāru'ṣ Ṣanādīd*, in his account of Delhi notables, gave enthusiastic notices of Sayyid Ahmad Barelvi and his close associate Muhammad Ismā'īl, the two Wahabi leaders killed at Balakot on the Afghan frontier in 1831. He states that till fourteen or fifteen years after that event, *mujāhids* were still going from different parts of the country to the Afghan frontier. (See the comprehensive edition of *Āṣāru'ṣ Ṣanādīd*, Delhi, 1965, pp. 491–95, 548–54). Syed Ahmad Khan obviously saw no contradiction between his loyalty to the British and his admiration for the Wahābīs' cause of *jihād*, probably because the Wahābīs' effort was directed until then not against the British but the Sikhs. As Iqtidar Alam Khan has argued recently, their role in the 1857 Uprising has often been overstressed.

16 Such, for example, was Munir Khan of Nagina, district Bijnor, who 'becoming a jihadi', assembled 400 men and marched off to Delhi, where he himself was killed in the fighting (Sayyid Ahmad, *Sarkashi-i Zila'-i Bijnor*, pp. 147–49; nowhere does Sayyid Ahmad suggest any Wahabi affiliation for Munir Khan).

17 Percival Spear, *Twilight of the Mughals*, Cambridge, 1951, pp. 207–08.

18 Rizvi (ed.), *Freedom Struggle in Uttar Pradesh*, Vol. II, Lucknow, 1958, pp. 155–56, 159. The entire pamphlet is translated, pp. 150–62.

[19] Rizvi (ed.), *Freedom Struggle in Uttar Pradesh*, Vol. I, p. 453.

[20] The rebel-period issues with some omissions are preserved in the National Archives, New Delhi. I have used a rotograph copy of the file in the library of the Department of History, Aligarh University. See also Shireen Moosvi's article on this newspaper in *People's Democracy*, 23–29 April 2007.

[21] Translated in S.N. Sen, *Eighteen Fifty-seven*, Delhi, 1957, pp. 382–83. I regret I have not been able to trace the original Hindustani text.

[22] See the original Urdu text, reproduced in Sen, *Eighteen Fifty*-seven, between pp. 74 and 75.

[23] Frederick Engels in his report, printed as a leading article in *New York Daily Tribune*, 1 October 1858, said of 'Ummer Singh' that 'he shows rather more activity and knowledge of guerrilla warfare [than other rebel leaders]; at all events, he attacks the British whenever he can, instead of quietly waiting for them' (*Karl Marx on India*, edited by Iqbal Husain, New Delhi, 2006, p. 203).

[24] The fact of the strength of the resistance in Oudh was acknowledged by Canning's notorious Oudh Proclamation, issued in March 1858 after the fall of Lucknow: 'This resistance, begun by a mutinous soldiery, has found support from the inhabitants of the city and of the province of Oude at large.' On this basis it went to announce that 'the proprietary right in the soil of the province is confiscated to the British Government' (Rizvi (ed.), *Freedom Struggle in Uttar Pradesh*, Vol. II, pp. 41–42). In a subsequent letter to the Secret Committee of the Court of Directors, London, Canning admitted that 'the rising against our authority in Oude has been general, almost universal' (ibid., p. 353).

[25] For a photo reproduction, see Rizvi (ed.), *Freedom Struggle in Uttar Pradesh*, Vol. I, Plate No. 19; a translation would be found on pp. 451–52.

[26] Translated in Rizvi (ed.), *Freedom Struggle in Uttar Pradesh*, Vol. I, pp. 453–58. Original text not published.

[27] Ibid., p. 463.

[28] Kaye, *History of the Sepoy War*, Vol. II, London, 1881, pp. 270–71.

The Coming of the Revolt in Awadh

The Evidence of Urdu Newspapers

Faruqui Anjum Taban

In most of the works on the Rebellion of 1857, there is an excessive, if not exclusive, reliance on the official English sources. As a consequence, the indigenous perception of the Revolt has often been casually treated, where it is not entirely ignored. It is proposed here to present the indigenous evidence regarding Awadh on the eve of the Revolt of 1857, as can be gleaned from Urdu weekly newspapers of the period: *Tilism* (Lucknow), the *Sadiq-ul-Akhbar* and the *Dehli Urdu Akhbar*.

Written in rhyming prose and published from Lucknow, *Tilism* is the most informative for the present theme. Its editor and publisher, Muhammad Ya'qub, belonged to the well-known theological house of Firangi Mahal in Lucknow. Forty-one issues of *Tilism*, beginning from 25 July 1856 and ending with 8 May 1857, with one issue (No. 37) missing, are preserved at the Centre of Advanced Study in History, Aligarh Muslim University. Attention to this weekly was first drawn in English by Iqbal Husain.[1]

The *Sadiq-ul-Akhbar*, also a weekly newspaper, was edited and published by Saiyad Jamiluddin Khan from Delhi. The National Archives of India has only four issues, from 26 January 1857 to 19 March 1857;[2] it is a disconnected series and many issues of the paper are missing. There is one issue (No. 11 of Vol. 2, dated 19 March 1857) that bears the same title but has a different editor and publisher, and belongs to a different series. The editor and publisher of this issue is mentioned as Saiyid Muhammad 'Abdul Qadir.[3]

The printer and publisher of *Dehli Urdu Akhbar* was Saiyad Abdullah. The National Archives has fifteen issues of this newspaper. The earliest available issue is No. 10, Vol. 19 (8 March 1857) and the last, No. 37, Vol. 19 (13 September 1857). Though most of the issues relate to the period of the Revolt, there are a few (Nos 10, 19 and 20 of Vol. 19) in the series that describe the events in Awadh in the period just before the outbreak of the Revolt of 1857.[4]

It appears from these papers that the Annexation of Awadh in February 1856 led to widespread resentment among the people of Awadh. Contrary to the 'official' view that prior to the outbreak of the Mutiny on 30 June 1857, there were no apparent indications of discontent in Awadh against the British over the Annexation,[5] these papers reveal a growing sense of resentment that ultimately found its most bitter expression in the Revolt. Towards the close of April 1857, the editor of *Tilism* informs us that sepoy mutinies had broken out at Amausa and Mandiyaon in Lucknow.[6] In the early part of May 1857 a cantonment (*chhawni*) in Lucknow was set on fire causing extensive damage to the residence of a major sergeant and the death of several Indian foot-men' (*Piyadas*).[7]

It is certain from these newspapers that discontent against the British was not confined to the sepoys, but was also widespread among the civil population. On 23 February 1857, in a riot in Faizabad, the rioters seriously injured an English officer and some of his soldiers.[8] Resentment against the British Annexation, naturally, was more pronounced among the erstwhile ruling classes and the landed families, whose attachment and loyalty (*namakhalali*) to the deposed ruling house is lavishly praised in the Urdu newspapers. The *Sadiq-ul-Akhbar* reports that in January 1857, some Rajput women of Awadh, by way of a 'joke' (*mazaq*), beat up a servant of the Company so seriously that he almost died. The *thanedar* arrested the women and, to get them released, their menfolk attacked the police station, killed four constables (*barqandaz*) and injured several others. In this riot, reports the paper, there were in all a dozen fatal casualties.[9] *Tilism* informs us that the son of a high noble at the court of Awadh, Ihtimam-ud-daula, refused to accept service under the Company nor did he accept its pension, out of what it describes as feelings of 'loyalty' (*namakhalali* and *janfishani*) for the deposed ruling house. 'He is one of the many', says the editor, 'who are not well-disposed towards the government, nor do they like its way of doing things.'[10]

Interestingly, these papers also reveal the role of scholars and saints in spreading disaffection. Maulvi Ahmadullah, a scholar-saint, is mentioned in *Tilism* as preaching *jihad* (holy war) against the Company to his followers. The Company had to post troops at his residence to prevent them from visiting him. Later, when he shifted from Lucknow to Faizabad, the government had him arrested.[11] Earlier, another saint of Lucknow, Qadir Ali Shah, was alleged to have been hatching a conspiracy against the Company and was arrested, to be released later for want of sufficient evidence.[12]

One major factor for this kind of hostility was a sense of strong emotional attachment towards the erstwhile Awadh ruling family: the deposition of the king was not simply a matter of concern but a major calamity. *Tilism* says: 'Close your eyes for a second and your turban [*pagri*] is gone. Gentlemen [Mir Sahib], these are difficult times. Hold your turban [*dastar*] by both hands . . . from the date the *sultanate* disappeared, the city has degenerated and things are let loose.'[13]

Events concerning the royal family naturally find a place of prominence in these papers. The visit of the queen mother, Malika Kishwar, to London is described in great detail in *Tilism*;[14] it is also mentioned in *Sadiq-ul-Akhbar*.[15] Both these papers also refer to debates in the parliament that concerned the British Annexation.[16] The editor of *Sadiq-ul-Akhbar*, perhaps too optimistically, believes that Queen Victoria was against the Annexation and desired restoration of the dynasty. The paper informs its readers that the queen of Awadh had filed a representation at the office of the Court of Directors, for the return of loans taken by the Company from the state of Awadh. The Company, it says, owed the ruler of Awadh Rs 3 lakh in 1834, Rs 17 lakh in 1839, Rs 12 lakh in 1840, and Rs 46 lakh (inclusive of arrears and interest on arrears) in 1843.[17] In language that is clearly intended to incite the readers, *Tilism* describes in detail the forceful manner in which the British tried to occupy the royal palaces, the ruthlessness with which they forcibly evicted the ladies of the harem, and the oppressions they inflicted on the royal servants to recover arms and ammunition belonging to the deposed house.[18] Quite obviously, these references that describe the developments concerning the erstwhile Awadh kingdom reflect the grief and concern of the people of Awadh – especially the influential landowning classes who were the chief subscribers of *Tilism* – over the Annexation. However, there were also influential individuals who deserted the Awadh kingdom and joined the service of the English Company. Bashir-ud-Daula and Dayanat-ud-Daula, high nobles in the court of Awadh, are two such individuals mentioned in *Tilism*. For them and many others like them, *Tilism* says:

> These are bad days. Every friend is now a stranger. Those on whom we place our trust, they do not help us in times of need. We have seen so many times that on occasions when they are needed, they are to be found nowhere. Ostensibly, they accept allegiance ['ita'at] but in testing times they run away.[19]

Rising prices and unemployment are other important factors cited in these papers as responsible for the growing discontent against the British rule. *Tilism* says:

> As it is, the city is already deserted by unemployment. To make matters worse, owing to the negligence of the white officials, the prices of grains have been persistently increasing. The hearts of the poor and the miserable are melting (from starvation) – millet *bajra* sells at the price of wheat.[20]

The Annexation led to a decline in the income of the ruling classes. This in turn appears to have led to a drying-up of patronage to mosques, *madrasas* and other religious institutions, for the Company was not willing to provide any worthwhile assistance to them. *Tilism* informs us that the scholars and saints, having lost their sources of income, are leaving Awadh in search of livelihood.[21] It further appears that the government established a few *madrasas* to provide livelihood to the scholars, and though these could hardly compense for all those who had lost their livelihood, for those who found employment in these *madrasas* it appeared as if, says *Tilism*, 'help has come from the skies'.[22] The shrinking patronage to religious institutions took away much of the fervent charm religious functions enjoyed earlier. *Tilism* reports:

> Look at the faithfulness of the skies. See the darkness of the times. The *Muharram*[23] at Lucknow was famous all over the world. The brightness of illuminations (in *Muharram*) could be seen from far away . . . from the first (of the month of *Muharram*) the *Imam-baras*[24] were illuminated. Free food and

sweets were distributed. The poor and the deserving used to come from far-off places. This time, look at the turn of fortune, see the arbitrariness of the revolutionary times. The doors of fortune are closed. The fire of suffering is at its height. The *Imam-baras* look deserted.[25]

The Annexation indeed caused widespread disruption in the social and cultural life in Awadh, especially of its elites, for whom once the mosques, *madrasas* and *Imam-baras* were deserted, the whole city appeared gloomy and haunted: 'Lucknow was once a garden that saw to autumn. Whoever lived there was like a nightingale in the garden of flowers. . . . The angels used to dance in ecstasy. These days it appears deserted, reminding all that this world is a place of warning.'[26]

The editor of *Tilism* takes issue with the English Company on its justification for the Annexation.[27] The grounds for Annexation, he says, rest on six allegations: (i) Awadh was mismanaged (*be-intizam*); (ii) the Kingdom (*Sultanate*) of Awadh was dependent on the will of the Company; (iii) by the treaty of 1801, the kingdom of Awadh could not exist without the consent of the Company; (iv) the aforesaid treaty gave the Company undisputed control over the kingdom of Awadh; (v) the Company had no choice in view of the deteriorating administration but to annex the kingdom; (vi) the treaty of 1837 was invalid because it was not satisfied.

The editor then points out that the primary justification for Annexation rests on the deterioration of the administration, for which two instances are specially cited by the English. One is the desolation of the *pargana* of Nanpara which was originally paying revenues of above Rs 3 lakh per annum and is now paying almost nothing. The second instance is that of a person by the name of Bholanath who arrested his servant Kishanlal and so severely harassed him that he set his own house on fire, killing his wife, sons and his own self. These instances, asserts *Tilism*, have been wrongly reported, but even if it is assumed that they took place, before accepting them as grounds for Annexation, the Company should first set its own house in order. The paper then cites six instances of deterioration of law and order in Calcutta.

(i) A zamindar arrested the daughter of a Brahman who owed him rent and insulted her in the open market.
(ii) On the banks of river Nil, an Englishman who had his mansion there forcibly stopped the boats and exacted money from the passengers, and even arrested some of them to force them to work as labourers on his estate.
(iii) To extract confessions from suspected criminals, the police in Bengal severely tortured them and, as if this was not enough, even their families.
(iv) A zamindar forcibly dragged the wife of his agent (*gumashta*) out of her house and molested her when he suspected that his daughter was interested in the *gumashta*. When the *gumashta* took the matter to the court, the Assistant Magistrate ruled in favour of the zamindar.

(v) The Englishman aforementioned in (ii) kidnapped a Brahman's bride, who stabbed herself to protect her honour.

(vi) A zamindar got so enraged with his 'Muslim rai'yat' that he forced them to drink the blood of pigs and eat pork.

One can discern in the choice of instances cited that they were meant to touch the deepest susceptibilities of the people of Awadh. They were also intended to forewarn the state of things to come in Awadh under the Company's rule. Above all, by citing these examples the editor was seeking to expose the shallowness of the English Company's claim that the Annexation offered the only way out to the growing lawlessness in the kingdom of Awadh.[28]

It is a persistent argument in both *Tilism* and *Sadiq-ul-Akhbar* that lawlessness, if any, has only increased after the Annexation. Instances of riots and plunder, murder, arson, thefts and dacoity find detailed narration in both the papers.[29] Presumably, there is an implied argument here that the British justification for Annexation on grounds of the deteriorating law and order situation were based on shallow claims. Referring to the failure of the British administration to arrest a dacoit by the name of Fazl Mir, the editor of *Sadiq-ul-Akhbar* suggests that the Company should, 'like the deposed ruler of Awadh', tie down all such dacoits to the 'network of favours and patronage', and fix a stipend fee for them. This is how, he says, the deposed king kept a large number of people obliged to him; and by benefiting them from his network of patronage, he prevented them from becoming criminals.[30] One can discern here a conscious attempt to compare the law and order condition in the post-Annexation period with the Nawabi period.

The papers provide interesting details about the British measures to combat the growing lawlessness. In March 1857 the *kotwal* of Lucknow ordered all dancing girls (*tawaif*) to furnish the following details about their visitors: (i) name, (ii) present residence, (iii) former residence, (iv) place of birth, (v) age and description, (vi) profession and amount spent.[31] On 23 September 1856, the Commissioner issued a long list of instructions, as given below, to the *thanedars*[32] and *faujdars*[33] of Lucknow with the intention of speeding up criminal justice:[34]

1. The reports of investigation submitted by the *thanedars* should be brief. 'Their task is to make investigations concerning the crimes committed and the cases registered in the court, not to write detailed reports'.

2. Cases placed before the court should be immediately presented and there should be no delay in the recording of statements.

3. In cases that are placed before the police-post (*thanas*), the *thanedars* should without delay record the statements of the plaintiff (*mudai*) and the witnesses. The clerks (*ahkaran*) should make all the investigations as to the veracity of the statements recorded. In cases of dacoity, robbery and theft, an estimate of the value of the goods stolen should also be recorded.

Perhaps with a similar intention of controlling the deteriorating law and order situation, a detailed list was prepared of the number of houses and *chowkidars* in each locality (*mohalla*).[35]

In so far as the revenue administration was concerned, it appears from *Tilism* that the land revenue demand was fixed very high. Raja Man Singh failed to meet the revenue demand, and, consequently, his entire property and belongings were confiscated and auctioned. His wife's repeated pleas, says *Tilism*, for a little more time were not heard.[36] In an attempt to collect as much revenue as possible, the Company encouraged the practice of revenue-farming, but when it was found to be counter-productive, an order was passed in August 1856 that in the settlement of revenue demand, the interests of existing proprietors (*qabizan-i hal*) would be duly considered. Those village proprietors who had lost their land to revenue farmers (*mustajirs*) could reclaim their land but by bidding a higher revenue.[37] From the *Sadiq-ul-Akhbar* it appears that the British revenue administration fostered new conflicts among the rural classes, especially between the *taluqdars* and the village proprietors (zamindars). The paper says: 'These days the market for legal suits is up. Every man is filling a suit against the other. They are wasting their money and filing the coffers of the government.'[38]

Another important aspect of British revenue administration that emerges from these newspapers is that the British farmed out the revenues from the markets.[39] The tax-farm did not always go to the highest bidder: one Sharaf-ud-Daula had his lower bid accepted as against the higher bid of an agent of the former Wazir, Ali Khan.[40] Merchants and traders were hard hit by the exactions of these farmers (*mustajirs*). In August 1856, an order was passed prohibiting the farmers from exacting illegal cesses.[41] Yet, in all probability these orders were not too effective. In August 1856 the traders and shopkeepers protested against the realization of cesses (*mahsul*) at two outposts, one in the city and the other at a place called Bahramghat, for the same commodities. When the Company refused to pay heed to their complaint, all the shopkeepers closed their shops in protest.[42]

Such organized protest action was displayed on another occasion too. We are told by the *Sadiq-ul-Akhbar* that in March 1857, when the English arrested a few moneychangers (*sarrafs*) on the charge of bribery, the shopkeepers staged a 'hartal' in their favour.[43]

The Urdu newspapers provide us with many fresh details about the conditions in Awadh on the eve of the outbreak of the Revolt of 1857. They indicate that resentment against the British government was widespread in Awadh. They also show that the British justification for the Annexation on grounds of deterioration in the law and order situation was far from credible. Contrary to the Company's claim that they improved law and other conditions in Awadh, our evidence shows that there were few bitter memories of the kingdom of Awadh and much resentment against the new order.

Notes and References

[1] Iqbal Husain, 'Lucknow between the Annexation and the Mutiny', *Journal of the Uttar Pradesh Historical Society*, Vol. 1, 1983.

In a subsequent work, Rudrangshu Mukherjee (*Awadh in Revolt, 1857–58: A Study of Popular Resistance*, Delhi, 1984) quotes from *Tilism*, but all his references appear to have been borrowed from Iqbal Husain's paper.

[2] National Archives of India (NAI), Mutiny Papers Collection Nos 4–6.

[3] Ibid.

[4] Rotocopies at the Centre of Advanced Study in History, Aligarh Muslim University, Aligarh.

[5] J. Murray, *A Lady's Diary of the Siege of Lucknow written for the perusal of Friends at Home,* London, 1858, p. 73.

[6] *Tilism,* Vol. 1, No. 41, 1 May 1857, pp. 1–2; ibid., Vol. 1, No. 42, 8 May 1857, pp. 1–2.

[7] *Dehli Urdu Akhbar,* Vol. 19, No. 10, 10 May 1857, p. 2.

[8] Ibid., Vol. 19, No. 10, 8 March 1857, p. 3.

[9] *Sadiq-ul-Akhbar,* Vol. 3, No. 4, 26 January 1857, p. 26.

[10] *Tilism,* Vol. 1, No. 26, 16 January 1857, p. 4.

[11] Ibid., Vol. 1, No. 28, 30 January 1857, pp. 1–2; ibid., Vol. 1, No. 33, 6 March 1857, pp. 1–2.

[12] Ibid., Vol. 1, No. 6, 29 August 1856, pp. 1–2.

[13] Ibid., Vol. 1, No. 26, 16 January 1857, pp. 1–2.

[14] Ibid., Vol. 1, No. 12, 10 October 1857, pp. 5–6.

[15] *Sadiq-ul-Akhbar,* Vol. 3, No. 4, 26 January 1857, p. 28.

[16] *Tilism,* Vol. 3, No. 4, 25 January 1857, p. 5. The queen mother's visit to London is also mentioned by Maulvi Masihuddin Khan Bahadur in *Oudh: Its Princes and its Government Vindicated* (1857), edited by Safi Ahmad, Meerut, 1969.

[17] *Sadiq-ul-Akhbar,* Vol. 3, No. 4, 26 January 1857, p. 28. *Tilism* also makes a reference to this in its detailed account of the queen's visit to London (Vol. 1, No. 12, 10 October 1856).

[18] *Tilism,* Vol. 1, No. 5, 22 August 1856, pp. 1–2; ibid., Vol. 1, No. 7, 5 September 1856, pp. 1–2; No. 8, 12 September 1856, pp. 1–2.

[19] Ibid., No. 7, 5 September 1856, p. 4.

[20] Ibid., Vol. 1, No. 22, 19 December 1856, p. 2.

[21] Ibid., Vol. 1, No. 25, 10 January 1856, pp. 1–2.

[22] Ibid.

[23] A religious festival of the shias to mourn the martyrdom of Imam Husian, the grandson of the Prophet of Islam.

[24] *Imam-bara* is a place where the image of the shrine of Imam Husain is kept and is visited with great veneration.

[25] *Tilism,* Vol. 1, No. 8, 12 September 1856, pp. 2–3.

[26] Ibid., Vol. 1, No. 22, 19 December 1856, pp. 1–2.

[27] Ibid., Vol. 1, No. 5, 25 August 1856, pp. 2–5.

[28] See, for example, W.H. Sleeman, *Journey through the Kingdom of Oude in 1849–50: The private correspondence relative to the annexation of Oude to British India and C.,* 2 Vols. D (London 1858), reprint, Lucknow 1989.

[29] *Tilism,* Vol. 1, No. 2, 1 August 1856, pp. 1–2; ibid., No. 6, 29 August 1856, pp. 2–5; ibid., Vol. 1, No. 11, 30 August 1856, p. 2; ibid., No. 12, 10 October 1856, pp. 1–2, 3–4 and *Sadiq-ul Akhbar,* Vol. 3, No. 12, 23 March 1857, p. 93.

[30] Ibid.

[31] Ibid.

[32] Officer incharge of the police post.

[33] Commandant of a territory, incharge of law and order.

[34] *Tilism,* Vol. 1, No. 15, 31 October 1856, p. 4.

[35] Faruqi Anjum Taban, 'Population of Lucknow in 1857: From Records in contemporary Urdu Newspapers', *Proceedings Indian History Congress, 55th Session,* Aligarh, 1994.

[36] *Tilism,* Vol. 1, No. 5, 22 August 1856, p. 6.

[37] Ibid., Vol. 1, No. 3, 8 August 1856, pp. 2–3.

[38] *Sadiq-ul-Akhbar,* Vol. 3, No. 11, 22 March 1857, pp. 84–85.

[39] *Tilism,* Vol. 1, No. 1, 25 July 1856, p. 3.

[40] Ibid., Vol. 1, No. 2, 1 August 1856, p. 5.

[41] Ibid., Vol. 1, No. 3, 8 August 1856, pp. 2–3.

[42] Ibid., Vol. 1, No. 5, 22 August 1856, p. 5.

[43] *Sadiq-ul-Akhbar,* Vol. 3, No. 12, 23 March 1857, p. 93.

Rebel Press, Delhi 1857

Shireen Moosvi

The hostility to the 'native press' that the British gave vent to after the outbreak of the Revolt may, by itself, be taken as indicative of the significant role played by the vernacular press in spreading disaffection towards the foreign government and, later on, in exhorting the rebels to persevere in their cause. Thomas Munro declared that 'free press', by its very nature, was 'antagonistic, above all, to foreign domination', since 'a free press, and the dominion of strangers, are things which are quite incompatible, and which cannot long exist together'.[1] Canning, in his complaint in June 1857, was more specific, alleging that, on the pretext of publishing news, the 'native press' was cleverly and craftily spreading seditious sentiments among the Indian people.[2]

There should, therefore, be no need to offer a special justification for a study of the Urdu newspapers published from Delhi before and during the Rebellion. The press, as well as its readership, of this erstwhile capital of the Mughals, had by then undergone the experience of British administration for over half a century. Also, the educated classes had received a whiff of the air of the Bengal Renaissance, and the establishment of the Delhi College in 1825, naturally became a conduit for modern ideas.

Quite a few newspapers began to be printed at Delhi after the liberalization of the press by Charles Metcalfe in 1835.[3] Out of these, only two, namely *Dehli Urdu Akhbar* and *Sadiq-ul-Akhbar* continued to be published regularly till the fall of Rebel Delhi in September 1857. The number of extant issues of both, however, are disappointingly few – a fact not, perhaps, surprising, given the savage reign of terror that was unleashed on Delhi by the British after their victory.

Of the *Dehli Urdu Akhbar*, which began to be issued from 1836 and appeared regularly until 13 September 1857, copies of only sixteen issues from 1857 have survived; these are available at the National Archives, New Delhi.[4] In addition to these, the Archives have issues of this paper for just one year, from 26 January to 12 December 1840.[5] More than one newspaper bearing the name *Sadiq-ul-Akhbar* was published from Delhi during the 1840s and 1850s, successively as well as simultaneously. This matter has been carefully explored by historians of Urdu journalism.[6] The National Archives have ten issues (all from 1857) of the *Sadiq-ul-Akhbar* edited by Jamiluddin Khan, and a copy of one issue of *Sadiq-ul-Akhbar* of 19 March 1857 which is very different in appearance from Jamiluddin Khan's paper. While Jamiluddin's *Sadiq-ul-Akhbar* was issued every Monday, the *Ishtihar* (Public Notice) of this *Sadiq-ul-Akhbar* from 19 march 1857 notifies that it was issued every Friday.[7] Atiq Ahmad Siddiqui rendered yeoman service to research on 1857 by publishing the transcriptions of all the issues of the Delhi weekly newspapers issued during the Mutiny as are available in the National Archives. These included the *Siraj-ul-Akhbar* (a Persian gazette issued by the Court) of 11 May, thirteen issues of *Dehli Urdu Akhbar* and seven issues of the *Sadiq-ul-Akhbar*.[8]

Given that so much work has already been done in respect of these newspapers, it is strange that William Dalrymple should make the following statement:

> No less exciting was it to discover that Delhi's two principal Urdu newspapers, the wonderfully opinionated *Dihli Urdu Akbhar* (sic!) and the more staid and restrained Court Circular, the *Siraj ul-Akbhar* (sic!), had continued publication without missing an issue throughout the Uprising, and that the National Archives contained almost complete sets of both.[9]

Very few assertions here are correct. The Court Gazette *Siraj-ul-Akhbar*, noted for its chaste Persian, was not an Urdu publication, and therefore could not have been one of the 'two principal Urdu newspapers'. With a copy of only one issue of this publication being available there, it is remarkable that a claim has been made that the National Archives have 'an almost complete' set of its issues. In this paragraph at least, Dalrymple forgets entirely the *Sadiq-ul-Akhbar* – the real Urdu rival of the *Dehli Urdu Akhbar*.[10]

Since the file of the *Dehli Urdu Akhbar* is the fullest among the extant Delhi newspapers from that period, I will first briefly discuss what we know about its history, and then offer an analysis of its contents during the time that the Rebels held Delhi in 1857.

The *Dehli Urdu Akhbar* began to be issued from 1837. By 1857, it came to be owned and edited by Maulvi Muhammad Baqir, a well respected Shi'ite scholar and a member of Delhi's educated elite, with access to the Court and much familiarity with the leading lights among the Urdu literati. Particularly friendly relations existed between him and the famous Urdu poet, Zauq. According to the print-line on all the surviving issues of 1857 it was 'printed and published' by Sayyid Abdullah, the Manager of the Dehli Urdu Akhbar Press. The press was located at Baqir's own house in Guzar Aitiqad Khan, near Panja Sharif. From a glance at the three pre-Mutiny issues, it appears that the *Dehli Urdu Akhbar* followed the practice of other contemporary Urdu newspapers (like the *Tilism* of Lucknow), in providing news drawn from government gazettes, other newspapers – both in English, such as the *Englishman*, and in Urdu, such as *Jam-i Jahannuma*, with unpaid freelancers supplying reports or information from other places by letters sent to the editor. In its issues of 1840 it also quoted the Bengali paper

Samachar Darpan, through the Calcutta-based Urdu paper *Jam-i Jahan Numa*.

Its coverage of news in the pre-Mutiny period was not confined to India. The extant issues from 1840 show the adoption of a fairly critical attitude towards British imperialism, which it clearly shared with parts of the Calcutta 'native' press. It admired the defiance exhibited by Muhammad Ali Pasha of Egypt against the British;[11] it proclaimed the wide unpopularity in Afghanistan of Shah Shuja, the puppet king installed by the British at Kabul[12] and criticized Britain's opium trade with China as well as her preparations for war with that country over the same issue.[13] At the same time, it welcomed the arrival of modern science and learning, and commended the graduates of the Delhi College on their success.[14] It also hailed advances made in modern medicine.[15] Even an examination of the three pre-Mutiny issues of March–May, 1857 shows the paper's concern not only with the events in the neighbouring countries of Kabul, Qandhar and Egypt, with England's war with Iran getting prime attention, but with events taking place in Europe (Firangistan) and England (Englistan) as well, keeping its readers informed on such matters as changes in the personnel of the British cabinet[16] or an attempt made on the life of the King of France.[17] Therefore, Dalrymple's statement that the paper remained concerned only with 'local political and religious matters' is absolutely erroneous.[18]

It is true that from the issue of 17 May, with Delhi having been cut off from the rest of the country by the English, and the postal system having been destroyed, the paper, naturally enough, could only report on events taking place in and around Delhi, or such other places about which the editor was able to learn either from people who had arrived from there or had sent communications by hand. This, of course, was not by choice: The issue of 17 May reports, in an account of the Cantonment, that the Englishmen looking after the postal system had been killed. Again, on 24 May, the editor laments that no arrangements for *dak* (postal system) had yet been made (by the rebel regime), so that it was difficult to get information from outside.

The three pre-Mutiny issues reflect, through some rather cursory reports, that a sense of popular disquiet prevailed. An abortive attempt at a sepoy uprising in Burma is reported in a rather neutral manner,[19] but an account of the happenings at Barrakpore and the disbanding of the 19th Native Infantary on 31 March 1857 on the basis of reports in the *Englishman* and letters from freelancers, are given in considerable detail.[20] The columns of 'Miscellaneous News' in all the three issues are full of reports of mysterious burnings of barracks, residences and stores of the Company at various places and the refusal of sepoys at different stations and outposts to accept the greased cartridges.

Even the issue of 17 May (published six days after the Rebel takeover) takes care not to explicitly reveal on which side its sympathies lay, but it is still exceptionally important because it contains the editor's detailed eyewitness (as well as hearsay) account of the events that took place in Delhi on 11 May and on the following days. The report is preceded by extracts from the Quran, and Persian and Urdu quotations on how God can make totally unforeseen events take place. The initial reaction to the Mutiny, as revealed by the first two issues of 17 and 24 May is, indeed, one of gleeful surprise on so sudden a turn of events that had led to the fall of the mighty English. There is no sympathy or compassion shown for the English, even for their women and children who were killed. In fact, a certain degree of unabashed pleasure is perceptible in the report on the killing of Nixon, the head of the 'Chancellery' and Taylor, the Principal of the Delhi College.[21] The terms used are almost invariably *Angrez* for the English and *Tilanga* for the rebel Sepoy. Yet, there is still no sense of the people of Delhi identifying with the Sepoys. There is a grudging approval of the Tilangis as they attacked and killed the English,[22] but also disapproval of their trigger-happy conduct when they killed a Khatri horseman or injured a vegetable vendor in Chandni Chauk.[23] The paper complains of the helplessness of the City Kotwal in maintaining law and order in the presence of the army of 'the Tilangis' that had descended upon Delhi. Reflective of this attitude is the poem that was composed by Muhammad Baqir's son, Muhammad Husain Azad (who, unlike his father, survived the Rebellion to join British service and become the first historian of Urdu literature). This was printed on the first page of the issue of 24 May, with the editor's special commendation, under the title 'Chronogram for this Instructive Revolution'. Recalling how great rulers and conquerors like Soloman and Alexander, cruel tyrants like Hajjaj, Chengiz, Halaku and Nadir, great epic heroes and sages, have all disappeared, the poem glories in the fact that, similarly, the English too, once so knowledgeable, so mighty, so cruel, have had their day. 'Nothing came of their knowledge, skill, wisdom and character: The *Tilangs* of Purab (present-day eastern U.P.) have done to death all of them here.' The wonder is: 'How every trace of the Christian rulers, despite their wisdom and foresight, has all of a sudden disappeared from amongst the people (*khalq*).'

However, from 14 June both the vocabulary and the attitude of the paper change. There is now a positive, even full-hearted, support for the Rebels. The *sipah-i diler* ('the brave army') the *Tilingan-i nar sher* (the lion-like Tilangis) are being enjoined, if Muslims, to take the name of Allah and the Prophet, and, if Hindus, to pray to Parmeshwar and Narain, while conducting their noble fight. The Sepoys are to follow the examples of Bhim and Arjun, of Rustam, Chingez, and Halaku, along with Timur and Nadir Shah, and defeat the English. Thus, the initial simple sense of wonder is now replaced by a great sense of sympathy with the Sepoys, and there is also a great anxiety to encourage them, in the name of both Hindu and Muslim traditions, in their battle against the English.

The terminology continues to change in accordance with the new spirit as the days pass: The Rebel Army becomes the *sipah-i-Hindostan* (the Army of India) and there are appeals to 'fellow countrymen' (*ahl-i watan*), 'dear compatriots' (*aziz ham-watan*), with specific exhortations for a united rallying of Hindus and Muslims. The English being Christians and so believing in the Trinity of God are held to be polytheists and infidels (*kafir*), while the Hindus being believers in 'Adi Purush' share the basic belief in One God with Muslims and so are close to them.[24] In view of this close proximity in belief, both Hindus and

Muslims are called upon to unite and fight and destroy the Christian English.

The next issue of 21 June recalls various grievances against the English: the utter lack of any respectable or gainful employment for Indians. The English rulers were not only of a different religion but also of a different race and speaking a different language. They cornered for themselves all the high offices and hoarded wealth which they did not spend in 'our country', but took it away to their own country, thus depriving 'our Hindustan' of its own wealth. It goes on to bemoan the lethargy and lack of industry on the part of the Indian upper classes, their practice of looking down upon business and artisanal professions and their reluctance to move out from their native places in search of better opportunities. It hopes that things will change and as the Rebel government expands its area of control, all competent persons will duly find employment under it.

The issue of 5 July is of special importance. It reproduces as the first item a copy of the *Ishtihar* (Public Notice) that was pasted on the Jama Masjid, allegedly by agents of the English, to 'threaten and mislead the citizenry and the army'. The Notice called upon Muslims to wage a 'holy war against Hindus', for the Christians were the natural allies of Muslims as 'People of the Book' according to the *Shariat*. It asserted that the rumour about the use of pig-tallow in the greased cartridges was totally false. The *Dehli Akhbar* declares this notice to be a conspiracy, the handiwork of enemies of both 'Dharm' and 'Iman' (the faith of Hindus and Muslims). The paper provides a point-by-point rebuttal of the pamphlet, sarcastically stating that the English should not try to deceive any one by invoking the *Shariat*.

In its later issues too the paper strongly espouses the perception that all Indians are one, while the English are absolute aliens.

Here it is necessary to correct certain misleading remarks made by Dalrymple about the reason behind the appeals for unity and resistance printed in the *Dehli Akhbar*. He tells us that 'Maulvi Muhammad Baqir included in his columns a call for the Hindus of the city not to lose heart – which of course implied that they were beginning to do just that'. He then goes on to give a passage in translation from a 'remarkable letter aimed at his Hindu readers'" published in the *Akhbar's* issue of 14 June.[24] The fact is that the appeal was addressed to *both* Muslims and Hindus, and Dalrymple's translation of the passage is doctored, deliberately omitting all references to Muslims. Without bothering about small inaccuracies, I reproduce below his translation, inserting in *italics* what he has omitted.

> O my countrymen, Looking at the strategy and devious cleverness of the English . . . and their overflowing treasuries you may feel disheartened and doubt that such a people could ever be overcome. But *those who are my Muslim brothers by faith, let them consider – if they are anxious and concerned out of worldly considerations –* to look at *their* [not 'your'] religious books, *such as the Qur'an, the Tafsir and Hadis,* and those who belong to the Hindu dharm [not 'my Hindu brothers'], let them [not 'you'], *by the light of their gyan (wisdom) and*

dharm (faith), illumine their hearts [not 'look into your Holy books'] *and first see* that except the Adipurush, the primaeval Deity, nothing is permanent."[25]

It can be seen from the above reproduction of what the paper actually wrote, that there is no sanction for the inference drawn by Dalrymple about the Hindus alone being addressed and, by implication, being suspected of a weaker commitment to the Revolt than the Muslims.

Even a lay reader would find, even in the last issue of the paper (13 Muharram = 13 September), the same spirit of defiance, and not the depressed resignation that Dalrymple ascribes to it.[26] The issue actually exists in two separate prints. Of one only the front page has survived. In both the prints, the news is carried that everywhere, from Banaras to Muzaffarnagar, the rebellion is enjoying successes. The readers are urged not to be demoralized from 'the long period' (*tulkashi*) of the struggle, a phrase used in both prints.

Dalrymple also quotes an English report (date not mentioned) purporting to be a translation of a letter from Muhammad Baqir to the effect that he had been persuading Bahadur Shah Zafar to make peace with the British, which Hakim Ahsanullah Khan was preventing. In this letter he is also reported as mentioning that there was much outrage among Muslims at the killing of five butchers by Hindu sepoys.[27] Whether such a letter was actually sent by Baqir or not cannot be established, since it is only an unsubstantiated allegation; but as far as the English are concerned, they did not treat him as their informer: he was seized and hanged, while Hakim Ahsanullah flourished.[28] The Rebels knew well enough that the Hakim was in league with the English. In the issue of 18 Zilhij/ 9 August, just after the Idu'z Zuha when the cow-slaughter issue came up, there is a report at the bottom of page 3 of the *Dehli Urdu Akhbar* that Hakim Ahsanullah Khan had been proved to be an agent of the English and so was arrested by 'the Victorious [Rebel] Army'.[29]

The *Sadiq-ul-Akhbar*, the other Urdu newspaper, was published by Sayyid Jamiluddin Khan at his own press, the Jamil Press, situated in Jamilpura alias Chauriwal, within the walled city. He was the owner–editor as well as the printer and publisher, according to the bottom line and the opening *Ishtihar* (Public Statement) appearing in every issue. Little is known about Sayyid Jamiluddin Khan except that earlier, in the early 1850s, he was associated with the Delhi branch of Lucknow's Mustafai Press (known for its newspaper *Tilism* published from Lucknow) as a scribe. Mustafa Khan, the owner of the Mustafai Press, brought out a newspaper called *Sadiq-ul-Akhbar* most probably in 1851 from Delhi, but it closed down some time in 1853. It seems that after the closure of that paper, Jamiluddin Khan established his own press and started his own paper under the same name in early 1854.[30] His paper's ardent support for the Rebels led to his being sentenced to three years of rigorous imprisonment after the fall of Delhi.[31] Nothing is known about his later years. Indeed, whether he survived his imprisonment – conditions were usually inhuman for such prisoners – cannot be ascertained.

Sadiq-ul-Akhbar was introduced in the trial of Bahadur Shah Zafar[32] and this bears testimony to the importance attached by the British to its role. The prosecution witness Chunni Lal described the paper as 'the most leading newspaper of Delhi, the articles in it were better written, and some being extracted from papers published in English, had more interest for the Mahommedans ... copies of it sold were certainly much more numerous than of any other native paper'. He also stated that 'it had an equal circulation amongst all classes capable of reading without distinction of caste'. Chunni Lal also characterized *Sadiq-ul-Akhbar* as the newspaper most hostile and inimical to the British.[33]

While the 'charge' of being anti-English is fully borne out by a perusal of the surviving issues of the paper from the Rebel period, the fact that all the issues of the newspaper after 20 April and before 6 July have been lost and that the last extant issue is that of 17 August makes it difficult for us to establish its initial reaction to the Rebellion and the changes in its attitude as the Rebel regime at Delhi took root – in the way we can do in the case of the *Dehli Urdu Akhbar*. However, one can say with some certainty that it remained consistent in two positions throughout the later stage of Rebel regime at Delhi: its loyalty and devotion to Bahadur Shah and its hostility to the British rule. It is possible that its resentment against British rule had earlier origins. In its issue of 26 January 1857, well before the outbreak of the Rebellion, it reports on the Anglo-Iran War and gives expression to a wishful expectation that the British would encounter failure in their military enterprise there. All the four extant pre-Mutiny issues are full of the Anglo-Iran War and comment on Russia's growing influence in Afghanistan and the support it might extend to Iran. It gleefully reports on the reverses suffered and the problems faced by the British in China as well as in Burma, by drawing upon the reports of the *Englishman*.

Within India, it gives a full account of Behrampore incident[34] and the resistance of the sepoys to the use of greased cartridges. It reports the occurrence of mysterious fires at the barracks and sepoy hospital at Ambala, extracting the report from a contemporary paper, *Koh-i-Nur*.[35]

The *Sadiq-ul-Akhbar*'s sympathy towards the deposed king of Awadh is made clear by the details it reports of the visit of the queen-mother to London, hoping for a favourable result. In its issue of 26 January it meticulously records the amounts borrowed by the Company from the deposed ruler of Awadh from 1833 to 1843, along with the rates of interest, and is apprehensive that perhaps Queen Victoria would only order the return of debt and not the throne.[36] It is very respectful in the words it uses for the ruling house of Awadh, in contrast to the *Dehli Urdu Akhbar* that merely refers to Wajid Ali Shah as the deposed *Gaddi Nashin* (occupant of the *gaddi*).

In its issue of 20 April 1857, the *Sadiq-ul-Akhbar* speaks up for the freedom of the vernacular press. It says: 'The mofussil English paper like the *Agra* and *Bombay Gazette* and others, have in all jealousy written that Indian newspapermen should not be allowed press freedom because they do not have sufficient knowledge and so kindle a fire which it is difficult to put out, that some manly sepoys after reading the *Sadiq-ul-Akhbar* become still more assertive; and so just as there are different laws for the English and Indians in many other matters so too there should be one in this regard as well.' After commending the *Englishman* for not subscribing to this view, the paper explains: 'Whatever news the *Sadiq-ul-Akhbar* publishes, exercising its freedom, is read by all, who can discriminate between truth and falsehood. If it was prevented from doing so by official prohibition, the news would nevertheless have spread as secret and done more harm...' On the very next page it carries a report on the sepoy unrest at Ambala and Sialkot, extracted from *The Friend of India*.

Owing to the absence of issues of the paper from the early days of the Mutiny, we can only track the opinions expressed by the paper from 6 July onwards. By now the Sepoys had apparently received some pay and were no longer a source of unruliness in the City. Whether the *Sadiq-ul-Akhbar*, in the early days of the Mutiny, had ever said, like the *Dehli Urdu Akhbar*, that the sepoys should be stationed outside the city walls, one cannot know. But now, in the later days of Rebel occupation, the paper found the Sepoy presence within Delhi very welcome, as providing 'splendour' to the city markets. In its 6 July issue the sepoys were still being referred to as *Tilangan-i Shahi* or *Sipah-i Sultani* or Royal Sepoys; but in August they are designated the *Sipah-i Hindustani* (Indian army) and *Afwaj-i Hindustan* (the Army of India).[37] This too corresponds with what occurred rather early on in the columns of the *Dehli Urdu Akhbar*. There is also much praise for Bakht Khan, the Rebel general of Delhi. In its issue of 27 July the paper describes him as 'the administrator of the age, General Bakht Khan, unrivalled in the dispensation of justice and equity, statesmanship and administration', and welcomes the fact that he had been made, by the order of the king, 'our gracious commander'.

The *Sadiq-ul-Akhbar* of 20 July relishes the fact that the English were overthrown not by others but by their own sepoys and, interestingly, adds that the royal charter (*theka*) given to them by Queen Victoria was, in any case, going to be terminated. It is strange that the editor of the paper should have been able to predict the fall of the Company which came about only the next year.

The English are dubbed *kuffar* (infidels), and all the *ahl-i watan* (fellow-countrymen) *ahl-i Hind* (people of India) and *Hindustani Bhai* (Indian brothers) were enjoined to destroy them and expel them from the country. The *Sadiq-ul-Akhbar*, in its issue of 3 August, records its sense of relief on the peaceful passing of the Idu'z Zuha and the fact that the issue of cow slaughter did not interfere with the amity between Hindus and Muslims as the English had hoped it would. Under the heading 'Thanks' (*Shukriya*) it writes:

> A thousand thanks to Almighty God that the auspicious day of the Id-i Qurban passed peacefully, despite the machinations of the mischievous opponents of religion, the irreligious English, and no dispute arose between Hindus and Muslims on account of cow-slaughter. Both communities remained united, like milk and sugar.

It gives all the credit, however, to Hakim Ahsan-ullah Khan for bringing about the prohibition of cow-slaughter, which eased the situation. (Rebel documents, preserved in the National Archives, however, show that it was Bakht Khan who strictly enforced the prohibition).[38]

From the issue of 27 July, the Christian era dates, so far carried along with the Hijri era dates by the paper, are replaced by the Samvat calendar and Hindi months – a deliberate attempt not only to shun any English connection but also to adopt a system of dating more familiar to the common people. The more intellectually oriented *Dehli Urdu Akhbar* had already, from 2 August onwards, shifted to using Hijri dates (alone) for its issues.

The last extant issue of the *Saddiq-ul-Akhbar* is that 17 August, a month ahead of the English occupation of the proud city. It still contains hopes of victory, and assures its readers that eighty thousand soldiers (*lashkar*) (thirty thousand from Bombay, three Companies from Punjab, an army from the hills, a contingent from Indore, the Gwalior contingent and sepoys from other directions) were getting ready to reach Delhi and once they arrived the English would be destroyed. One may dismiss this today as wishful talk, resulting more from a desire to encourage the Delhi rebels than any real belief in its truth. But it is possible that by now the paper's editor really believed it impossible for any sepoy to have remained loyal to British or indifferent to the fate of the Delhi rebels. The hope for succour from the Gwalior Contingent, at least, was not unreal: only the march of that famous Contingent was delayed, and, with the fall of Delhi, it turned back towards Kanpur where it overthrew General Windham in a famous battle.

The eventual fall of Delhi casts a tragic shadow over these rebel newspapermen (their editors and their usually anonymous freelance reporters) and their readers. Their demise and destruction marked not only the end of Rebel Delhi, but also the end of the Delhi Renaissance that had produced these early pen-pushers of freedom.

Notes and References

[1] Margarita Barns, *The Indian Press*, London, 1940, p. 251 (quoted from the Minutes of Lord Elphinston, Governor of Bombay, dated 24 June 1857.

[2] M. Donogh, *History of Law and Sedition*, New York, 1952, p. 183.

[3] Nadir Ali Khan, *Urdu Sahafat Ki Tarikh, 1822–57*, Aligarh, 1987, pp. 73–159 mentions six newspapers: *Mazhar-ul-Haq, Akhbar Fawaid-ul-Shaiqeen, Siyad-ul-Akhbar* and *Geti Numa*, besides *Dehli Urdu Akhbar* and *Sadiq-ul-Akhbar*, the papers that have been studied here.

[4] The extant issues available at the National Archives of India (NAI) are of following dates: 8 March, 12 April, 10, 17, 24 and 31 May, 14 and 21 June, 5, 12 and 19 July, 2, 9, 16 and 23 August and 17 September. Four of these, beginning from 12 July, appeared under the changed name *Akhbaruz Zafar* written on top in ornamented hand with *Dehli Urdu Akhbar* inscribed below it, the last three issues, from 16 August onward, no more carry the previous name and only bear the title *Akhbaruz Zafar*.

[5] The transcribed texts of these issues of 1840 have been published by Khwaja Ahmad Farooqi, *Dehli Urdu Akhbar*, Delhi, 1972. Files for 1851–54 are available at Adabiyat-i Urdu, Hyderabad (Muhammad Atiq Siddiqui, *Suba-i Shumali wa Maghribi ke Akhbarat wa Matbuat*, Aligarh, 1963, p. 102).

[6] M. Atiq Siddiqui, *Hindustani Akhbar Nawisi*, Aligarh, 1957.

7 NAI, *Mutiny papers 1857*, Collection No. 4–6. The ten issues are of the following dates: 26 January, 16 and 23 March, 16 April, 6, 20 and 27 July and 3, 10 and 17 August.

8 M. Atiq Siddiqui, *Atthara Sau Sattawan ke Akhbarat wa Dastawezin*, 17, 24 and 31 May, 14 and 21 June, 5, 12 and 19 July, 2, 9, 16 and 23 August and 13 September.

9 *The Last Mughal: the Fall of a Dynasty*, Delhi, 1857, p. 14.

10 Dalrymple refers it only once, *Last Mughal*, p. 215.

11 Khwaja Ahmad Farooqi, *Dehli Urdu Akhbar*, Delhi, 1972, p. 78.

12 Ibid., p. 103–04 and passim.

13 Ibid., p. 90.

14 Ibid., p. 192.

15 Ibid., p. 230.

16 *Dehli Urdu Akhbar*, 12 April 1857.

17 Ibid., 10 May 1857.

18 *The Last Mughal*, p. 86.

19 *Dehli Urdu Akhbar*, 8 March 1857.

20 Ibid., 12 April and 10 May.

21 Ibid., 17 May.

22 Ibid., 23 May (Account of the City).

23 Ibid.

24 Ibid., 14 June.

25 *Last Mughal*, pp. 268–69.

26 Ibid., p. 346.

27 Ibid., pp. 301–02.

28 Ibid., pp. 375–76.

29 The report was true. The Hakim was, however, released at the intervention of Bahadur Shah.

30 *Nadir Ali Khan, Urdu Sahafat Ki Tarikh*, Aligarh 1987, pp. 402–03.

31 Muhammad Atiq Siddiqi, *Hindustani Akhbar Nawisi*, Aligarh, 1957, pp. 143–44.

32 *Trial of Mohd. Bahadur Shah, Ex-king of Delhi*, Government Press, Lahore, 1928 (reprinted as *The Trial of Bhadur Shah Zafar*, ed. Pramod K. Nayar, Hyderabad, 2007). Ten out of the fourteen extracts of newspapers produced by the prosecution were from different issues of the *Sadiq-ul-Akhbar* (out of these issues those of 19 March, 11 May and 24 August are no more available) and three are from the *Dehli Urdu Akhbar*.

33 Ibid., pp. 141–42.

34 *Sadiq-ul-Akhbar*, 16 March 1857, p. 84.

35 Ibid., p. 85.

36 Ibid., 23 March 1857. It may be mentioned here that besides its freelance correspondents it mentions (in its Pre-Mutiny issues) official gazettes and other English and Urdu newspapers such as *Friend of India, Morning Chronicle, Englishman, Lahore Chronicle, Central Star* (Lucknow), *Kashiful Akhbar, Jam-i Khurshid* (Meerut) and *Koh-i Nur* as sources of its news.

37 Ibid., 10 August.

38 Order of Bakht Khan dated 8 *Zil hij* 1273 (30 July 1857), facsimile and transcription published in, Atiq Siddiqui, *Atthara Sau Sattawan Akhbar Aur Dastawezin*, p. 315.

The Rebel Administration of Delhi

Iqbal Husain

The Revolt of 1857 in Delhi has been a subject of much interest among historians of modern India. Some of them have, rather incidentally also discussed the rebels's efforts at establishing a working administration of Delhi. Perceive Spear has assigned some pages in his *Twilight of the Mughals* to the travails of the rebels within Delhi. A detailed study of the administration of Delhi under the rebels, is, however, long overdue. An attempt is made here, to discuss the type of administration the rebels set up in Delhi by setting out whatever information is available, in a chronological order. Unless directly relevant to our theme, details of Court politics and intrigues by princes and other members of the Royal family, have been avoided.

Delhi was occupied by the rebel sepoys on 11 May. The rebels foisted upon Bahadur Shah the responsibility of administering the country.[1] Indeed, the need for firm administration immediately asserted itself. Taking advantage of the sudden disappearance of British rule from Delhi, the bad characters and plunderers began to loot the people in the guise of sepoys. Five of them were apprehended and thrashed by the rebel sepoys and were sent to jails.[2] Some of the sepoys also seem to have joined in the plunder of the jewellers, *baniyas* and even petty shopkeepers such as sweetmeat sellers, as there was no leadership to control them.[3] Many of the plundered people appealed to the King for protection.[4] The developments were so rapid and unprecedented that it was beyond the capabilities of Bahadur Shah, already bereft of power and resources, to control declining law and order in the city. On 12 May the condition of the city worsened. Munshi Jiwan Lal, the British spy, tells us that the unwilling king was distracted by the cries and petitions. The servants of the Europeans, shopkeepers, rich people whose houses had been plundered, all appealed to him for redress.[5] Bahadur Shah was keen to restore order and summoned Mirza Ziauddin Ahmad Khan, Aminuddin Ahmad Khan and Hasan Ali Khan (uncle of the nawab of Jhajjar) to form an Executive Council to maintain law and order in the city. Hasan Ali Khan's direct refusal foiled the King's attempt at restoring order in the city.[6] As an alternative, Mirza Moinuddin Hasan Khan, on the recommendation of Hakim Ahsanullah Khan[7] was directed to restore order in the city and its suburbs.[8] These measures were hardly enough to satisfy the terrified people, specially the shopkeepers, to resume their occupations. On being persuaded (or rather pressed) by the rebels, Bahadur Shah personally visited the city, making appeals and giving assurances to the shopkeepers for their safety and asking them to resume their business.[9] The King's personal appeals also did not restore the confidence of the shopkeepers and they kept their shutters down.[10] On the other hand, disputes between the rebels from Meerut and Delhi over the distribution of plunder posed a new problem. The King on returning from a round of the city found the agitated sepoys occupying the courtyard of the *Diwan-i Khas*.[11] The rebels, unaware of the Court's etiquette, addressed the King in a manner, which was deemed disrespectful.[12] The behaviour of the rebels and their conduct in the city led Mirza Ghalib to explain that they (rebels) reduced to dust both the honour and mansions of those who were distinguished for their wisdom and good name, while those who had neither power nor pelf shot into prominence. Men of valour were scared of their own shadows, and mere troopers ruled over all and sundry.[13]

On 13 May, Mirza Moinuddin Hasan Khan was appointed Kotwal of Delhi and head of the Commissariate in the city. But this was a mere formality. Reports of rapine and plunder continued to come into the fort. Bahadur Shah shut himself up and refused audience to all on 14 May.[14] Delhi remained at the mercy of the individual rebels and plunderers in the guise of rebels. Similar conditions prevailed even within the Fort, the King's abode. A regiment of Native Infantry occupied the fort and placed its own guards without an officer to command them.[15]

On 15 May, another effort to raise a police force of 100 men for the 'safety' of the city failed to yield any result.[16] Yet Bahadur Shah, with all his limitations, was trying to restore order and punishing the offenders connected with the imperial service.[17] To strengthen the city administration, he appointed Qazi Muhammad Faizullah and Abdul Hakim as city Kotwal and Naib Qazi for the administration of justice.[18] These attempts fell short of the requirement to control the plunder as well as reining in some of the sepoys, who were openly disobeying the orders of the civil authorities.[19] Apart from attempting to strengthen the city administration, endeavours were also being made to raise troops. Accordingly, on 15 May, orders were issued to recruit horsemen at a salary of Rs 30 and infantry at Rs 10 per mensem.[20]

The fast declining law and order situation necessitated the formal involvement of the princes in undertaking military responsibilities in order to contain the uncontrolled elements in the city. Bahadur Shah assigned various offices to them.[21] Mirza Muhammad Jawan Bakht was appointed wazir of the empire (perhaps on paper, practically he did not function), and Mirza Zahiruddin Bakht (Mirza Mughal) was appointed 'Commander-in-Chief' of the forces (infantry, cavalry and other branches of army). Mirza Abul Hasan alias Abdullah, Mirza Sohrab, Mirza Muhammad Khizr Sultan, Mirza Kochak Sultan and Mirza Muhammad Abu Bakr were assigned different military positions.[22] The expectation, perhaps, was that their royal prestige would enable the princes to enforce authority over the rebels. But none of the princes had the ability to discharge the responsibility with competence. Moreover, soon intrigues and conspiracies among the rival factions of the princes further distracted the fledgling administration. The princes began to exert such authority as they obtained, by proceeding to violate all norms of regular administration. In the meantime, the sepoys captured the King's private office. They placed guards on the *Diwan-i Khas* and substituted the King's personal staff with their own.[23] Bahadur Shah was thus surrounded by the sepoys.

It is not yet clear that how the princes reacted to the new situation. Their silence, however, suggests their connivance behind the capture of the King's office.

Armed with new authority, the princes' greed for money encouraged their troopers to exact money from the leading bankers of the city. In one of the petitions, two *mahajans*, Jugal Kishore and Sheo Prasad, drawing the attention of the King urged him to prohibit all the princes, particularly Mirza Mughal, Mirza Khizr Sultan, Mirza Abu Bakr and Mirza Abdullah, from deputing *Tilangas* or sepoys to their residences for realizing money. They also requested the King for deputing soldiers (*Najibs*) for their protection.[24] Though the King ordered Mirza Mughal to comply with the request,[25] its implementation, however, seems doubtful.

On 16 May 1857 the King appointed Mufti Yusuf Ali Khan, Mir 'Adl Bahadur, Captain Dildar Ali Khan Bahadur, Saiyid Sharif Ali Khan *Faujdar* and Nazrul Khan Bahadur to assist the administration.[26] But the law and order condition of the city remained far from satisfactory giving annoyance to the King. Even the King's servants, such as Kashi Nalei, a *thanedar*, pressurized the shop-keepers to pay him bribes. On receiving complaints, he was ordered to be sent to the prison.[27]

On 18 May, another attempt was made to placate the princes by defining their ranks. The princes, Mirza Mughal, Mirza Khizr Sultan, Mirza Abu Bakr and Mirza Abdullah were appointed to different commands over the rebels.[28]

On 21 May, some of the city bankers raised a sum of Rs 1 lakh for payment to the sepoys.[29] Still the plunder of the people continued for they were supporting different princes. Even the King's servants, were not spared. The princes remained indifferent despite continuous complaints. Bahadur Shah was shocked over this state of affairs.[30] The passive attitude of the princes, whose responsibility was to maintain law and order in the city, added to the miseries of the people. Faced with the continuous disorderliness of the sepoys, Bahadur Shah gave orders to Mirza Mughal to direct them not to move within the city.[31]

On 24 May, Bahadur Shah was informed of the plight of the English prisoners under the control of the sepoys. Expressing his helplessness over the prevailing conditions he asked Mirza Mughal, Mirza Abdullah and Khizr Sultan to ensure the release of the prisoners and to look after them properly[32] as their execution was contrary to the religious texts expounded by the Prophet.[33]

A number of the rebel soldiers had collected a considerable amount of wealth through loot and plunder during the rebellion in Delhi. Some of them left the city with their booty, but because of being looted on the way, they returned once again, only to add to the existing problems.[34] Those who stayed in the city began to change their silver into gold coins for the purposes of hoarding. This resulted in a doubling of the price of gold coins in Delhi, from Rs 16 to Rs 32. Many soldiers, in their attempts to change their silver coins with gold ones, were duped. Counterfeit gold coins gained wide circulation in the market and the government had to issue a proclamation asking the soldiers to desist from making such purchases. The duped soldiers, much chagrined over the loss of money, began to plunder innocent people to recoup themselves.[35] The princes only saved such rich persons as bribed them, and the general population was thrown at the mercy of the plunderers.[36] Bahadur Shah once again expressed the desire to retire to the tomb of Khwaja Bakhtiyar Kaki at Mehrauli.[37]

In the prevailing state of confusion and disorder, Bahadur Shah issued a proclamation by the beat of drum that a *batta* would be levied on Company's coins (*Putti Shahi*). The residents of Delhi were also warned not to give shelter to mischief mongers in their houses; and in case of any incidents, the offenders were threatened with being blown through the guns.[38] On 25 May, coins in the name of Bahadur Shah were introduced under the care of Munshi Ayodhya Prasad and a mint was established at Kara Mashro.[39] By 31 May, the *Dehli Urdu Akhbar* reported that some order was restored in the city due to the exertion of the Kotwal.[40]

Most of the sepoys being out of their regiments, they began to mount pressure for the payment of their salaries. On 28 May a sum of Rs 1,75,000 arrived from Rohtak. Orders were issued to pay the salary of the sepoys. But Mahbub Ali Khan's attempt to pay Rs 9 and 7 against the promised Rs 30 and Rs 10 to the cavalry and infantry resulted in violent protests from the troops. The situation was saved by the timely intervention of the King's servants. Later on, the cavalry was persuaded to agree to a payment of Rs 20 per month.[41]

While the affairs of the soldiers were to some extent settled, the civil servants working in different branches of administration had little relief. At the end of May, there was no indication of disbursement of their salaries. The *Dehli Urdu Akhbar*, heralding their views, urged the government to arrange payment of their salaries and to save them from hunger. It also appealed to the government to keep the *Tilangas* (sepoys) under control.[42] The Imperial treasury remained empty and the government faced acute financial difficulties. On 1 June, Girdhari Lal and Girwar Singh, the two leading bankers, were asked to advance a loan of Rs 3 lakhs. They yielded to the demand for fear of their lives and property.[43] Still the amount fell far short of what was needed. On 3 June, all the *mahajans* of the city were summoned to the Fort. The houses of those who avoided to respond the summons were surrounded by the troopers.[44] Under compulsion, the bankers paid Rs 1 lakh and promised to advance another sum of Rs 1 lakh within four days.[45] Salik Ram, Zor Awar Singh, Raja Bhole Nath, Aramji Ramji Mal, Gaurwala, Munshi Sultan Singh and Mathura Das assured the king that a regular supply of money would be provided in the future.[46]

Apart from the normal functioning of the administration, the city municipal administration also suffered on account of increasing filth and lack of hygiene.[47] The worst affected *mohallas* were Kucha Raiman, Ballimaran, Kucha

Malik Attar etc. The miseries of the people were further increased when the water carriers stopped attending to their regular duties.[48] The grocers and grain merchants added to the miseries of the people by creating an artificial scarcity of food-grains and other essential commodities. The prices of all the essential goods were skyrocketing. The *Dehli Urdu Akhbar* laments over the state of affairs, quoting the rates of various commodities and complaints of adulteration in ghee, oil and flour etc.[49]

Bahadur Shah was regularly receiving such distressing news. Fed up with the total breakdown of the administrative machinery, he summoned the princes and wished to proceed to Mecca for *haj* and pass his remaining life there. The princes, apparently moved by the King's gesture, assured him of their sincere involvement in restoring normalcy to the administration.[50] The situation however, did not improve. On 1 July, Jugal Kishore and Sheo Prasad, mahajans, petitioned to the King for protection against the princes.[51] The King ordered Mirza Mughal to desist from such acts in future. But the King's orders were, as usual, ignored.[52]

In the meantime, Bakht Khan,[53] appeared on the scene on 2 July 1857. He was 'an artillery subahdar of 40 years experience' who had served in the first Afghan War. It appears that he had entered Delhi soon after the revolt and had become a regular visitor to the Court. He had established his position among the sepoys and to some extent, also enjoyed the confidence of Bahadur Shah. He was honoured with the title of 'Bakht Baland Khan'.[54] Yet the circumstances were such that Bakht Khan always suspected the King and the princes of dealing secretly with the English. He, therefore, persuaded the King to send the princes on expeditions so as to keep them away from the court.[55]

The collapsing civil and military administration needed immediate reform. The more responsible elements in the army, undoubtedly influenced by the British army organization and institution, set up a 'Court" to eliminate mismanagement and restore order. How far Bakht Khan was responsible for the formation of the Court is not hard to understand. The Court was to function on a written twelve-point programme. According to this programme, the Court was to consist of ten 'members' (*membran*). Of them, two were to be elected from each of the three wings of the army, i.e. the infantry, cavalry and artillery. The Court was to have one 'President' (*Sadr-i Jalsa*) and a 'Vice-President' (spelt *vais-president* and also styled *naib-Sadr-i Jalsa*), who were to nominate two members (one by each of them). The English words used for these two officers of the Court are noteworthy. The President, enjoying the right of a casting vote (literally, two votes) had a clear edge over other members including the Vice-President. The members of the Court were to work selflessly for the welfare of the people and the Empire. It was to function under the care of 'Commander-in-Chief', Mirza Mughal (the English word 'Commander-in-Chief' is used). All decisions were subject to his assent. In case of disagreement on any matter, the decision of the King was to be considered final and binding upon all. The King had the right to attend the meetings of Court. All decisions concerning civil and military affairs were to be taken by a majority of votes.[56] The Court thus clearly represented the influence of English constitutional ideas on the minds of the sepoys.

In the beginning, Bahadur Shah seems to have had high hopes from this court. To meet the expenses of the army, Prince Mirza Mughal was pressing Bahadur Shah for money, who politely declined to meet the demand due to an empty treasury and lack of sources of income. He wrote to the Prince that he expected a decision soon by the Court on financial matters to run the administration.[57]

But it seems that to a large extent the Court also remained a paper organization. It could hardly successfully exercise its powers to maintain law and order. Prince Mirza Mughal, being the President of the Court and Commander-in-Chief, continued to interfere in the affairs of the Court and violate its orders. Under these conditions, Bakht Khan's offer to enforce general discipline was greatly valued by Bahadur Shah. Bakht Khan held a long meeting with Mirza Mughal and secured for himself the appointment of 'Commander-in-Chief' (whereby he also became President of the Court). Mirza Mughal was elevated to the position of 'Adjutant General'.[58] A proclamation was issued directing all officers to obey the orders of Bakht Khan.[59] Realizing that the princes would continue to interfere in administrative affairs, Bakht Khan secured the king's mandate to deal with them severely if they once again indulged in plunder.[60] On the same date, the King issued elaborate instructions to Bakht Khan directing him to take the following actions. First, to destroy the position of the English; second, to remove the infantry and cavalry occupying the fort and the city forbidding them sternly from plunder and rapine; third, to find out an immediate solution for the disbursement of salaries of the old (*qadim*) and new (*jadid*) servants; fourth, to make suitable arrangements for revenue collection and setting up of *thanas* outside the city for checking plunder; and fifth, to punish the sepoys and imposters moving in the garb of sepoys and committing plunder of the houses of the gentry (*shurafa and najaba*).[61]

Bakht Khan made vigorous efforts to restore law and order. His task was difficult. The rebellion had evoked great apprehensions among the former *jagirdars*, pensioners and *madad-i ma'ash* holders residing in and around Delhi. Most of them, therefore, secretly sympathized with the English, and some of them were also working as the enemy's spies. Bakht Khan immediately issued an order allaying their fears and assuring them that their grants and daily allowances would be maintained even after the rebels' victory. He also assured them that all the losses which they suffered at present would be made good. However, he warned them of severe punishment if caught spying or supplying provisions to the enemy.[62] Bakht Khan also attempted to allay the fears of the shopkeepers via a proclamation, made to the beat of a drum, asking them to keep arms at their shops. Shopkeepers having no arms were asked to obtain them from the headquarters. Severe punishment, such as severing of limbs, was prescribed for sepoys caught thieving and plundering. The general public was advised to surrender their arms, failing which they were threatened with punishments. Bakht Khan also inspected the magazine and ordered the stores and materials to be arranged properly.[63]

Bakht Khan's initiative greatly impressed Bahadur Shah. On 3 July 1857, he gave him absolute authority to make arrangements for civil and revenue administration. To make the work easier, the princes were relieved of all military duties. The emergence of Bakht Khan to such prominence, however, made the princes jealous, for they were in no mood to concede to his authority. A letter with the King's forged signature was sent to Bakht Khan, censuring him. But the King's denial of having written such letters (11 July) cleared the misunderstanding between them.[64] Though Bakht Khan enjoyed absolute power in revenue affairs, a levy of eight *annas* per maund on sugar was imposed without his knowledge (12 July). He got the tax withdrawn on the ground that it was bound to affect regular supplies to the city causing great distress to the people and soldiers.[65] Similarly, he got the salt tax abolished.[66] These steps were clearly intended to secure the confidence of the people.[67]

The administrative reforms, however, did not bring adequate income to the exchequer to meet the financial difficulties. Bahadur Shah remained under constant pressure from the sepoys to provide them salaries. Despite financial problems, Bahadur Shah was unwilling to raise the income through 'irreligious' means. He, therefore, did not allow Ayodhya and Thakur to set up wine shops in Delhi (19 July).[68] On 23 July, he also rejected the proposal of Moti Ram to re-impose taxes on salt (Rs 1 per maund), edible oil (12 annas per maund), burning oil (4 annas per maund) and sugar (8 annas per maund).[69]

The British, expelled from Delhi after 11 May 1857, were striving hard to recapture power. Their agents became quite active in Delhi as the festival of *baqar-id* approached. Rumours gained wide circulation among the Muslims alleging that the sepoys, majority of whom consisted of Hindus, were objecting to Muslims calling for *azan* (prayers) from the roadside mosques, and that they would not allow the performance of their obligatory practice of slaughtering of big animals. Such rumours fuelled communal tensions and led to a breach in communal harmony in the city and its suburbs, resulting in the killing of four butchers. To maintain communal harmony proclamations were issued prohibiting cow slaughter, warning the offenders of severe punishment.[70] The proclamations were resented by a section of the Muslims. Considering it an act of interference in their religious freedom, they declared a holy war. But they were persuaded by Bahadur Shah to withdraw their agitation through the efforts of Mufti Sadruddin (31 July 1857).[71]

The prevalence of disorder in Delhi adversely affected trade and commerce. In one of the petitions to Bahadur Shah, some traders of Delhi (Haider Baksh, Haji Moula Bakhsh and fifteen others) pointed out that due to the rebellion, they had suffered heavy losses, their trade with places such as Kanpur, Banaras, Calcutta, Ambala and Lahore etc., had already been ruined and they had become destitutes. Over and above this, Mirza Mughal had demanded Rs 50,000 from them and upon their expressing the inability to pay, he placed guards outside their houses, blocking their movements. They were not allowed even to offer their 'Eid' prayers.[72]

On 28 August, from four rich persons of Delhi, Ramsee Mull (brother of Umed Singh, the Mir Munshi of Indore state), Sa'adat Ali, Agha Jan (former Mir Munshi of Rajputana) and Zorawar Chand (*sahukar*) money was demanded, and to make the demand effective, their water and food supplies were stopped pending compliance.[73] Ironically, Bakht Khan could not forge discipline and order in the army ranks owing to the underhanded intrigues of the princes. Conflict between 'General' Sidhari Singh (under the influence of Mirza Mughal) and Bakht Khan divided the army in Delhi. It was further weakened due to conflict between the Sikh soldiers and the sepoys, most of whom came from eastern U.P. and western Bihar – generally called *Purabia*.[74]

By the end of August, several attempts had been made to reform the administration through transfers and adjustments of the powers of the princes and that of Bakht Khan. Theoretically, Bahadur Shah commanded supreme authority, but in practice, he held very little power. Regular defiance of Bakht Khan's orders and the failure of the attempted reforms kept Delhi in the grip of disorder. A petition sent by the members of the Court to Bahadur Shah reveals how the princes were exacting money from the *mahajans* and interfering in the affairs of the Court. The members of the Court urged Bahadur Shah to direct the princes to not violate the Court's order in future.[75]

Efforts made by Bahadur Shah, the Court and Bakht Khan to restore administration and introduce reforms were foiled by the princes' self-interest. Bakht Khan lost much of his time and energy in checking the princes' intrigues, who were often oblivious to the grave danger to which the rebels were exposed. Although, theoretically, Bakht Khan enjoyed absolute power to deal with the princes, he remained hesitant to take any action against the princes fearing further problems. Bakht Khan might have succeeded in providing a more viable administration in Delhi had he been free from such constraints. The wonder is that despite these difficulties, Bakht Khan and his sepoys offered such a spirited defence of Delhi, for such a long time. As for the citizens' loyalty to the rebel cause, it needed no better certificate than the general slaughter of them decreed by the victors.

Notes and References

[1] Cf. G.B. Malleson, *The Indian Mutiny of 1857* (reprint) Delhi, 1977, p. 84. However, Abdul Latif, *1857 Ka Tarikhi Roznamacha*, edited by K.A. Nizami, Delhi, n.d., pp. 119–20, says that the British Resident asked Bahadur Shah to assume responsibility in order to restore order in the city.

[2] *Dehli Urdu Akhbar*, 24 May 1857, reproduced in Atiq Siddiqui, *1857 ke Akhbar aur Dastavezen*, Delhi, 1965, p. 45; *Roznamacha*, p. 23; Moinuddin Hasan Khan, in *Two Native Narratives of the Mutiny of Delhi*, translated by C.T. Metcalfe, Delhi, 1974 (reprint), pp. 41–53.

[3] Abdul Latif, *1857 Ka Tarikhi Roznamcha*, p. 123; Metcalfe, *Two Native Narratives of the Mutiny of Delhi*, pp. 41–53.

[4] Abdul Latif, *1857 Ka Tarikhi Roznamcha*, p. 123.

[5] Jiwan Lal, in Metcalfe, *Two Native Narratives of the Mutiny of Delhi*, p. 86.

[6] Ibid., p. 85. Abdul Latif says that Miyan Nizamuddin, Khan Jahan Khan, Iradat Khan, Mufti Sadruddin Khan and Karam Ali Khan were also present in the meeting. See Abdul Latif, *1857 Ka Tarikhi Roznamcha*, p. 123.

[7] A renowned physician of Delhi since the days of Akbar Shah II. Bahadur Shah raised his honours conferring several titles. Peoples of Delhi looked upon him with suspicion. He gave evidence against Bahadur Shah. See H.L.O. Garret, The *Trial of Bahadur Shah Zafar*, 1932, pp. 256–82.

[8] Abdul Latif, *1857 Ka Tarikhi Roznamcha*, p. 123.

[9] *Dehli Urdu Akhbar*, 17 May 1857, refers to the appointment of Mufti Sadruddin as *Sadr-i 'ala*, Maulvi Abbas Ali and Karam Ali Khan as Munsif criminal and civil court.

[10] Metcalfe, *Two Native Narratives of the Mutiny of Delhi*, p. 86.

[11] *Dehli Urdu Akhbar*, 17 May 1857.

[12] Jiwan Lal says that the King was addressed, 'Are buddhe sun'; (O! oldman, listen) etc. See Metcalfe, *Two Native Narratives of the Mutiny of Delhi*, pp. 86–87. The *Dehli Urdu Akhbar* in its issue of 17 May 1857 reported that the Red Fort looked like a military cantonment.

[13] *Dastanboo*, cited by K.M. Ashraf in *Rebellion of 1857*, edited by P.C. Joshi, Delhi, 1957, p. 249.

[14] Metcalfe, *Two Native Narratives of the Mutiny of Delhi*, p. 89.

[15] Ibid., pp. 55–56; *The Dehli Urdu Akhbar*, 17 May 1857.

[16] Metcalfe, *Two Native Narratives of the Mutiny of Delhi*, p. 91.

[17] Ibid.

[18] Ibid., p. 92. Abdul Latif writes that Qazi Faizullah was appointed Kotwal on 17 May, Abdul Latif, *1857 Ka Tarikhi Roznamcha*, pp. 124–25.

[19] Metcalfe, *Two Native Narratives of the Mutiny of Delhi*, pp. 57–58. On 24 May 1857, the *Urdu Akhbar* published the news of the plight of the people of Delhi who continued to suffer at the hands of the plunderers, who moved freely in the guise of Tilangas.

[20] Delhi Proclamation, May 1857, cited in Charles Ball, *The History of Indian Mutiny*, Vol. I, 1859, p. 495. Also in, *Freedom Struggle in Uttar Pradesh*, Vol. I, Lucknow, 1957, pp. 438–39. Jiwan Lal writes that the infantry was to be paid Rs 5 per month. See, Metcalfe, *Two Native Narratives of the Mutiny of Delhi*, p. 92. It may be pointed out that before the revolt, the salary of a sepoy serving the Company was Rs 7 and a cavalry man got between Rs 21 and Rs 30 (S.N. Sen, *Eighteenth Fifty-Seven*, Delhi, 1958, p. 22) at a later date the King, under the pressure of the rebels, issued a proclamation inviting the services of sepoys and cavalry in the Company's employment offering Rs 30 and Rs 50 per month. See Metcalfe, *Two Native Narratives of the Mutiny of Delhi*, pp. 60–61.

[21] Earlier (on 11 May) the King had directed Mirza Mughal, Mirza Abdullah and other princes to help restore order in the city. See *Siraj-ul Akhbar*, 11 May 1857, pp. 11–12, Delhi.

[22] *Press List of Mutiny Papers*, National Archives of India (NAI), Delhi, Vol. 13, No. 1, May 1857, pp. 16–22. Jiwan Lal gives two more names, viz. Mirza Bakhtawar Shah and Mirza Sidu Beg. See, *Two Native Narratives of the Mutiny in Delhi*, p. 58. Sen refers to Mirza Mughal only. (S.N. Sen, *Eighteen Fifty Seven*, p. 74).

[23] Metcalfe, *Two Native Narratives of the Mutiny of Delhi*, p. 60.

[24] *Press List of Mutiny Papers*, NAI.

[25] Abdul Latif tells us that the King being unhappy over the conduct of the princes asked them to work for the welfare of the people as ordained by God. See, Abdul Latif, *1857 Ka Tarikhi Roznamcha*, p. 124.

[26] Metcalfe, *Two Native Narratives of the Mutiny of Delhi*, p. 93.

[27] Ibid., pp. 93, 94–95.

[28] Ibid., p. 96. On 24 May 1857, the *Dehli Urdu Akhbar*, published a detailed report of prevailing disorder in Delhi.

[29] Metcalfe, *Two Native Narratives of the Mutiny of Delhi*, p. 99.

[30] Abdul Latif, *1857 Ka Tarikhi Roznamcha*, p. 126.

[31] *Akhbar Deorhi Khan Darbar-i Mualla*, 22 May 1857, *Press List of Mutiny Papers*, No. 2, SN, 22, NAI.

[32] Abdul Latif, *1857 Ka Tarikhi Roznamcha*, pp. 127–28.

[33] *The Dehli Urdu Akhbar*, 31 May 1857; Metcalfe, *Two Native Narratives of the Mutiny of Delhi*, p. 100; *Press List of Mutiny Papers*, No. 2, SN, 22, NAI.

[34] Abdul Latif, *1857 Ka Tarikhi Roznamcha*, pp. 127–28.

[35] Metcalfe, *Two Native Narratives of the Mutiny of Delhi*, p. 101.

[36] *The Dehli Urdu Akhbar*, 24 May 1857; *Press List of Mutiny Papers*, Call No. 1, No. 21, NAI; Abdul Latif, *1857 Ka Tarikhi Roznamcha*, pp. 127–28, refers to the King's conversation with the princes advising them to win the goodwill of the subjects by good work.

[37] Abdul Latif, *1857 Ka Tarikhi Roznamcha*, p. 129; Metcalfe, *Two Native Narratives of the Mutiny of Delhi*, p. 122; *Dehli Urdu Akhbar*, 24 May 1857.

[38] *The Dehli Urdu Akhbar*, 24 May 1857.

[39] Abdul Latif, *1857 Ka Tarikhi Roznamcha*, p. 129. The coins so minted carried the couplet:
Sikka zad dar jahan ba fazl-i Ilah
Shah-i Hindustan Bahadur Shah.

[40] *Dehli Urdu Akhbar*, 31 May 1857.

[41] Ibid.

[42] *The Dehli Urdu Akhbar*, 31 May 1857.

[43] Metcalfe, *Two Native Narratives of the Mutiny of Delhi*, p. 111.

[44] *Press List of the Mutiny Papers*, No. 63, SN 4, dated 3 June 1857, NAI.

[45] Metcalfe, *Two Native Narratives of the Mutiny of Delhi*, p. 113; Abdul Latif, *1857 Ka Tarikhi Roznamcha*, pp. 133–34.

[46] Abdul Latif, *1857 Ka Tarikhi Roznamcha*, p. 134.

[47] *Press List of the Mutiny Papers*, No. 61, SN 43, NAI; *Dehli Urdu Akhbar*, 14 June 1857.

[48] *Dehli Urdu Akhbar*, 14 June 1857.

[49] Ibid.

[50] Ibid.

[51] He belonged to Sultanpur (Awadh), Uttar Pradesh. Jiwan Lal refers to his conversation with Bahadur Shah where Bakht Khan traced his descent to the Awadh rulers. During the revolt, Bakht Khan joined the rebels, abandoning his employment with the Company. His rapid rise caused jealousy among the princes. He distinguished himself during the siege of Delhi and fought with great determination. When the British forces surrounded the city and the fall of the city became imminent, he suggested that Bahadur Shah accompany him in order to continue the struggle from outside. After the fall of Delhi, he disappeared and could not be caught despite the best efforts by the British forces. See Metcalfe, *Two Native Narratives of the Mutiny of Delhi*, pp. 146–47; Ghulam Rasul Mehr, *1857 Ke Mujahid* (Urdu), n.d., pp. 104, 119; Intizamullah Shahabi, *East India Company aur Baghi Ulema*, Delhi, n.d., pp. 72–76; S.N. Sen, *Eighteen Fifty Seven*, Delhi, 1958, pp. 83–84.

[52] According to S.N. Sen and Percival Spear, Bakht Khan appeared before the King on 2 July 1857 (S.N. Sen, *Eighteen Fifty Seven*, p. 83; *Twilight of the Mughals*, reprint, Delhi, 1969, p. 208). However, Abdul Latif mentions his date of arrival as 26 May 1857 which is incorrect. Bakht Khan moved from Bareilly after 31 May 1857 (see Abdul Latif, *1857 Ka Tarikhi Roznamcha*, p. 129).

[53] See Metcalfe, *Two Native Narratives of the Mutiny of Delhi*, p. 130.

[54] *Press List of the Mutiny Papers*, Bundle No. 539–40, No. 57, NAI. Sen suggests that the Court was formed in the second week of May (Sen, *Eighteen Fifty Seven*, p. 75). Documentary evidence, however, suggests that the Court was established much later. See *Press List of Mutiny, Papers*, No. 57 (Misc.), No. 35, NAI. For a detailed discussion of the Court's functions see Talmiz Khaldun (pseudonym of Sourin Roy?) '*The Great*

Rebellion', edited by P.C. Joshi, *Rebellion 1857 – A Symposium*, Delhi, 1957, pp. 36–62. The author of this paper is, however, in disagreement with some of the conclusions drawn by Khaldun about the Courts' functioning.

55 *Press List of Mutiny Papers*, No. 153/1, 8 July 1857.

56 *Press of Mutiny Papers*, No. 146, SN 16, NAI. Also see, Abdul Latif, *1857 Ka Tarikhi Roznamcha*, pp. 142–43.

57 Jiwan Lal writes (2 July) that the 'King said it was no use his giving orders, as they were not obeyed, and he had no one to enforce them. . . .' Metcalfe, *Two Native Narratives of the Mutiny of Delhi*, p. 134.

58 Ibid., pp. 134–35; *The Dehli Urdu Akhbar*, 12 July 1857 reported that the King also granted a sum of Rs 4,000 to Bakht Khan for sweetmeats (*shirini*).

59 Metcalfe, *Two Native Narratives of the Mutiny of Delhi*, p. 134. Spear says that the title of 'Lord Governor General' *Sahib-i Alam Bahadur*, was also inferred on him. See, Spear, *Twilight of the Mughals*, p. 213.

60 Ibid., pp. 134–35.

61 *The Dehli Urdu Akhbar*, 12 July 1857. Jiwan Lal says that Bakht Khan informed the Kotwal of the city that 'if any plundering took place he would be hanged' (Metcalfe, *Two Native Narratives of the Mutiny of Delhi*, p. 135).

62 *The Dehli Urdu Akhbar*, 12 July 1857.

63 Metcalfe, *Two Native Narratives of the Mutiny of Delhi*, p. 135. *Sadiq-ul Akhbar*, dated 6 July 1857, reported that the appointment of Bakht Khan greatly increased the confidence of the people. The shopkeepers began to open their shops and there was no scarcity of provisions due to regular supply from outside the city. The city administration also became active. The Kotwal and *thanedars* took regular rounds of the city.

64 Metcalfe, *Two Native Narratives of the Mutiny of Delhi*, p. 144.

65 Ibid., pp. 149, 152.

66 Ibid., p. 152. Zakaullah says that Bakht Khan also offered five *bighas* of land to the descendants of soldiers who laid down their lives in fighting against the British. See, *Tarikh-i Uruj-i Sultanat-i Englishia Hind (Urdu)*, Delhi, 1904, p. 682. Jiwan Lal elsewhere says that Bakht Khan had obtained the King's assent that the wounded soldiers should receive pension as well as grant of land. See Metcalfe, *Two Native Narratives of the Mutiny of Delhi*, p. 146.

67 Bakht Khan's popularity is reflected from the fact that, *Sadiqul Akhbar*, 27 July 1857, gives a historical *masnavi* praising Bakht Khan.

68 Abdul Latif, *1857 Ka Tarikhi Roznamcha*, pp. 149–50.

69 Ibid., p. 150. On 25 August, Baldeo Singh's request for securing the *mahals* of Delhi on farm, with promises of regular supplies and payment to the imperial servants was rejected (ibid., p. 165).

70 The ban orders were vigorously enforced. See, the proclamations of Bahadur Shah and Bakht Khan reproduced in original in S.A.A. Rizvi, *Swatantra Dilli* (Hindi), Appendices 1, 2, 3, 5, 7 and 8. Sen is doubtful about the implementation of the prohibition order (Sen, *Eighteenth Fifty Seven*, p. 93, n. 67). Also see Abdul Latif, *1857 Ka Tarikhi Roznamcha*, pp. 153–54, for some details of the communal issue raised at the time.

71 Jiwan Lal, the British spy, says that on 19 May 1857 some of the local Muslims in Delhi attempted to raise the standard of holy war, to the great annoyance of Bahadur Shah. See, Metcalfe, *Two Native Narratives of the Mutiny of Delhi*, p. 95; Abdul Latif, *1857 Ka Tarikhi Roznamcha*, pp. 153–54.

72 *Press List of Mutiny Papers* (n.d.), No. 166/377, NAI.

73 Ibid., No. 19, SN 5, 8 August 1857.

74 *Press List of Mutiny Papers*, No. 19, SN 5, 8 August 1857, NAI.

75 Jiwan Lal, vide Metcalfe, *Two Native Narratives of the Mutiny of Delhi*, p. 183.

76 *Press List of Mutiny Papers*, No. 57, SN 352, NAI.

The Profile of a Saintly Rebel: Maulavi Ahmadullah Shah

Saiyid Zaheer Husain Jafri

Maulavi Ahmadullah Shah happens to be a well-known figure of the Rebellion of 1857. British Officers who had performed the task of crushing the uprising in the province of Awadh speak in respectful terms of his personal qualities and organizing capacity. Apart from these memoirs, the dispatches of British officials on the day-to-day occurrences bear out the exceptional courage and valour displayed by him during the years 1857–58.[1] Most modern studies tend to rely heavily on these accounts.[2] Little attempt had been made, however to utilize his versified biography[3] in Urdu composed by Fath Muhammad Taib, who became a disciple of Ahmadullah Shah in 1856 and thus came to have a substantive idea of his career during those years. Similarly, the reports in the contemporary newspapers and the short notices in the lesser known works of his contemporaries have also escaped the notice of historians.[4]

From the documentary and literary evidence available in Arabic and Urdu one can reconstruct Ahmadullah Shah's life and obtain many details, otherwise not known, of his role in the Rebellion. This will also be helpful in understanding the popular uprising.

I

Saiyid Ahmad Ali Khan alias Ziauddin, titled Dilawar Jang, was a son of Nawab Muhammad Ali Khan of Chinapattan (Madras). Born in the second decade of the nineteenth century, he received, as a prince, the best education of the time. We are told that during his childhood he won warm commendations from his teachers for his exceptional memory, intelligence and industry. After the completion of studies in the classical languages and traditional Islamic sciences, he received extensive training in the art of warfare.[5] He seems to have acquired some knowledge of English as well. As an enterprising young prince his fame reached far and wide. He visited Hyderabad as a guest of the Nizam in connection with some marriage proposal, and though the proposed marriage did not take place, he stayed in the city for quite some time. His biographer tells us that he undertook an expedition on behalf of the Nizam to coerce some rebellious Raja into submission. The details of the expeditions are revealing, as they indicate his preference for deceptive methods of warfare.[6] But such spectacular success also earned him a number of enemies. In a surprise move, the jealous courtiers planned an attack on his person, but fortunately he escaped unhurt.[7] The British officers at Hyderabad formally requested his father to allow him to visit England. Thereafter, he proceeded to London, where he had the opportunity of meeting the King as well as the notables of that kingdom. His biographer, Fath Muhammad Taib has not provided the details of his stay at England, except the fact that he was allowed to display his skill in the use of arms at his own request.[8] On his way back to India, he stopped at Mecca[9] and Medina, then passing through Iraq, he reached Iran, where the king wanted him to join his service, but he declined the offer and proceeded to India.

By the time he was back in India, he became inclined towards mysticism and after an intense search for a *sufi* guide, became a disciple of Saiyid Furqan Ali Shah, a saint of the *Qadri* order at Sanbhar (Rajasthan).[10] He remained with his *pir* for some time to get initiated into the doctrines of the order. From here he was directed by his spiritual guide to proceed to Gwalior. Now, he was called Ahmadullah Shah by his Shaikh, the title by which he became known afterwards.

At that time Gwalior happened to be in the 'jurisdiction' (*wilayat*) of another *sufi* saint of the *Qadri* order, Mehrab Shah Qadri.[11] After some initial hesitation, Ahmadullah Shah was initiated by him in the creed a second time. In the company of the new *pir* he spent at least four and a half years, roaming in the vicinity of Gwalior since the new initiation entailed practical training and the propagation of *jehad* or 'Holy War', as part of a new strategy, and was directed to go to Agra. Mehrab Shah is said to have given him a new name, Waliullah, but this did not gain currency.

Probably as part of a strategy, audition parties were arranged in a big way so as to attract crowds and preach the call for *jehad*. Although the *Qadris* are averse to the very idea of audition parties, we find that sermons were delivered after these parties were over calling upon people to be ready for *jehad*.

Another contemporary testimony about his activities in Agra is worth reproducing:

> (Ahmadullah Shah) arrived at Agra with a large number of *murids*. He took a palatial house at rent, kept *naqqaras* at the gate, the drums were beaten five times a day. As his popularity grew, many more became his *murids*. Audition parties (*majalis-i qawwali*) were arranged. I also became a frequent visitor at his place.[12]

It was generally believed that 'neither fire can burn his disciples, nor sword can do any harm to them'. During the course of these audition sessions, the Shah was fond of practising meditation for long durations by way of holding his breath (*habs-i dam*). It was on one such occasion that Shah told the author of *Khawariq-i Mastan* that, 'from this date after six months, there will be great disturbance in the territories of the government'.[13]

From Agra, Shah left for Aligarh to meet Raja Mursan. He stayed in the 'sarai of Ratan Lal and the Raja made an offering (*nazr*) of two hundred and fifty rupees in cash, one highly prized horse and two hunting dogs. The author of these lines 'too had the occasion to visit Aligarh and meet Shah there'. Shah told him about his intention to go to Lucknow, 'where he will sit on the throne and issue his own coins, the whole army will obey him and the treasure will also be under his control'.[14]

It seems that at Agra he was very vocal in pleading for *jehad*, hence complaints were lodged with the British authorities to the effect that, 'he is a *derwesh* only in name, actually he is a prince and is preparing the masses to wage a war against the government'. No action was initiated against him, instead the complainants themselves were made to suffer.[15]

Sometime afterwards he went back to Gwalior to discuss the future course of action. By this time, the incidents at Hanumangarhi and the assassination of Maulavi Amir Ali in course of his call for *jehad* had come to be widely known and this might have influenced Ahmadullah Shah. In any case, he decided to proceed to Lucknow, the capital city of the recently annexed kingdom of Awadh, where he arrived in November 1856. His arrival in the city was reported in *Tilism*, the weekly newspaper of Lucknow, on 21 November 1856, in the following manner:

> These days a person called Ahmadullah Shah in disguise of a *faqir* but having all paraphernalia of royalty has arrived in the town and stayed in the *sarai* of Mutamad-ud Daulah, now has shifted to Ghasiyarimandi. . . . People of the town visit him in a large number on Mondays and Thursdays to take part in the mystic gatherings (*majalis-i-hal-o-qal*). A number of feats are performed in midst of these gatherings . . . such display takes place every morning and evening for the viewing of the masses. . . .[16]

The impact of these gatherings on the population of Lucknow can be gauged by the next report of *Tilism* which appeared two months later. On 30 January 1857 it was reported that:

> Ahmadullah Shah in Ghasiyarimandi is very fearless in saying whatever he wishes to say and a large crowd is always there, often Maulavi Amiruddin Ali is remembered. Although he is unable to do anything, orally he always pleads for *jehad*.[17]

It appears that in January 1857, alongwith a group of chosen followers, he decided to launch a surprise attack on the Christians when all of them gather together on a Sunday (in a Church?). But his followers could not adhere to the time schedule. The plan failed and the news was leaked to the British.[18] The *kotwal* was sent to him asking him to give up the call of *jehad* and to surrender the arms and ammunitions. But the Shah replied:

> Since you (*kotwal*) are also a Muslim and if you follow the *shari'at*, then *jehad* is obligatory even on you. Likewise, I also consider *jehad* obligatory for me, but for want of means (to carry on the struggle) I have not been able to undertake it. Otherwise I am quite ready for it.[19]

The *kotwal* was not convinced, and the British administration thought it necessary, to post some sepoys to check the inflow of the visitors and to record their names as well.[20] At the same time, orders were issued to the *thanedar* of Chinibazar for putting curbs on his activities. Finally, Shah was forced to leave the town and to go elsewhere along with his arms.[21] Such an order was not resisted by him, although we are told by Taib that 'Thousands of *Telingas* (sepoys) used to come there (in the audition parties) and have a discussion with him and go away'.[22]

Ahmadullah Shah now left Lucknow, apparently for Bahraich, along with ten or twelve men (in other reports only with five or seven men). A stop was made at Fyzabad, where he stayed in the *chowk sarai*. Here, once again, he started preaching for *jehad*.[23] Hardly two or three days had passed since he began delivering the sermons, that the authorities got alarmed as a '*chuprase* informed the magistrate of the rather dangerous nature of this man's doings. Accordingly, the officer incharge of the city issued the necessary orders for his arrest. The principal terms demanded from the Maulavi were that he and his armed followers (numbering about seven), should give up their weapons, which should be kept in safe custody. . .; further, that all this preaching and distribution of money, so conducive to disturbing the peace, should be put to an end. A deliberate refusal was afforded to every attempt of coercion, early next morning an infantry company . . . attacked them . . . these fanatics fought fiercely.'[24]

Ultimately, the Shah was arrested and placed under guards in the cantonment as he was considered too dangerous a character to be kept in the city jail. After a brief trial he was imprisoned in the district jail at Fyzabad.[25]

II

With the outbreak of mutiny at Fyzabad on 8 June 1857, the gates of the prison were broken open and Ahmadullah Shah was chosen by the mutineers as their leader, the notables of the town presented themselves before him and offered *nazar*. On assuming leadership, he issued orders for the destruction of the temples of Hanuman garhi, reportedly built on the orders of Wajid Ali Shah, the deposed king of Oudh at the site of a destroyed mosque. The Mahants of Hanuman garhi are reported to have offered the British assistance and 'exerted themselves to keep the troops steady'.[26] It was natural for the Hindus to feel alienated, therefore they thought of withdrawing their support to him as, 'just now he is planning for the destruction of *garhi*, nothing can be predicted for the future'. The difference of opinion among the officers of the sepoys over the question of leadership was also made known to Shah. Therefore, he left for Lucknow. Nevertheless, at the final reckoning, forgetting these apprehensions the sepoys joined Ahmadullah's forces. Consequently, at the time of the battle of Chinhat, he commanded both the Hindu and Muslim sepoys of Fyzabad.[27]

With the Battle of Chinhat began the second phase of the Shah's career. Now, he was a busy commander of forces, planning the attacks on the British positions and strengthening rebel defences. Since most of these details are quite well known and, moreover, Syed Mouinul Haq has fully utilized the information of Taib's *masnavi*, there is little need to repeat these facts; still there are quite a few aspects which should be highlighted in order to understand his mission.

The first engagement of the Shah with the British forces took place at Chinhat when the British made a surprise attack in the morning hours of 30 June 1857. The columns were hurriedly organized and Ahmadullah Shah and his contingent distinguished themselves in hand-to-hand combat, they even captured many assault guns. In inflicting a crushing defeat on the British, the Shah played a very significant role. He wanted to take full advantage of the confusion in the British camp, but other leaders failed to realize the importance of such a strategy. The Shah's contingent was left alone to pursue the enemy. Taib bitterly complains that it was due to the lack of joint action at the decisive moment that the English were able to consolidate their position. Regardless, the Shah led an assault on the English fortification (Residency) and suffered a bullet injury. But he remained undeterred, yet 'there was need for the cannons and the balls, not of the lances and swords; therefore, the Shah had to beat the retreat and fixed his quarters at Tara Kothi. This continued to be his headquarters for quite some time'.[28]

Taib also pointed out the reasons for the early estrangement between Shah and Prince Birjis Qadar. He recalls that as a result of the military victory against the British, the sepoys as well as the army commanders had become very arrogant, causing many hardships for the inhabitants of the city, and even the people of means were being plundered indiscriminately. This lawlessness on the part of the sepoys was objected to by the *mujahideens* who brought the matter before the Shah. Thereupon it was decided that a leader should be chosen to check the indiscipline and disorderly conduct of the sepoys. Quite contrary to his expectations, the army leaders decided in favour of prince Birjis Qadar. The Shah reacted sharply to this. His plea was that since *jehad* could be conducted only under the leadership of an *imam*, it was necessary that the creed of the *imam* should be the same as that of *mujahideens*; moreover, *jehad* is not obligatory for the *shias*, so by declaring Birjis Qadar as the leader, the most important ingredient of a *jehadi* was missing. Therefore, the fight against the British could no longer remain a battle waged for religion. The *mujahideens* could fight only in self-defence. Further, since the *mujahideens* had offered the stiffest resistance to the British, they had an inflated sense of self-importance. Also, the Shah had arrived to fight at the behest of his *pir*, and the leadership should have been conferred upon him.[29] However, this seems have been only a theoretical position taken by the Shah, for, practically speaking, he did lend full support in attacking the Residency. At the request of Barkat Ahmad, his disciple and the commander of the Fyzabad contingent, he personally participated in an assault on 'Baily Guard'. In this attack, a bullet pierced his right hand.[30]

Taib broadly confirms the general impression that at Lucknow, the British position was threatened by two separate factions having conflicting and even contradictory interests. The military leaders frequently changed sides, and shifted their loyalties from one camp to another. But after the British capture of Lucknow, the Shah became the main rallying point of the anti-British forces, so a joint venture to fight the British was proposed by prince Birjis Qadar. The Shah readily agreed. In the ensuing fight, halfway through, the forces of the prince withdrew, leaving the *ghazis* to face the cannon fire of the English. Ultimately, the Shah was forced to retire to the palace at Gaughat. In this battle also he was severely wounded and one of his disciples, Nur Ahmad, had excelled in the fight.[31]

The occupation of Gaughat probably gave some kind of strategic edge to Shah over the rival camp. Consequently, a siege was laid on his position by the prince's forces, but he refused to fight these 'new adversaries as he never wanted to fight Indians, since he thought of himself as their leader and guardian. The siege went on for ten days, without affecting the morale of the *mujahideen*, the prince's army commander made another plea that treasure was buried in the palace and its vacation will help the distribution of the salaries of the soldiers. The request was readily conceded though it is needless to point out that treasure story was a hoax'.[32]

The common soldiers had the utmost respect and consideration for the Shah, and whenever he thought of going somewhere else, they prevailed over him to change his mind. The entire responsibility of opposition to him, lay with the sepoy leaders.

At the same time, it must be conceded, that the unruly mob of sepoys was hardly under any one's control. Sharaf ud-daulah, one-time prime minister of Awadh was suspected of treachery, and so the sepoys arrested him and wanted to execute him. The Shah did not approve of this, therefore, for the time being he was put in prison. However, he was killed there. Taib absolves the Shah from any responsibility of his murder and says that had this been his intention, none of the conspirators would have escaped.[33]

A murderous assault was made on the Shah during his morning walks. However, the target was missed. And in spite of the Shah's wishes to the contrary, the assassin was killed by his bodyguards.[34]

Unable to hold ground at Lucknow, Ahmadullah Shah decided to withdraw with his small following towards Sitapur and establish his quarters at Bari. Hazrat Mahal (the mother of Birjis Qadr) also thought it expedient to join him. Although the initial response of the Shah was cautious, ultimately he agreed. Taib insists that after reaching Bari, prince Birjis Qadar had the honour of offering *bay'at* (spiritual allegiance) to the Shah. The arrangement put the entire management in the Shah's hands, he forced the officers of the Begum to part with their wealth. This would certainly have caused some resentment. Therefore, when the Shah decided to make a surprise attack on the Gorkha army of Nepal returning after much plunder, his new allies ditched him. As a result, the *mujahideens* were left alone in the assault. One Sa'adullah distinguished himself during this assault. Many acts of valour and chivalry were performed by his supporters.[35]

After suffering considerable losses at Bari, the Shah was forced to retire to Muhammadi. Here a last bid was made to take a firm stand against the British. Although his health was deteriorating very fast, he remained the guiding spirit behind all the planning and execution done by the army. But Taib says that here he demanded the total support of the sepoys and the army commanders before deciding upon any future course of action. He sought to arrange the supply of the ammunition for his forces. Accordingly, an envoy was sent to Nawab Bahadur Khan of Bareilly for the supply of lances. Although, we are told, the envoy was received courteously, lances were not arranged as they were needed by the Bareilly regiment itself.[36]

At Muhammadi the Shah declared himself to be the independent ruler. The coronation is said to have taken place on 15 March 1858, and coins were also struck with the following legend:

> The slave of Mehrab Shah struck his
> Coins in the seven countries;
> A supporter of the faith of Muhammad is
> King Ahmadullah.[37]

No such coins seem to have survived. The measure was probably announced to boost the sinking morale of the fighting forces. We also hear that at Muhammadi he received many rebel leaders, like Azimullah Khan, prince Firoz Shah, Nawab Bahadur Khan of Bareilly, and one Ismail Khan under the banners of the Shah. Besides these generals some sixteen thousand sepoys also gathered there.[38]

Taib has given many details of the military campaigns of Ahmadullah Shah in the Rohilkhand region.[39] Finally, we have a first-hand account of the death of the Shah at Pawayan and the consequent situation in the region. Offered by Maulana Fazle Haq Khairabadi, who was an eye witness on the occasion, it is worth reproducing:

> With the innocent *amil*[40] (Ahmadullah Shah) most treacherous game was played by an infidel (*kafir*) rustic *zamindar*. On oath he had promised that when both the armies came face to face (Shah's army and the British forces) he would support the Shah along with a contingent of four thousand brave soldiers. As a result, the guns and the cannons sprayed fire from the front, while stabbing was done at back by this treacherous, hypocratic *zamindar* and his contingent. In fact, they were acting at the behest of the Christians. They had become friends of the Devil. Consequently, that God worshipping *amil* attained martyrdom in the battlefield itself, and many of his supporters followed the suit. After the martyrdom of these (brave men), the cowardly supporters fled from the battlefield only to be slaughtered by their Christian pursuers. Hence, all the inhabitants became obedient to the Christian rule. Two faithful commanders gave a very tough battle inspite of the fact that they did not posses the sufficient war material, still the enemy was killed in thousands. . . . This was the last of the saddest incidents, and heralded the end of the war. . . .[41]

A large number of documents have been reproduced by Abrar Husain Farooqi relating to the assassination of the Shah by Raja of Pawayan, from the reports of the British officers, one gains an impression of the sense of relief they obtained after receiving the news. The Raja received a cash reward of Rs 50,000.[47]

Before the outbreak of the mutiny, Maulavi Ahmadullah Shah carried forward a systematic propaganda to emphasize the need for *jehad* in the United Provinces and Awadh. This call to wage a religious war had a considerable impact on the popular mind. We know for certain at least about Agra, Aligarh, Lucknow and Fyzabad. At the same time, he cannot be considered a lone preacher, for, certainly, a significant role must have been played by people like Saiyid Furqan Ali Shah and Mehrab Shah Qadri in this direction. Unfortunately, very little is known about these figures. Such an intense propaganda bore the desired result, as all the English officers were unanimous in saying that the most 'fierce fight was given by the fanatics or the *jehadees,* who entered the battle field crying *din! Din!*'.[43]

Notes and References

[1] See for example, G.B. Malleson, *A History of the Indian Mutiny,* Vol. III, London, 1878–80, pp. 541–44; J.W. Kaye, *History of the Sepoy War in India 1857–58,* London, 1880; J.J. MacLeod Innes, *Lucknow and Oude in the Mutiny,* London, 1896; G. Hutchinson, *Narrative of the Mutinies in Oude,* Calcutta, 1859.

[2] S.N. Sen, *Eighteen Fifty-seven,* New Delhi, 1957; Rudrangshu Mukherjee, *Awadh in Revolt, 1857–58, A Study of Popular Resistance,* Delhi, 1984. A biographical sketch has been attempted by Gautam Bhadra, 'Four Rebels of Eighteen Fifty-seven', *Subaltern Studies IV,* edited by Ranajit Guha, Delhi, 1985, pp. 263–75, but like R. Mukherjee he too was not aware of an important versified biography of the Shah.

[3] Fath Muhammad Taib, *Tawarikh-i Ahmadi,* Lucknow, 1925. The author of this *masnavi* (composed in AH 1280/AD 1863) was a landed aristocrat of Lucknow and had become a disciple of Ahmadullah Shah in 1856. On the instruction of Mehrab Shah Qadri of Gwalior, the spiritual guide of the author's *pir,* he composed this *masnavi.* The work is divided into 40 sub-sections, and the main discussion on the activities of Ahmadullah Shah is confined to sections 11 to 35, but the verses are numbered in continuation. For the purpose of precise reference, the numbers of the verses have been cited. This edition has been reprinted with extensive notes and a useful introduction by Abrar Husain Farooqi, as *Mirat-i Ahmadi,* Hardoi, 1973.

[4] Although, in English works, Ahmadullah is invariably referred to as Maulavi or Maulavi of Fyzabad, to be in tune with Taib the epithet 'Shah' has been retained in this article. Syed Moinul Haq, in *The Great Revolution of 1857,* Karachi, 1968, made full use of Taib's account but unfortunately had no access to the weekly newspapers located in Indian archives and libraries. Similar is the case with a number of important Urdu works, for example, Intizamullah Shahabi, *East India Company our Baghi Ulema,* Delhi, n.d.; Ghulam Rasool Mehr, *Atharah Sau Satawan ke Mujahid,* Lahore, 1957, Mufti Intizamullah Shahabi, *Ghadr ke Chand Ulema,* Delhi, n.d. Abrar Husain Farooqi, in his *Masir-i Dilawari,* Lucknow, 1965, utilizes all the evidence about Maulavi Ahmadullah Shah with a number of photoplates of rare documents. See also Muhammad Ayub Qadri, *Jang-i Azadi 1857 Waqi'at aur Shakhsiyat* (Urdu) Karachi, 1976, pp. 525–40 for a fairly comprehensive account of the Shah's activities.

[5] Taib, 7: 551–67.

[6] Ibid., 8: 580–96. It is said that on reaching the territory of the defiant chieftain (the name of the Raja and area could not be ascertained) he left the soldiers in the neighbouring forest across the river and entered the territory of the Raja in the disguise of a wandering ascetic. Soon the fame of the 'holyman' reached the Raja who paid a number of visits to him. Thus, he was able to persuade him to go for an outing in the neighbouring forest, where the army was camping. The Raja was made captive and could secure his release only after submission.

[7] Ibid., 8: 597–632.

[8] Ibid., 9: 644–66.

9 Ibid., 9: 674–90.

[10] Saiyid Furqan Ali Shah belonged to a family of *madad-i maash* holders of Sanbhar, since the Mughal period. For sometime, he had been in the service of Maharaja Ram Singh of Jaipur. He was initiated into the mystic order of the *qadris* by one Shah Hafizullah of Khatav (Nagpur district), who in turn was a disciple of Shah Habibullah Qadri of Lahore. (This information was obtained by one Mirza Abdul Hafiz Beg, Superintendent Rajasthan *Waqf* Board, Jaipur during the course of a field survey conducted in November 1969.) Cf. Abrar Husain Farooqi, *Mirat-i Ahmadi*, pp. 323–27.

[11] Mehrab Shah Qadri was a soldier in the contingent of some Maratha *sardar*. But due to strong mystic tendencies he resigned after sometime and, we are told, opted for a life of meditation and contemplation. It is also said that he preached *jehad* against the British to all his disciples. The special favours shown to Ahmadullah Shah were due to the fact that he too had an extensive training in the art of warfare, hence he was considered quite capable of leading the *jehad* movement in practical form. However, it is not known whose disciple Mehrab Shah Qadiri was. The *Shajra-i Manzooma* of Ahmadullah Shah (reproduced in Farooqi) is of no help in this respect due to its rather incoherent nature. The *dargah* of Mehrab Shah still exists in good condition and is situated at Jiwajiganj, Laskar, Gwalior. See Abrar Husain Farooqi, *Masir-i Dilawari*, pp. 284–92.

[12] Maulana Mohammad Akram Faiz, *Khwariq-i Mastan*, Agra, AH 1317, p. 29. The author's sympathies are ultimately with the 'victors' as he praises the British for 'providing stability' and having 'established the tenets of justice for high and low', also they were unmatched as 'they possessed an excellent army'. To please the new masters further, he says that at Aligarh the Shah had made him an offer of appointing him the as the *imam* of the army, realizing 'the futility of the cause' (the Shah was going for) he had refused the offer.

[13] Ibid., p. 32.

[14] Ibid., pp. 32–33. The author further says that thereafter the Shah left for Lucknow and the author went to Moradabad. The mutiny reports confirmed all the predictions that the Shah had made. Although he showers all his praise for the bravery and valour displayed by the Shah, but he does hasten to point out the futility of the whole venture. During the course of events, 'our author had moved away further to Bachrayun where things were peaceful and no harm was done to him'. Ibid., p. 33.

[15] Taib, 14: 1016–29.

[16] *Tilism*, No. 18, dated 21 November 1856. This paper was edited by one Maulavi Mohammad Yaqub Ansari of *Firangi Mahal*, Lucknow during 1856–57. The last issue of this paper was published on 10 May 1857. For a discussion on the importance of this newspaper see Iqbal Husain, 'Lucknow between the Annexation and the Mutiny', *UP Historical Review*, Allahabad, Vol. II, No. I, pp. 40–51. R. Mukherji and G. Bhadra, both have used this article to discuss the early career of Ahmadullah Shah.

[17] *Tilism*, No. 28, part 1, dated 30 January 1857.

[18] Taib, 14: 1034–47. In fact, one verse is very clear, where Taib says, as he had been ordered (by his pir) to fight the Christians, he preached the idea (*jehad*) to every one. Cf. Syed Moinul Haq, *The Great Revolution of 1857*, p. 592.

[19] *Tilism*, No. 28, 30 January 1857, p. 1; also in Taib, 14: 1047–57.

[20] Tilism, No. 29, 30 January 1857, p. 1.

[21] Ibid., No. 32, 27 February 1857, pp. 1–2.

[22] Syed Moinul Haq, *The Great Revolution of 1857*, p. 60.

[23] *Tilism*, No. 32, explicitly asserts that the he was leaving for Bahraich, and he stayed at Fyzabad simply as a passenger. For details of Fyzabad happenings, see Taib, 15: 1065–97.

[24] Hutchinson, *Narrative of the Mutinies in Oude*; cf. Syed Moinul Haq, *The Great Revolution of 1857*, p. 61. The incident of Fyzabad became widely known and all the leading newspapers reported it in detail. See *Tilism*, No. 33, 4 March 1857; *Dehli Urdu Akhbar*, No. 10, 8 March p. 3; *Sahr-i Samiri*, No. 17, March 1857. The editor,

Raghubir Narayan 'Aysh notes that 'he is the same person who had established himself at Ghasiyarimandi, but considering him a dangerous person, the *kotwal* had expelled him . . . earlier Maulavi Amir Ali had also led a *jehad*, inspite of the opposition of the king he was able to enroll many, but in the end every body met destruction, they were beheaded when they came face to face with the soldiers'.

[25] Taib, 15: 1065–97. Shah was not just aimlessly roaming from place to place, but in fact his preachings and sermons had a considerable impact upon his disciples. The testimony of Hutchinson is worth noting: 'This man (Ahmadullah Shah) after passing through a vast number of cities and stations under our rule, in all parts of India, and establishing his disciples therein reached Fyzabad in February 1857, subsequent investigations elicited that everywhere he had preached *jehad*, or religious war against the *kafirs*, or infidels, as the Europeans were politely designated. From some places he had been summarily ejected, but in others evaded expulsion, meeting with no real check until he came to Fyzabad' (Hutchinson, *Narrative of the Mutinies in Oude*, p. 292).

[26] H.R. Nevill, *Fyzabad: A Gazetteer*, Allahabad, 1920, p. 165. See also M.H. Fisher, *A Clash of Culture: Awadh, the British and the Mughals*, Delhi, 1987, pp. 231–32.

[27] Taib., 16: 1135–55.

[28] Ibid., 1170–1236.

[29] Ibid., 18: 1234–88. The arguments set out by Taib over the question of *imamat*, on the role of *mujahideen* and on the necessity of *jehad* find strange corroboration from the arguments on these issues in a pamphlet called *Risala-i Fath-i Islam*. Although the authorship of the pamphlet is yet to be determined, one can fairly conclude that it is the most representative piece of writing on the ideology and organization of the *mujahideen*. It is divided into two portions. The first portion contains a discussion of a highly academic nature about the necessity of *jehad*, the role the *mujahideen* and the *ghazi* were meant to play, the difference between plunder and distribution of *ghanimah* (the war booty), the appointment of an *amir* and the necessity of offering him *bayat* on the specific issue of *jehad*, the wisdom of the sages behind the theory of the *Quraish* descent of the *imam* and its impracticability in the then prevailing circumstances, and last but not least, an appeal to Hindus to join the struggle against the common enemy. Apart from this, certain practical measures were also suggested to continue the struggle. The second portion of the pamphlet was in the form of an *ishtihar* 'meant for the Hindus and the Muslims of India, so that they should think over, and should prepare themselves for the slaughter of the English in order to protect their *din* and *dharma*'. This call was to be popularized among the masses by the *maulavis* and the *pundits*. But by its very nature, the *itshtihar* was meant for public consumption in the form of propaganda literature for the rural poor.

In fact, when one compares the British describing the 'rebels and their leaders as scoundrels, *badmash*, *shuhda*, riffraffs', and the *mujahideens* as 'a debased class of the people and fanatics', and also employ the most abusive language (which they never did for the Irish rebels or for Australian convicts, or during the American war of Independence) in their dispatches and reports throughout the course of the events of 1857–59, one can understand why this pamphlet uses 'the most insulting language to describe the British especially Queen Victoria', which has injured the sensibilities of modern scholars such as R. Mukherjee, *Awadh in Revolt, 1857–58, A Study of Popular Resistance*, p. 148. While Gautam Bhadra is not very happy with such an 'abusive condemnation' of the 'whole chain of British colonial authority from the crown to the common soldiers and administrators'. For him the image of the 'good Queen' Victoria appears to have been ideal. Bhadra, 'Four Rebels of Eighteen Fifty-seven', p. 271. The lack of any 'sensitivity' among these 'subalterns' about the way British wrote and behaved during this phase is really unfortunate.

In fact the *mujahideen* and their leaders offered such stiff resistance to the British and had shown such ruthless valour that after the suppression of the events of 1857 the entire class of the *ma'afidar* had become suspect in the eyes of the British. As during the course of the first regular settlement, each confirmation of the *ma'afi* was subject to their *ma'afidar* having displayed 'loyalty during 1857'. As for those who were hostile to the British or had supported the rebels or even remained neutral, their grants were summarily confiscated or drastically reduced. For the role of the *mujahideen* in 1857, see K.M. Ashraf, 'Muslim Revivalists and the Revolt', in P.C. Joshi (ed.) *Rebellion, 1857*, New Delhi, 1957, pp. 71–102. An English translation of *Risala-i Fath Islam* can be found in S.A.A. Rizvi (ed.), *Freedom Struggle in Uttar Pradesh* (FSUP), Vol. II, Lucknow, 1958, pp. 150–62. However, here the original *Risala* has been used.

[30] Taib, 19: 1293–1311.

[31] Ibid., 21: 1377–1418.

[32] Ibid., 23: 1553–70.

[33] Ibid., 25: 1737–49.

[34] Ibid., 25: 1724–27.

[35] Ibid., 26: 1766–1812.

[36] Ibid., 28: 1883–1909 for the versified account of the *farman* dispatched to the Nawab of Bareilly and verse nos. 1910–40 for the versified version of the *'arzdasht* of the Nawab in reply to the *farman*; see also Farooqi, *Mirat-i Ahmadi*, pp. 133–36.

[37] Taib, 30: 2024–65, for coins and the dispatch of *farman* to various rulers, See Syed Moinul Haq, *The Great Revolution of 1857*, p. 544 & n.

[38] For his activities in Rohilkhand region, see Taib, 29: 1941–2023; and 31: 2066–2145. The British officers were equally concerned about his movements, they too kept themselves informed about everything the Shah was doing. In this connection, a letter from the Chief Commissioner of Oudh to the Secretary Government of India is worth mentioning: 'the defeat of the rebels at Bareilly and Shahjahanpur drove Moulvi Ahmadullah Shah with his followers back into Oudh, where he was joined by Nurput Singh of Rohia. After reconnoitering the Palace with a strong body of sawars, the Moulvi with nine guns and seven thousand men made a movement on the Thane of Palee, which he entered on the 22nd instant. From Hence he marched on to Sandee, and immediately threatened the position of the Commissioned Colonel Clarke at Dhurmpur.

The circumstances in which Colonel Clarke found himself thus suddenly placed, fully justified him in withdrawing all his civil officers to Futah Gurh at once before their retreat was cut off'. Letter No. 373 (1858) dated 29 May 1858, *Foreign Secret Consultations*, Nos. 56–57, 25 June 1858, National Archives of India, New Delhi (NAI).

[39] The best account has been provided by Syed Moinul Haq, who has utilized the account of Taib fully. See Haq, *The Great Revolution of 1857*, pp. 544–50.

[40] It is quite interesting that the Shah was designated simply an *'amil* by one of his chief supporters. Does it mean that the claim of independence by the Shah posed no challenge to the authority of Birjis Qadar?

[41] Fazle Haq Khairabadi, *Al Thaurat-al Hindiya* (Arabic) edited with comprehensive notes and a useful introduction by Abdul Khan Sharwani as, *Baghi Hindustan*, Bijnore, 1947. Urdu translation of the text has also been provided into parallel columns, at the end. See pp. 409–413; also compare with Haq 'The story of the war of Independence, 1857–58', *Journal of Pakistan Historical Society*, Vol. V, Pt. I, [January 1957], pp. 21–57, especially pp. 48–49.

Maulana Fazle Haq of Khairabad (1797–1862) is one of the most fascinating and a multifaceted persons of his times. Belonging to the well-known family of the scholars of Khairabad (Awadh), after perfecting his knowledge of the traditional and rational sciences at his fathers *madrasa*, he came to Delhi. He came during a period when some of the most bitter theological controversies were taking place that resulted in a vertical division within the *sunnis* on purely hypothetical issues, such as the question of the intercession of the Prophet (*shifa'at*) and the finality of the Prophethood (*imitina'at*). A man of his genius could not remain a mute witness to such debates even if it involved some polemics. He proved to be one of the most bitter critics of Maulavi Shah Ismai'l of Balakot fame on the question of *jehad*. But strangely enough, during 1857, he changed his position and caused the leading theologians and the divines to issue a *fatwa* for *jehad*. A detailed study of his intellectual environment is worth analysing in order to understand the ideological trends of this period better. For his role in 1857, see Iqbal Husain, 'Fazle Haq of Khairabad. A Scholarly Rebel of 1857', *Proceedings Indian History Congress (PIHC)*, 48th session (1987), pp. 355–65.

[42] Farooqi, *Mirat-i Ahmadi*, for the photographic reproduction of various application reports and orders alongwith their transcripts see pp. 192–243.

[43] It is strange that the scholars working on this period have seldom touched upon this important aspect. This, inspite of the fact that there is no dearth of material giving the point of view of the 'vanquished', these proclamations, letters and intelligence reports afford a glimpse of the 'rebels' point of view'. Apart from Syed Moinul Haq and K.M. Ashraf, in recent years Iqbal Husain has taken up this subject seriously. For his important contributions see 'Bakht Khan – A Leading Sepoy General of 1857', *PIHC*, 46th session, 1985, pp. 371–86; Iqbal Husain, 'Fazle Haq of Khairabad. A Scholarly Rebel of 1857', *PIHC*, 48th session, 1987, pp. 355–65.

The Gwalior Contingent in 1857–58

The Organization and Ideology of the Sepoy Rebels

Iqtidar Alam Khan

Dilating on Disraeli's view (put forward in his speech in the House of Commons on 27 July 1857) that the violent events triggered all over North India by the 'sepoy mutiny' at Meerut were nothing short of a 'national revolt', Marx had suggested in his article published in the *New York Daily Tribune* of 14 August 1857 that the rebelling sepoys were in reality acting as the 'instruments' of the Indian peoples' upsurge against British colonial rule.[1] According to him, by creating the 200,000 strong native army British rule had brought into existence 'the first general centre of resistance' which the Indian people ever possessed.[2] In 1857, it was this center, comprising the peasants and artisans in uniform, that was apparently seeking to act, with all its ideological and organizational failures, as the vanguard of the spontaneous people's uprising.

Marx's own subsequent information as well as the detailed researches of the later writers have fully upheld these early insights into the character of the 1857 Revolt: that all the sections of the native army, including some of the exclusively Sikh corps were affected by the rebellious sentiments;[3] that in many places the sepoy revolts were followed by the stirring into action of the artisans and other poor sections of the urban populace;[4] that in the northern subdivisions of the Muzaffarnagar districts the rival *khaps* of the Jats peasantry had come together, defying the English authority, under the leadership of a Mewati Muslim; that the Jat peasantry of the same Muzaffarnagar district had also aligned itself with 'the petty Muslim gentry elements', then fighting last-ditch battles against the advancing English troops;[5] that the *zamindars* and other landowning groups in Awadh as well as in other parts of the then North-Western Provinces and central India, at least initially, not only looked with approval at the rebellious acts of the sepoys, but, in many cases actually participated in the rebellion;[6] that the so-called *wahabis* armed with a consistent anti-British ideology and also having at their disposal a network of organized centres spread all over northern India, were in the forefront of the struggle in all the main centres of the Revolt;[7] are now well known and almost universally recognized as the general features of 1857 rebellion that testify to its character as a national or people's uprising spearheaded by the sepoys. But within this broad framework of a national or people's revolt there remain unanswered many important questions. Some of them relate to the roles played by the diverse social interests and ideological influences discernible among the rebels[8] and have a bearing on the military and organizational failures of the rebels.[9] For example, it still remains to be fully investigated as to whether the sepoy rebels of 1857 were really always as devoid of any organizational cohesion and discipline or were as incapable of clearly defining their long and short-term military as well as political aims, or were as hopelessly lacking in efficient planning as has been generally assumed. This paper has been aimed primarily at gaining a better perspective on these questions by examining the motivations of smaller groups among the rebels of the Gwalior contingent as well as the symbols of political legitimacy that they had a tendency to rally around.

I

The Gwalior contingent, which was at the centre of the revolt in the Gwalior territory, was created in 1844 after the disbanding of a major part of Scindia's army. This arrangement was made under the provisions of a treaty imposed upon Scindia by the East India Company's government, following the defeat of the Gwalior army near Dholpur.[10] Originally the Gwalior contingent consisted of a regiment of 400 cavalry and 200 Marhatta horse, 52 *gulundaze*, 2 nine pn. (percussion), guns and 2 twenty-four pn., a howitzer and an infantry regiment of 600 men. At the time of its creation the contingent was commanded by a brigadier and six other English officers, two of cavalry, three of infantry and one of artillery.[11] In addition to these seven English officers, a number of 'native' – commissioned as well as non-commissioned – officers were recruited into the contingent from the regular corps of the Bengal Army.[12] A distinctive feature of the Gwalior contingent was the high rates of salaries paid to its sepoys. These rates – 30 Chanderi rupees per month to a cavalryman and 7 Chanderi rupees per month to an infantryman – were perhaps higher than those of Bengal Army and were conceived as a means to give 'the officer a strong hold' over the troops.[13]

The expenses on the maintenance of the contingent were to be met by Scindia but its command and management was entirely in the hands of the English officers, headed by a brigadier. The latter, took his orders from the commander-in-chief and ran the day-to-day affairs of the contingent in consultation with the political agent residing at Gwalior.[14] Scindia had ceded to the British several 'districts' including those of Chanderi, Kachwahagarh, Shander and Orai, the revenues of which were to be used for the maintenance of the contingent.[15] From 1844 onwards, it was the undeclared policy of the East India Company's government not to allow Scindia to increase the number of troops, particularly, of infantry. Throughout this period, as and when it was felt necessary to have a 'larger force of infantry' for maintaining order in Gwalior, the strength of the contingent was increased. And, simultaneously, more revenues were sought to be taken away from Scindia's charge for the maintenance of these additional troops.[16] It would appear that between 1844 and 1857, the strength of the contingent was steadily increasing. By 1857, the size of the cavalry and infantry had grown from

600 each to 1,158 and 6,412 respectively. Similarly, there was a sharp accretion in the contingent's firepower with a rise in the number of its gunners from 52 to 74 and that of guns from 4 to 26.[17] With this increase in the strength of the contingent, the number of its commissioned as well as non-commissioned officers had also grown. This should also apply to the number of Englishmen serving as the officers of the different corpses of the contingent.[18]

As it steadily expanded during 1844–57, the Gwalior contingent appears to have gained, by and large, the same composition, in terms of caste, regional and religious groups present, as that of the Bengal Army.[19] From the random mention in records of Muslim names or references to some of the sepoys or to the sepoys joining a body of *ghazis* on the eve of the rebellion or to the sepoy rebels swearing 'on the Ganges water and Koran to stand by each other', go to indicate that a sizeable section of sepoys and officers of the contingent were Muslims. They were perhaps present in the cavalry in much larger strength. The infantry and artillery, on the other hand, were apparently, predominantly manned by the *poorbeahs*, who were mainly Brahmans and Thakurs recruited from the eastern parts of Awadh and the adjoining districts of Bihar.[20] The presence of a considerable number of horsemen belonging to the caste *Kychee* in the contingent's cavalry[21] was, however, another important point about its composition that deserves to be noted. It goes to show that unlike the Bengal Army, men in the Gwalior contingent were not exclusively high-caste people. At least some of them in the cavalry were known to have belonged to a comparatively lower caste (of the *Kychees*).

In addition to the Gwalior contingent, there were present in the Gwalior territory in 1857 three other bodies of troops, each one of which also participated in the Revolt to a limited extent. These bodies were (a) Scindia's regular troops, (b) troops attached to Baiza Bai, the widow of Daulat Rao Scindia, (c) the irregular troops maintained by the chiefs, mostly Rajputs, subjugated by Scindia. Scindia's regular troops were limited by the Treaty of 1843 to 3000 infantry, 6000 cavalry (including bodyguards of *paigah*) and 2000 were some kind of policemen. A large number of officers commanding these troops were Scindia's Marhatta *sardars*. Apparently, in Scindia's cavalry there were present a large number of Muslim horsemen recruited from British territories, possibly from Rohilkhand. This is suggested by a reference in Macpherson's Report (of 10 February 1858) to the presence of '800 of Scindia's Mahomedan Horse from our provinces' among the rebel sepoys who proceeded from Gwalior to Agra in September 1857. In the same group, Macpherson also notes the presence of 'several hundred Wilayatees in the service of Baiza Bai', which would indicate that on the eve of the Revolt a large body of horsemen was attached to Baiza Bai as well. Perhaps these troops had come with her from her earlier stations Satara, Nasik and Ujjain where she was staying before this time as a virtual fugitive from Gwalior.[22] The *wilayatis*, as is well known, were Afghan mercenaries recruited from different places in north-western India and were famous for being fiercely loyal to their employers. Lastly, so far as irregular troops commanded by the chiefs paying allegiance to

Scindia were concerned, their total strength is estimated to be around 17,540 men.[23] As may be imagined, these irregular troops were dispersed all over the Gwalior territory. The role of this otherwise large body of troops was also restricted by their parochial outlook and lack of proper organization. They were fit only for serving as watchmen or in the escorting parties.

At the time of the outbreak of sepoy revolts at Meerut and Delhi in the second week of May 1857, the Gwalior contingent, and to a slightly lesser extent Scindia's troops as well, shared the general discontent and resentment of the sepoys and the native officers of the Bengal Army.[24] This discontent, fanned by superficial issues like greased cartridges etc., seems to have stemmed basically from the growing economic distress and pauperization of the peasants and urban masses from amongst whom the sepoys of both the Bengal Army as well as the Gwalior contingent were recruited. Moreover, the Muslim sepoys and officers of the contingent, as also the Rohilas and Wilayatis among Scindia's and Baiza Bai's troops, appear to have been widely influenced by the revivalist appeal of the *Wahabi* doctrines prescribing an anti-British *jehad* under the leadership of an *imam*.[25] The phenomenon of many of the sepoys opting, after the contingent's revolt on 14 June 1857, to join the freely roaming *ghazi* bands, goes to testify the impact of *Wahabi* propaganda on the minds of the Muslim troops at Gwalior. Surviving evidence does suggest the possibility of some kind of centre preaching *jehad* being present at Gwalior for a number of years before this time.[26]

In May 1857, the contingent was headed by brigadier Ramsay who, with the help of sixteen or more English officers, was administering its affairs quite efficiently.[27] Before the news of the revolts at Meerut and Delhi reached Gwalior, the sepoys of the contingent were, apparently, quite content and on the best of terms with their English officers as well. Around this time, while the main body of the contingent was at Gwalior, a number of its infantry regiments were stationed at Neemuch (7th Regiment), Seepree (3rd Regiment), Agra (5th Regiment), Sultanpur (6th Regiment), Burhanpur (a company of the 6th Regiment), Jabalpur (another company of the 6th Regiment) etc. From this pattern of deployment of the contingent's regiments one gets the impression that in addition to being an effective instrument for maintaining order inside the Gwalior territory, by then, it had also come to be used for bolstering British authority in a large part of central India. In the given situation, therefore, a revolt at Gwalior could have created a very difficult situation for the already endangered military position of the East India Company's government in the North-Western Provinces and central India.[28]

It speaks of the efficient management of the affairs of the contingent by brigadier Ramsay and also of fairly close ties existing till then between the sepoys in general and their English officers, that despite the growing signs of general discontent against the colonial regime and the presence of *Wahabi* elements among the sepoys, there was no flare-up at Gwalior throughout May and the first half of June. As late as 23 May, Lieutenant-colonel H.M. Durand, the officiating agent of the Governor-General in central India went out of his way to state in one of his dispatches that 'the conduct of the contingent troops has hitherto been so exemplary'.[29] The British authorities were so confident of the loyalty of the contingent at that time that soon after getting the news of outbreaks at Meerut and Delhi, Macpherson had mooted the idea of sending it to Agra to reinforce the English troops there. This proposal, however, was dropped owing to Scindia's opposition on the grounds that the contingent's moving away from Gwalior would encourage the local chiefs to rebel against him. However, on 13, 17 and 19 May small detachments of troops mainly those of the contingent's cavalry were sent to reinforce Agra. This movement of troops which commenced after the news of the revolt at Delhi had already reached Gwalior, was not opposed by any section of the sepoys or their native officers. Then again on 20 May, on the Lt. Governor's request, troops belonging to the contingent's infantry and one hundred horsemen of Scindia's bodyguard marched to Etawa under Major Hannessy who was able to restore the district magistrate's authority in that place.[30]

Partly, at least, this 'exemplary' behaviour of the contingent, for about two weeks after the news of outbreak of rebellion reached Gwalior, was prompted by the deliberate impression that was sought to be given to its sepoys and native officers by Scindia that if they would refrain from joining the revolt, henceforth, their position would be at par with those in his direct employment. Major Macpherson himself indirectly contributed to strengthening this impression by depositing with Scindia, around this time, rupees 4.5 lakhs meant for meeting the expenses of the contingent which were collected from the ceded district of Orai. It was a continuation of the same posture on Scindia's part that, after the outbreak at Jhansi (7 June), he took over the administration of the ceded districts, of Kachwahagarh and Chanderi 'which were assigned for the expenses of the contingent'. This posture of Scindia, which he seemingly adopted with the full approval of Major Macpherson, gave to the men of the contingent, particularly to those who either from doctrinal considerations or on account of their feelings of solidarity with the rebelling sepoys of Meerut etc., were averse to being counted on the side of the British, the psychological satisfaction of no longer being in the service of the British military authorities without actually resorting to rebellion.

In this context, it is worth remembering that down to the end of May, neither the main body of the contingent at Gwalior nor any one of the regiments deputed to different neighbouring stations, with the sole exception of the Ist cavalry sent to Agra on 13 May, acted in an overtly rebellious manner. That the Ist cavalry was induced to revolt at Agra only under the influence of the rebellious elements of the Bengal Army indicates that it had revolted rather half-heartedly and also that it had acted in this manner without obtaining the agreement of the other units of the contingent. This is borne out by the following details gleaned from Macpherson's brief notice of this episode in his report.

On 19 May, the troops of Ist cavalry, the company of a wing of 9th native infantry, marched to Aligarh and captured the treasury there. Their moving to Aligarh suggested that, perhaps, they had planned to proceed to Delhi via Aligarh. But on reaching Aligarh and after having seized the treasury they seem to have changed their mind. From Aligarh they retired to Hathras where they tried to restore order by acting against a body of rebels who were plundering the place. Macpherson refers to their conduct at Hathras approvingly ('behaved-well' is the expression used by him). But on 23 May, a hundred men separated themselves from this group, and proceeded to Delhi – 'shouting *deen*'. Our records do not tell us as to what happened to the majority of the Ist cavalry of the contingent who had stayed back at Hathras on 23 May. These men were apparently having second thoughts on the advisability of their taking an active part in the rebellion. It was possibly this indecisiveness of the majority which led to a rift between them and a militant minority. The latter were, perhaps, not prepared for any slide-back from their earlier resolve to join the rebel forces at Delhi. When they felt that the majority was deliberately stalling their march to Delhi they decided to part company with them. It is possible that this sudden change in the attitude of the majority was caused by the advice that they might have received from the emerging leaders of the contingent at Gwalior. These leaders were, perhaps, in favour of stalling a decision on the question of their active participation in the fast spreading rebellion. They were, apparently, hopeful of eventually shaking off the authority of the English officers by simply persuading Scindia to take the management of the contingent into his own hands.

There does exist an interesting piece of evidence pointing to the emergence, as early as 16 May, of a leadership within the contingent who presumed to hold negotiations with Brigadier Ramsay as well as Scindia on behalf of the sepoys and the native officers. A communication of the political agent at Gwalior to the Governor-General, dated 16 May 1857, records Scindia's directive to the contingent that it should move towards Chanderi to suppress the chiefs of Chanderi, Rayaghur, Muadhungur, Komru and Bhadoara, who had come out against his administration. Apparently, this direction had the full approval of Brigadier Ramsay. But the sepoys were not prepared to comply with this directive. They excused themselves from immediately marching out to Chanderi. While not spelling out any reasons for their reluctance, they vaguely promised to proceed against the rebellious *rajas* 'after the rainy weather' which was nothing but a pretext, a play to cover up their unconcealed defiance.[31]

This evidence is of vital importance on a number of counts. Firstly, it shows that already by 16 May 1857, there existed within the contingent a set of leaders who were capable of acting as the spokesmen of the entire body of sepoys. These leaders, apparently, had come to the forefront in the course of prolonged discussions at the meetings of sepoys that were going on, according to Macpherson, 'more or less since the commencement of insurrection'.[32] It also indicates that, immediately after the outbreak of rebellions at Meerut and Delhi, the sepoys and the native officers of the contingent, in their collective wisdom, had come to resolve to not allow a large scale removal of their regiments from Gwalior. They agreed to the sending of small bodies of horsemen to Agra on 17 and 19 May and another small detachment of infantry to Etawah on 20 May, as this would not amount to large scale dispersal. But the moving away of the entire contingent towards Chanderi was something they could not but oppose. Brigadier Ramsay as well as Scindia were obliged to condone this development to the point of even entering into negotiations with the leaders of the sepoys. They eventually had to overlook the sepoys' polite refusal to comply with their directive. In the rapidly changing situation all over North India during the third week of May 1857, the leaders of the sepoys at Gwalior, apparently conceived the contingent as an organized body of professional soldiers whose basic allegiance was to their own organization. They seemed to be acting under the impression that their primary duty was to protect the collective interests of the contingent in every possible way. With this understanding of their role, the leaders of the sepoys this time around were not only opposed to the removal of the main body of the contingent from Gwalior, but they also appear to have been averse to making an overtly rebellious move that might endanger the existing organization of the contingent, of which the English officers were an important part. Thus, their attitude of flouting the directive to march to Chanderi without giving too much provocation to Brigadier Ramsay or Scindia. Apparently, the English officers at Gwalior, on their part, also vaguely appreciated this self-perception of the sepoys and their leaders. It is worth noting that despite this incident of 16 May, down to 23 May, the English officers continued to regard the conduct of the contingent as 'exemplary'.

From 26 May onwards, the situation at Gwalior suddenly tended to become very tense. This happened as a consequence of the arrival of the emissaries of the sepoys as well as ordinary deserters from the rebellious units of the Bengal Army located in different places all over North India ('our possessions' in Macpherson's words). The rumour that the flour and sugar 'mixed with pigs and bullocks bones had arrived for sale at Gwalior from Agra' first started circulating in the town on 22 May. Then started the arrival of deserters, emissaries, as well as letters from Delhi and other centres of rebellion. This development seems to have crystallized a body of opinion in the ranks of the contingent, pressing for the immediate overthrow of the English officers. This was a line of action which to begin with was not favoured by everyone. Many sepoys were, perhaps, not too sure of the advisability of giving up the cautious course adopted by them immediately after the outbreaks at Meerut and Delhi. These differences among the sepoys, however, were resolved through the long and tortuous discussions that followed. Macpherson has reproduced the information given to him by Scindia on 26 May on these discussions. According to this information, the sepoys 'administered' pledges to each other on Ganga water 'amid infinite boastings of destruction of the English power and all Christians'. Subsequent events go to show that these discussions finally led to a consensus among the sepoys of the contingent in favour of an uprising at an appropriate moment. Information conveyed by Scindia to Macpherson on 26 May clearly indicated that already by that date the sepoys of the contingent had 'ceased to be the servants of the government'.

All that we know of the contingent's behaviour between 26 May and 14 June, tends to suggest that unlike the revolts by the units of the Bengal Army at different stations in the North-Western Provinces and central India, the contingent's uprising of 14 June was a carefully planned action. It was executed, by and large, quite successfully, under an efficient leadership which was fully committed to keeping the entire establishment of the contingent intact after eliminating the English officers. During this period, the sepoys and the native officers of the 14th infantry regiment (some of whom had earlier played a conspicuous role in 'restoring order' at Etawah) emerged as the most active elements in the leadership. The manner in which the contingent's leaders were able to throw their English officers off their guard between 29 May and 14 June is an indication of the careful planning that had gone into organizing the revolt. Scindia and Macpherson are reported to have tried their best to convince Major Ramsay and other Englishmen serving under him that they could no longer trust the contingent. But these officers were not convinced. They continued to regard a majority of the contingent's sepoys as totally loyal to them. Despite repeated reports coming to the officers, from diverse channels, of the revolt being imminent and despite the false alarm on 29 May, they refused to shift to the Residency for protection.

That after 29 May the entire contingent was resolutely committed to staging an uprising is also borne out by the behaviour of its infantry brigades stationed at Neemuch and Sultanpur. After they revolted on 3 and 13 June respectively, these regiments, significantly enough, did not betray the same kind of hesitation that marked the conduct of the Ist cavalry at Hathras in the third week of May (19–23 May). This may be explained in terms of the prevailing consensus among the members of the contingent favouring immediate revolt which was perhaps missing earlier.

During the same period, the leaders of the contingent were, apparently, moving with great caution. While all the time preparing for an uprising, they also strived deliberately to strengthen the Brigadier's as well other English officers' illusions of the sepoys' continued loyalty to them. In an obvious attempt to put the English officers off their guard, on 29 May 'the 4th regiment, most suspected, formally petitioned to the Brigadier to be led anywhere against the rebels'. When on 7 June, the same regiment and 'Stuart's Battery' were ordered to proceed, under captain Murry, to Jhansi to put down the rebellion there, these troops readily abided by this order without giving the slightest indication of their already being committed to engineering a revolt at Gwalior itself. Many more such instances can be cited.

There was yet another noteworthy aspect of the behaviour of the contingent's disaffected sepoys present at Gwalior during this period (i.e. between 29 May and 14 June). Unlike the disaffected sepoys of Scindia's army, those of the contingent's seem to have avoided resorting to individual or group desertions. In this context, it is worth keeping in mind that actions like group or individual desertions, by their very nature, amount not only to severing ties of allegiance and service with the established authority but also tend to contribute to the dissolution of the organizations to which the deserters originally belonged. It is possible that the sepoys of the contingent desisted from deserting primarily on account of their strong feeling of self-identification with the establishment in which they were employed. But partly at least this may also be ascribed to the firm hold of the contingent's newly risen leadership over the rank and file of the sepoys and also to their anxiety to keep the English officers off their guards.

However, in the existing situation of mounting tension, the contingent's sepoys could keep up this charade of being loyal and obedient to their English officers only up to a point. There were certain kinds of orders which if given, would possibly have left the sepoys with no option but to disobey. One such order was issued on 13 June. Half a regiment of the infantry and the men serving two of the contingent's guns were ordered to proceed to villages Parso and Sakurwuree. This order as recorded by Macpherson in his report does not clearly spell out the aim of the proposed move. The next day (14 June), the sepoys refused to comply with this order which led to a general uprising.

III

The ouster of the English officers on 14 June was by all indications a well organized operation which enabled the leaders of the revolt to capture the entire establishment of the contingent intact and with minimum bloodshed. After the initial killings of a few officers and their families (7 officers, 6 sergeants and pensioners, 3 women and 3 children) on the night of 14 June, the rebel leaders were able to restrain the sepoys from committing further atrocities. It is no doubt true that among the rebels of Gwalior there were present elements who, possibly out of their religious fanaticism, ardently favoured a general massacre of the English. This bloodthirsty tendency was, however, sought to be kept under check by those who had led the uprising within the contingent on 14 June.

Commenting on this situation, Macpherson observes: 'Against our rule the contingent apparently acted as one man. They were so much divided as to the slaughter of the officers, that 4 out of 7 infantry regiments, 2 out of 4 Batteries of Artillery, and the 2 Regiments of Cavalry, excepting a party at Gwalior, killed none.' Then he goes on to give credit, though implicitly, for the restraint shown by a majority of the sepoys, to the leaders who organized the uprising in the following words: 'It does not appear to have been their plan to murder the women and children – at least next day, they sent off, after very insulting treatment, those who survived to the Maharaja.' At another place, he records the specific cases of English officers who were helped by the rebelling sepoys themselves to reach the Residency safely. Macpherson writes: 'The cantonment guards favoured or aided actively in escaping several officers and families. Thus of the 2nd regiment, 3 men escorted the Lieutenant and carried his wife in a litter 7 miles to the residency. And the guards of the Ist Regiment over the family of its absent commandant behaved admirably. The rearguard of the 4th Regiment protected most faithfully Captains Murry and Meade and their families while a party of the 2nd came to destroy them'. The same was the behaviour of the contingents at Neemuch and Sipree. The general pattern was that of sparing the lives of the English officers but at the same time they were made to leave the cantonment with enough violence and harshness to make them feel insecure at Gwalior.

Apparently, this treatment of the English officers was aimed at inducing them to leave Gwalior immediately. This is borne out by Macpherson's narrative. It seems that, as soon as he set out, on 15 May, from the Gwalior fort to proceed to Agra, even the most fanatical elements among the rebels lost much of their keenness to pursue and attack him. This is clearly brought out by Macpherson's account of his coming face to face, on 14 and 15 June consecutively, with a band of *ghazis* led by rebel leader, Jahangir Khan. On the night of 14 June, while he was being escorted by Scindia's horsemen from the Residency to Phoolbagh Palace, this band of *ghazis* (partly consisting of the sepoys belonging to the contingent) surrounded his carriage and demanded vehemently that they be allowed to kill him. The guards escorting Macpherson on that occasion saved his life by pretending as if they were carrying him as a prisoner of Scindia. But only twenty-four hours later the same band intercepted Macpherson again at the village Hingorah. Then he was proceeding towards Dholpur, taking with him all those Englishmen, women and children who had survived the massacre of the previous night. Interestingly enough, the attitude of the *ghazis* towards Macpherson and his party on this occasion was much less violent than what it was on the previous night. The leader of the band, Jahangir Khan, 'protested that he did not wish to injure' them. '(He) came to visit us', writes Macpherson, 'arrayed in green with beads fingered in ceaseless prayer. But in concert with him, a body of plunderers were assembled to attack us in the ravine fringing the river.' It is thus very obvious from Macpherson's own narrative that after it had become evident that the ousted English officers were moving away to Agra, even the most fanatical elements of the contingent's sepoys were no longer very keen to attack them. But they were of course very eager that the English party leave Gwalior territory as early as possible. It is significant that on 15 June Jahangir Khan did not try to block Macpherson's progress towards the ferry on Chambal which led to Dholpur. One cannot but attribute Jahangir Khan's changed attitude towards Macpherson and his entourage to the advice of the leaders who had captured power within the contingent a day earlier.

The rebel leaders of the contingent appeared to be endeavouring from the very beginning to prevent its dissolution into small bands headed by individual native officers. They could hope to ensure against such a possibility first and foremost by restraining the *Wahabi* elements present within the contingent from acting in a chaotic manner. The Muslim sepoys influenced by the *Wahabi* doctrines had the tendency to join the roaming bands of the *ghazis*. This naturally threatened to undermine the organization of the contingent. From Macpherson's description of the band led by Jahangir Khan on 15 June, one can infer that within twenty-four hours of the uprising hundreds of sepoys of the contingent had turned into *ghazis*. They had rallied round a person who was no longer an officer of the contingent.[33] It was precisely this trend that the rebel leaders of the contingent appeared to be very eager to thwart. They seem to have tried to keep the fanatical zeal of these elements within acceptable limits by discouraging excesses against the ousted English officers.

The policy of the rebel leaders in this respect appears to have met with wide approval among the Hindu as well as Muslim sepoys. But in one isolated case it did lead to a rift between the overzealous ranks and their officers, who possibly in pursuance of the accepted policy, tried to save the lives of the English officers. The sepoys of the 3rd infantry regiment, after their revolt on 17/18 June at Sipree, accused five of their Indian officers of helping the Englishmen and of accepting bribes from them. They took a collective decision to turn them out of the regiment.[34] This episode deserves notice as it brings to light the differences prevailing among the rebels over the treatment to be meted out to the ousted English officers. In the present context it must, however, be stated that despite such occasional difficulties, on the whole, the policy of checking excesses against the discomfitured Englishmen was abided by the rank and file of the contingent without much protest. This in turn helped in discouraging the chaotic behaviour of the unruly elements in general.

But another and far more effective devise which the rebel leaders adopted to keep the contingent intact was that of announcing the appointment of its new commanding officer who was given the designation of a general. This position went to Amanat Ali, till then a *subedar*-major of the Ist infantry regiment. Seemingly, Inayat Ali's rise to the position of the commanding officer of the contingent had the support of most of the leading elements among the native officers as well as that of the ordinary sepoys. The other high positions in the contingent vacated by the English officers were also filled in a similar manner.

This new team of officers seems to have directed the regiments stationed outside Gwalior to return to the headquarters after removing their English officers. This is suggested by the behaviour of the regiments stationed at Sultanpur (revolted 13 June), Seepree (revolted 17–18 June) and Agra (revolted 3–4 July). Each one of them came to Gwalior after overthrowing the English officers. In this respect, the behaviour of the 7th Regiment at Neemuch, who had revolted as early as 3–4 June, and, apparently, without consulting the rebel leaders at Gwalior, was an exception. Instead of coming to Gwalior, it marched, in the company of the Bengal Brigade, directly to Agra, participated in an inconclusive action against the force led by the brigadier there and then proceeded to Delhi.[35] This action of the 7th Regiment resembled the chaotic ways of the elements influenced by the *Wahabis*. But most of the other regiments stationed outside Gwalior, seem to have, by and large, followed the directions issued to them by the high command headed by 'General Amanat Ali'.

There also survives some evidence indicating that those who were managing the affairs of the contingent after 14 June took pains to keep its organization in good shape. Each regiment not only retained but carefully guarded its banners and other paraphernalia. Practices like the posting of guards, grand rounds, drills etc., were also carefully adhered to.[36] The artillery was kept in a fairly good state of readiness. Perhaps, steps were also taken to produce at Gwalior percussion caps charged with fulminating powder for use in the latest type of English handguns available with the contingent.

For the day-to-day management of the contingent and also for paying the salaries of its sepoys and officers, the rebel leaders needed a constant supply of funds which could be provided only by Scindia. Rs 4.5 lakhs collected from the ceded district of Orai, which were meant for meeting the expenses of the contingent, were deposited by Macpherson with Scindia only a few days before the uprising. That amount, regarded by the sepoys of the contingent as theirs, was still with him. On 11 June, Scindia demonstratively took over charge of the ceded 'districts' of Bhander and Kachwahagarh the revenues of which were also set aside for meeting the expenses of the contingent. Against this background it is quite understandable that the leaders of the contingent should expect Scindia to take the responsibility of maintaining the contingent. But despite such an expectation they were, at least to begin with, very clear in their minds that they should not agree to the contingent's taking up service under Scindia. This is borne out by the demands which the leaders of the contingent made upon Scindia immediately after the ouster of the English officers. The demands were: (a) that he should make over to them the Rs 4.5 lakhs deposited with him by Macpherson; (2) that he should lead the contingent in an attack on the fort of Agra which was then being defended by a small English force; (3) that the contingent, after it conquered Agra for Scindia, would be free to move wherever it preferred; (4) that in anticipation of this service Scindia should give to the contingent an additional sum of Rs 12 to 15 lakhs which it needed to replenish supplies and for the repair of equipments. These demands were not acceptable to Scindia, basically owing to their political thrust. It was obvious that the rebel leaders were trying to lure Scindia into making use of the contingent for regaining the territories that his predecessor had lost to the English during the preceding three decades. Scindia as well as many of his Marhatta *sardars* were, however, quite convinced in their minds that English authority would soon be re-established in the whole of North India. They did not see any real gain in the plan suggested by the rebel leaders.

Scindia turned the tables on the rebel leaders by formally announcing his acceptance of the entire contingent in his own service, which also implied a promise of regularly meeting the salary bills of the sepoys. This was a step which they were in no position to oppose, as a large number of the sepoys were bound to be attracted by the prospect of their salaries being paid regularly from Scindia's treasury. This arrangement, however, clearly tended to undermine the autonomous status that the contingent had acquired after the overthrow of the English officers. It also left little scope for it to play a significant role in the ongoing anti-English struggle to which the leaders as well as the sepoys of the contingent appear to have been deeply committed. For these leaders, taking up Scindia's service would have been sensible only if he was to come out openly on the rebels' side which they knew was an impossibility. That Scindia and his *Diwan* were having secret correspondence with the Political Agent and other English officials at Agra and

Jabalpur could not have remained a secret to them. Yet, in view of the promise of regular salaries that Scindia's service held out to the ordinary sepoys and to a lesser extent also for the advantage of finding a symbol of political legitimacy to rally round, they appear to have reluctantly agreed to the *fait accompli* of Scindia's announcement.

From Macpherson's report one knows that in offering to accept the contingent in his service, Scindia was not at all sincere. He was all the time in league with the British. Scindia had given a promise to Macpherson before the latter left Gwalior on 15 June, to resort to such a step as a stratagem aimed at keeping the contingent tied down to Gwalior till the end of September. The idea was to prevent it from intervening at any point in North India on the rebels' side before the English forces were able to turn the tide. Initially, the leaders of the contingent were, perhaps, partly taken in by Scindia's false pretensions. They failed to realize the full extent of his involvement with the British. The contingent's leaders hoped in vain that in the long run it would be possible for them to pressurize Scindia into acting against the British forces. Their experience of the next four months, while the contingent was at Gwalior, belied these hopes altogether. Scindia was too clever and too resourceful a prince to be handled in the same manner that the sepoy leaders had employed with Bahadur Shah in Delhi. His greatest strength lay in his 10,000-strong army. Many of his sepoys and officers, particularly his Rohilla cavalrymen shared the anti-British sentiments of the members of the contingent but they were not prepared to allow Scindia's personal humiliation. The contingent's artillery of course gave it a definite military advantage over Scindia. However, the actual use of artillery against Scindia's establishment inside the fort was not feasible. It could only be used for pressurizing him. A large-scale cannonading of the fort would have certainly turned Scindia's own army as well as a considerable section of the Rajput chiefs of the neighbourhood against the contingent rendering its own position at Gwalior difficult to maintain.

For the next four months, while the contingent was still at Gwalior, there continued a battle of wits between Scindia and the rebel leaders. While the rebel leaders again and again pressed Scindia to lead them against the British, he went on putting it off on various pretexts. During this period, there seems to have taken place a gradual transformation in the nature of contingent's leadership which also deserves notice.

As time passed, persons advocating a more militant attitude towards Scindia came to have a greater say in the leadership. Within the contingent, decisions on policy matters began to be taken in a more pronouncedly populist manner which was bound to push the professionalism of the leaders into the background. Macpherson, who was kept informed about these developments by Scindia as well as his regular news-writers, describes this situation succinctly. 'The troops', he writes, 'spent their whole time in councils, *punchayats*, courts and deputations'. Scindia had to daily receive in his palace large deputations from every corps. Each one of these deputations would be accompanied by thirty to a hundred 'private delegates who would be there to watch over the conduct of their representatives'. 'They menaced, beseeched, dictated, until they planted their batteries against him (Scindia).' But it is significant to note that these threats of cannonading Scindia's quarters were never translated into actual practice. Apparently, despite the growing populist pressure the professionally-inclined elements among the leaders still enjoyed sufficient clout to be able to dissuade the militants from taking such a step.

During the month of July, the situation at Gwalior tended to become rather difficult and complicated from the point of view of the rebel leaders. The most threatening aspect of this situation was the cropping up of serious differences with in the contingent's ranks on parochial lines. It seems that the *Porbees*, mostly high-caste Hindus, pleaded for the contingent to move away to Kanpur, which was located closer to the region from where they hailed. As against this, the elements from the 'North', mostly Muslims recruited from the Doab region as well as those hailing from Gwalior itself (among whom naturally would also, be included a large number of Marhattas) were insisting that it would be better to go to Agra, and from there, to Delhi. These differences were apparently so pronounced that Scindia, instigated by the English officers shut up in the Agra fort, tried to use one section of sepoys against the other. He went to the extent of offering bribes to the officers of the contingent and 'their priests' for instigating the sepoys to continue to press their respective views vehemently. This problem tended to become particularly serious after the arrival of the rebels of Indore and Mhow (mainly of Holkar's army) at Morar on 31 July. They were on their way to Agra and were very eager to persuade the contingent to accompany them. This was bound to aggravate differences between the Porbees and the rest. And then, around the same time, arrived at Gwalior sepoys of 6th infantry regiment, who were dispersed from Kanpur after Nana Sahib's flight from there on 15 July.

These fugitives from Kanpur started spreading a very defeatist view within the contingent's ranks. They reportedly argued that the leaders' plans to engage the British forces were impracticable and advised them to give up all such ideas. This defeatist view was of course rejected by the leaders as well as by all the sections of sepoys. But it had one rather negative impact. Advocacy of a defeatist line of action by one whole regiment appears to have created a sharp reaction among those groups who were demanding a more militant attitude towards Scindia from the very beginning. They became still more insistent on the demand to severe links with Scindia. It is likely that some of these elements were asked by Scindia to proceed against the Rajput *zamindars* of the area to the southeast of Gwalior, who were adopting an increasingly defiant attitude towards him since the outbreak of insurrection in the North-Western Provinces. According to Macpherson, on this occasion, the 2nd regiment simply refused to move out of Gwalior. After the commencement of insurrection at Meerut, this was, in fact, the second occasion that the contingent's sepoys showed their disinclination to get involved in operations directed against the Rajput *zamindars*. Earlier, the contingent had adopted a similar stance on 16 May. Evidently, the entire leadership of the contingent was firmly opposed to its being used by Scindia as an instrument of coercion against the local zamindars.

Despite these complications the rebel leaders were able to stick to their original line of action of trying to preserve the organization of the contingent with Scindia's help and of pressurizing him into aligning himself openly with the rebels. That the rebel leaders were able to have their way in rejecting formal offers brought by Nana Sahib's and Rani Lakshmi Bai's *Wakils* sometime in August for hiring the contingent's service in return for very high payments seems to suggest their firm adherence to this line of action. It is of course true that Macpherson ascribes the rejection of Nana Sahib's and Rani Laksmi Bai's offers to Scindia's propaganda and manipulations. But, in this regard, one must not lose sight of the fact that the final decision on these offers was taken by the rebel leaders themselves, in a situation when a sizeable section of the sepoys were already favouring the contingent's joining, without further delay, the rebel forces in the North. Thus one can see that roughly down to the end of August, despite general demoralization created by the rebels discomfiture at Agra and Kanpur and in spite of all the other complications, the rebel leaders of the contingent were still in command of the situation.

On the eve of the Indore rebels setting out from Morar for Agra (5 September), the position of the rebel leaders as well as the line of action to which they were sticking so stoutly for the preceding two and half months received a severe jolt. At this time, the differences within the ranks of the contingent seem to have grown to the point that a sizeable number of troops were encouraged to join the Indore rebels' camp. This amounted to opting out of the main body of the contingent by a large body of sepoys, a development which the rebel leaders were struggling so hard to avert.

Subsequent to the departure of the Indore rebels for Agra, the rebel leaders found it very difficult to keep the sepoys pacified. The sepoys refused to trust them for negotiations with Scindia. At a meeting with Scindia on 7 September (three days after the departure of the Indore rebels), the sepoy 'observers' became unruly. After pushing aside their representatives they came forward to tell Scindia that as he was still refusing to lead them against the British forces without further delay, they were now giving up service under him. On returning to their cantonment, the sepoys and their leaders announced the autonomous status of the contingent by planting green and white flags as the new rallying symbols for them.

During the next one and a half months, the contingent was perhaps busy making preparations for a march against Kanpur, which was already under British control. Apparently, once the sepoys had forced the decision to severe links with Scindia, the rebel leaders fell in line with them. They now took pains to ensure that the contingent was able to put up a good show in the impending struggle. That these efforts were not entirely wasted is borne out by the humiliating defeat that the contingent inflicted on the English force commanded by general Windham (a hero of the Crimean War) near Kanpur on 27 November 1857. On that occasion the contingent had also succeeded in briefly reoccupying Kanpur for the rebels. This was the only occasion during the 1857 rebellion when a rebel force was able to defeat an English army of matching strength in an open battle. Frederick Engels celebrated this victory of the rebels by writing a special article in the *New York Daily Tribune* of 20 February 1858 which was entirely devoted to this event; it was titled 'Windham's Defeat'. The credit for this remarkable achievement of the contingent should go to the heroism and dedication of its sepoys as well as to the professional competence of the men who were leading them after the ouster of the English officers. Even after its defeat on 6 December 1858 at the hands of general Campbell, the contingent succeeded in withdrawing to Kalpi without losing its formation and carrying with it a major part of its artillery. The contingent, however, ceased to exist following the disorderly withdrawal of the rebel forces from Kalpi in May 1858. But to be fair to the contingent and its leaders, one must not forget that the situation within the rebel camp at Kalpi was controlled not by them but by other powerful rebel figures and the utterly disorganized troops following them, who, it seems, did not give the contingent another chance to show their mettle once again.

Notes and References
[1] Karl Marx, 'The Indian Question', *New York Daily Tribune*, 28 July 1857, reproduced in Karl Marx and Frederick Engels, *The First Indian War of Independence*, Moscow, 1975, p. 48.
[2] Karl Marx, 'The Revolt in the Indian Army', *New York Daily Tribune*, 15 July 1857, reproduced in Marx and Engels, *The First Indian War of Independence*, pp. 36–37.
[3] Karl Marx, 'The State of the Indian Insurrection', *New York Tribune*, 31 July 1857, reproduced in Marx and Engels, *The First Indian War of Independence*, p. 50.
[4] *The Bengal Hurkara and Indian Gazettee*, 4 June 1875, commenting on the rebels' proclamations in Awadh that were couched in the most abusive language for those who were not joining them, observes: 'there are reasons to believe (these proclamations) are written by people who like Scottish robbers, would like to see the world turned upside down' (cited in A.A. Rizvi's *Freedom Struggle in Uttar Pradesh*, Vol. II, Lucknow, 1958, p. 83).
[5] Eric Stokes, *The Peasants Armed*, edited by C.A. Bayly, Oxford, 1986, pp. 216–27.
[6] For large-scale participation of the *zamindars* of Awadh, see Rudrangshu Mukherjee, *Awadh in Revolt, 1857–1858*, Delhi and New York, 1984. For a contemporary assessment, see also 'Letter from M.H. Court, Magistrate and Collector, Allahabad, to C. Chester, Commissioner, Allahabad Division, dated 21 July 1857', in Judicial File No. 3, year 1858, Allahabad Collectorate, Mutiny Records, State Archives of U.P., Allahabad; reproduced in A.A. Rizvi, *Freedom Struggle of Uttar Pradesh*, Vol. IV, p. 558. Court observes: 'There is a very general impression abroad that the *zamindars* and agricultural population generally are not against us, but with great reluctance, I declare my belief that this is a mistake'.
[7] Cf. K.M. Ashraf, 'Ghalib and The Revolt of 1857', in. P.C. Joshi (ed.), *Rebellion 1857*, New Delhi, 1957, p. 71.
[8] Frederick Engels, ('The Capture of Delhi', *New York Daily Tribune*, 5 December 1857, reproduced in Marx and Engels, *The First Indian War of Independence*), even after, conceding that 'some notions of scientific warfare had penetrated among the sepoys' goes on to suggest, without referring to any evidence, that the plan for the defence of Delhi bearing a close resemblance to the defence of Sebastopol in the Crimean War must have been prepared 'for the sepoys by some Europeans that are with them'.

[9] According to Frederick Engels, as late as December 1857, the sepoys of the Gwalior contingent 'were the only insurgent troops, the formation of which can be said to go beyond, that of companies', retaining 'something like organized battalions' ('Windhams Defeat', *New York Daily Tribune*, 20 February 1858, reproduced in Marx and Engels, *The First Indian War of Independence*, p. 117). It seems that down to May 1858, when the rebels were forced to abandon Kalpi, the contingent still retained its artillery as well as its regimental standards. These were captured by Major-General Hugh Rose on his entry into the fort of Kalpi (Major-General Hugh Rose's letter to Major-General W.M. Mansfield, dated 22 June 1858, reproduced in A.A. Rizvi, *Freedom Struggle in Uttar Pradesh*, Vol. III, p. 404).

[10] For the disorders at Gwalior resulting from Jayaji Rao's minority and Lord Endenborough imposing a treaty on Scindia after defeating the Gwalior army in December 1843, see H.H. Dodwell, *The Cambridge History of India*, Vol. V, 1929, p. 578. Cf. Foreign Department, Political Consultations, dated 23 March 1844, No. 568, National Archives of India, New Delhi (NAI), where details relating to the disbanding of the Gwalior army in 1844 are given.

[11] Foreign Department, 19 February 1844, I/C.A., NAI.

[12] Ibid.

[13] Ibid.

[14] Cf. Foreign Department, Secret Consultations, 28 August 1857, No. 133, NAI, contains a circular sent by H.M. Durand, Officiating Agent of Governor-General for Central India, dated 23 May 1857, stating that 'the General Order No. 677 of 14 May 1857, Military Department, is to be considered applicable to all sections of the contingent troops where British Officers commanded'. For the close consultations between the Political Agent and the Brigadier commanding the contingent in May–June 1857, see Major Charles Macpherson's report to R. Hamilton Rust, Agent of the Governor-General for Central India, dated 10 February 1858 in *Foreign Political Proceedings, 1–8 October*, p. 476ff (henceforth referred to as *Report*).

[15] Cf. *Report* and also Foreign Department, 23 March 1844, 716/C, NAI. Compare, Khushhalilal Srivastava, *The Revolt of 1857 in Central India-Malwa*, Bombay, 1966, p. 55.

[16] A Letter Addressed to Lt. Col. Sleeman, Agent of Governor-General for the affairs of Scindia's Dominions, Foreign Department, 23 March 1844, 723/ C.A., NAI.

[17] For the strength of the contingent in 1857, see John William Kaye, *A History of the Sepoy War in India*, Vol. III, London, 1880, p. 309, n.

[18] With the help of the *Report* and other records of the revolt at Gwalior, it is possible to prepare a list of sixteen Englishmen serving as officers in the contingent.

[19] According to Kaye, *A History of the Sepoys War in India*, Vol. III, p. 309, 'The contingent was little more than a local branch of our own military establishment.'

[20] See, for example, *Report*. For the fact that the first detachment of the contingent's cavalry consisted entirely of Muslims while in the artillery there one-fourth were Muslims see Macpherson's letter to Lt. Governor, dated 16 May 1857, in *Foreign Political Proceedings*, 1858, 1–8 October.

[21] Cf. Macpherson's letter to Lt. Governor, dated 20 May 1857 in *Political Proceedings*, 1–8 October, 1858, p. 534, 'The 70 horse under Major Rallis are Hindus of *Kychee* caste'.

[22] For Baiza Bee's antecedents see Srivastava, *The Revolt of 1857 in Central India-Malwa*, pp. 6, 32.

[23] Srivastava gives the strength of these irregular troops as 17,540. He apparently borrows this information from an official document missed by me (Cf. Srivastava, *The Revolt of 1857 in Central India-Malwa*, p. 90).

[24] According to Macpherson (see *Report*) the Marhattas and other officers of Scindia who were the survivors of the old wars, as well as his chief *sardars* believed in the invincibility of British authority. This seems to have been the main reason for their refraining from joining the rebels. Some of Scindia's troops, particularly the Mahrattas among them, were bound to be influenced by this state of mind of their officers. But the fact that several of Scindia's corps, manned by troops recruited from the North-

Western Provinces, became deeply disaffected following the revolts at Meerut and Delhi is borne out by a number of incidents recorded by Macpherson. One of these was the desertion, on 29 May, by Scindia's "chosen Mohammadan guards at the Residency', who reportedly escaped to Delhi. Subsequent to this event there were daily desertions from Scindia's army. Most of the men who deserted were those recruited from the North-Western Provinces and Awadh ('our provinces' in the words of Macpherson).

25 The evidence pointing to continuous desertions by Scindia's Muslim troops recruited from the British provinces as well as by the *Wilayatis* belonging to Baiza Bai's personal contingent, to join the rebels at Delhi may partly be attributed to the influence of the *Wahabi* doctrines on their minds. According to Macpherson (see *Reports*), on the second day of the revolt at Gwalior, i.e. on 15 May, a certain Jahangir Khan was able to raise a body of 200 *ghazis*, who were earlier serving in the contingent as well as other corps.

26 Ahmadullah Shah, who during the 1857 uprising, led a large *ghazi* band in Awadh 'gave himself out to be a disciple of Mehrab Shah a holy man of Gwalior'. Ahmadullah Shah himself was residing at Gwalior for a long time. Deposition of Wazir Khan, late Sub-Assistant Surgeon of Agra Dispensary, Foreign Political Proceedings, 30 December 1859, No. 310, NAI, cited in A.A. Rizvi, *Freedom Struggle of Uttar Pradesh*, Vol. II, p. 147.

27 *Report* mentions the following names: Brigadier Ramsay, Captain Meade, Major Henessy, Major Black, Hawkins and Stuart (officers of artillery corps whose ranks are not indicated), Captain Murry, Lieutenant Tomkinson, Seriff (rank not mentioned), Lieutenant Proctor, Lieutenant Pierson, Captain Alexander, Captain Hills, Major Macpherson, Lieutenant Cekbur, Sergeant (Dr) Jules.

28 For Lord Canning's remark in one of his dispatches to the court of Directors – 'if Scindia joins the rebellion, I shall have to pack off tomorrow' – see Ashok Mehta, *The Great Rebellion*, Bombay, 1946, p. 39.

29 Foreign Department, Secret Consultation, 28 August 1857, No. 133, NAI.

30 Cf. *Report*.

31 Political Proceedings: 1 October to 5 October 1858, p. 534, NAI.

32 *Report*.

33 Jahangir Khan was originally a *havaldar* in the contingent. After leaving the contingent, he became a Captain in Scindia's army. At the time of the uprising at Gwalior on 14 June, he had become 'a *ghazi* leader of the highest pretension of sanctity'. According to Macpherson's information, on 15 June, he was on his way to Delhi (see *Report*).

34 Letter from Scindia to Major S.C. Macpherson in *Political Proceedings*, 1 October to 8 October 1858.

35 *Report* and J.W. Kaye, *A History of the Sepoy War in India*, Vol. III, p. 383.

36 See letter from Major-General Huge Rose to Major-General W.M. Mansfield, Gwalior, 22 June 1857 included in *Selections from State Papers*, Vol. IV, 'Central India', pp. 82–103. According to him, till their defeat at Kalpi in May 1858, 'All the Sepoy Regiments kept up, carefully, their English equipment and organization, the words of command for drill, grand rounds, etc., were given, as we could hear, at night in English'. Cited in Rizvi, *Freedom Struggle in Uttar Pradesh*, Vol. III, p. 388. It may be suggested that this description would mainly apply to the regiments of the Gwalior contingent then present in the fort of Kalpi. As Engels remarked in his article in *New York Daily Tribune* of 2 February 1858 (reproduced in Marx and Engels, *The First Indian War of Independence*, p. 117), by this time, the contingent was the only rebel force 'the formation of which can be said to go beyond that of companies, as they had been officered by natives almost exclusively, and thus, with their field officers and captains, retained something like organized battalions'.

The Tribals and the 1857 Uprising

K.S. Singh

'Shut the mouth of slanderers, bite and eat up backbiters, trample upon the
    sinners, O the destroyer of enemies!
Kill the British, exterminate them, O Mother Chandi!
Let not the enemy escape, nor their wives and children, O Goddess Sanharaka
Show favour to Shankar, support your slave
Listen up the Mlechhas, make to delay
Now devour them, and that too quickly,
O Ghormat Kalika'.[1]

(Composed by Gond chief, Shankar Shah, Jabalpur)

The 1857 uprising has largely been studied in terms of the participation in it of
sepoys, particularly of the Bengal Army, and peasants who saw in this event an
opportunity to vent their grievances and assert their rights, led by a feudal
aristocracy which saw its privileges being threatened or taken away. The tribals
are not mentioned as such in the chronicles of the uprising, but the exploits of the
communities known as tribes today, have been documented. While the tribes and
peasants demonstrated many similarities in their response to the uprising, there
were also significant differences emanating from their specific social structures
and political systems. There was, in fact, a plurality of responses. The tribes
were not only fighting the colonial rulers, the enemy outside, but they also tried
to settle scores with the enemies within, the exploiters, the moneylenders, their
rivals in regional power structures and so on.

    The notion of tribes as we understand it today had not crystallized until
the end of the nineteenth century. The official records refers to the uprising of
these communities with such names as the Kols, Bhumij, Santals, Bhils or the
Khonds. However, the very mention of such names suggests the presence, at the
back of the officials' minds, of communities which were warlike, militant, prone
to violence, quick to take offence, rebellions, sensitive, remotely situated,
'backward' and waiting to be reclaimed to civilization – all the ingredients that
make up the notion of a tribe.

    For students of tribal history, the participation of such communities in
the 1857 uprising was the culmination of almost sixty years of their resistance to

colonial rule. The tribal movements in this phase, from the end of the eighteenth century to 1857, have been described as primary forms of resistance: elemental, spontaneous, violent, led by tribal or other chiefs, aimed at overthrowing the colonial authority that destroyed the old system. Most of these characteristics were present in the 1857 uprising.

II

Probably the best known episode of a tribal uprising in 1857 is offered by the Chero–Bogtah combination in Palamau, set against the background of the general uprising of *zamindars* and *jagirdars* in the Chotanagpur region. The glorious raj of the Cheros had ended in 1814 and the Chero *jagirdars* were unhappy and looking for an opportunity to re-establish their control. They rose in rebellion several times in 1800, 1817 and 1832. They were particularly suspicious of Rajput-Thakurais who they thought had colluded with the British in putting an end to their raj. The British were accused of supporting the Rajput-Thakurai *zamindars*.

In 1857, the Cheros were joined by the Kharwars or Bogtahs. Unlike the Cheros, the Kharwars were largely peasants, and there were very few *jagirdars* among them. One section (*gosthi* or clan) of these, the Bogtahs, occupied a strategically unassailable position in the area lying between the lowlands of Palamau and the uplands of Sirguja and possessed almost inaccessible mountain 'fastness'. They have been described by colonial authorities as lawless free-booters, whose predatory habits were somewhat repressed by the British government conferring a *jagir* on the two brothers, Nilambar and Pitambar Sahai, who shared the headship of the Bogtah clan after the death of their father, 'an outlaw'. It was customary for the colonial authorities around this period to describe tribals in such terms.

The mutiny of the sepoys in Ranchi and Hazaribagh was the signal for the 'turbulent tribesmen' of Palamau. Pitambar was reportedly at Ranchi at the time of the outbreak of the Ramgarh battle and he regarded the abandonment of the station by the officers as implying the end of the British Raj. The return of Pitambar from Ranchi to Palamau and the advance of the Hazaribagh regiment through Palamau towards Rohtas, provided the signal to the Bogtahs to 'arm, assemble and commence plundering'. The two brothers declared themselves independent chieftains.[2]

Another important development was the conclusion of the Chero-Bogtah alliance. The last Chero Raja, Churaman Rai, died childless, leaving behind a widow. There were three collateral branches of the family, represented by Babu Bhavani Bakhsh Rai of Bisrampore, Babu Ram Bakhsh Rai of Chukla and Babu Devi Bakhsh Rai of Luckna. On 26 September 1857, Babu Bhavani Bakhsh Rai came to Shapur (opposite Daltonganj, on the other side of the river Koel), the residence of the widowed Rani. A general meeting of all the Chero chiefs was convened there, either to elect a Chero Raja or to devise measures for the safety of the district. But whatever the purpose of the meeting, it was 'followed by a general rising both of Cheros and of Kharwars'. The first target of attack was

Thakurai Raghubar Dayal Singh, the common object of enmity for both the Cheros and the Bogtahs. The Commissioner of Chotanagpur (Captain E.T. Dalton) observed:

> I am convinced that this time the Bogtahs were not so fascinated with the idea of having a Chero dynasty rule over them as led them to join the Cheros for the sake of gratifying their old grudge against the Thakurai, but it is quite clear that the Cheros and others considered the destruction of the Thakurai and his party as essential to the success of their undertaking, because he was devoted to the interest of the British Government; he felt confident that Government would not be subverted and he opposed himself in every way to the movement in favour of the Cheros.[3]

An economic motive was also at work behind the tribal uprising in Palamau. The Chero rulers had created a class of Chero *jagirdars* by giving them land. Hence there was a large number of small Chero *jagirdars*. Being impoverished, they had mortgaged their small estates, and they wanted to escape from the inevitable consequences of their improvidence. Captain E.T. Dalton, the commissioner, held that many proprietors might have joined the insurgents with 'a hope of summarily avoiding such encumbrances'. As Sarkar says,

> Just as the Crusades were joined by many a debtor to escape from the clutches of moneylenders of medieval Europe, so the Palamau *jagirdars* might have been tempted to join the movement with a similar object. This throws a new light on the genesis of the movement and would show that it had a 'sordid aspect' as distinct from the lofty national impulse of freeing the country from a foreign yoke.[4]

An interesting feature of the Palamau uprising was the attempt by rebels to link up with the Shahabad forces of Babu Kunwar Singh and Amar Singh, as also with the compatriots from Hazaribagh. Palamau's ecology – its extensive forests and natural links with Shahabad explain the rebels' attempt to join hands.

Palamau became the haven and refuge not only for the mutinous Hazaribagh companies but also for many Ranchi mutineers who, after their defeat in October 1857, had made common cause with the Bogtah leaders Nilambar and Pitambar, Chero Devi, Bakhsh Rai and Paramanand of Kunda. During the last days of the year 1857, when the mutineers' cause was on the verge of collapse, the Bogtah chieftains Nilambar and Pitambar tried to get armed reinforcements from Amar Singh, brother of Kunwar Singh. After the repulse of the insurgents at the Palamau fort (22 January 1858) by the Commissioner and Lt. Graham, letters addressed to Nilambar and Pitambar Sahai and Nucleut (Naklaut) Manji were found with the baggage and amongst them were communications from Ummer Singh promising immediate assistance from Koer Singh. Though they failed to get this assistance, they were joined by 'a party from the Mirzapore hills' and were thus emboldened to pillage several villages in early January 1858. After the suppression of the movement in Palamau, several mutinous sepoys proceeded to

Shahabad district, which was still disturbed. But they were disheartened and disorganized, and were not considered to be a potential source of mischief. Further, the dispersion of the Shahabad mutineers was followed by their infiltration into Palamau under Amar Singh and Seadha Singh.[5]

To revert to the first outbreak in Palamau, which took place within one month of the general meeting of the Cheros at the Shapur palace, the combined Chero–Kharwar–Bogtah forces attacked Chainpur, Shapur and Leslieganj in quick succession. The attack on Chainpur (21 October 1857) directed against Thakurai Raghubar Dayal Singh and his cousin Thakurai Kishun Dayal Singh was repulsed. At Shapur they captured four guns of the Rani, attacked the *thana*, destroyed its records and shot dead a *thana barkandaz*. Leslieganj was plundered and its *thana* burnt down. By the end of November the situation had become critical, as the whole district of Palamau rose up in rebellion. Graham was besieged in the 'large' house of Raghubar Dayal, 'encircled by a strong wall' and containing three to four hundred Indian women and children. The rebels, at first numbering 2000, swelled to 6000 and plundered the neighbourhood, but refrained from assaulting the Thakurai's house either because its defences had been strengthened by Graham or due to some other reasons.[6]

On 27 November 1857, the insurgents (Bogtah) attacked Rajherwa, the station of the coal company. On 2 December, the *thana* at Monka and Chutterpore were burnt and all their records destroyed.

The capture of rebel leader Devi Bakhsh Rai marked 'the collapse of the rebellion' in Palamau. The insurgents lost heart. Released from the fear of insurgents, the 'well-disposed chiefs' openly joined the British. Thus, the rebels had lost some of their most daring leaders who had been either taken and hanged, or imprisoned. The Cheros for the most part abandoned their cause.[7]

On 22 December the British attacked Palamau fort in three columns, defeated the Cheros and Bogtahs, who fled the fort leaving behind their guns, ammunition, cattle, supplies and baggage, and also captured some of the leading insurgents. The same day, the Bogtahs, who had formed the bold design of checking the advance of the commissioner at a small *ghat*, were attacked and repulsed by Macdonnell's men, assisted by seven *jagirdars*. Many Chero *jagirdars* now joined the British and were prepared to fight against the Bogtahs. The suppression of the Bogtahs, now isolated from the Cheros, became a comparatively easy affair, taking only a fortnight (8–23 February). The retreating Bogtahs fought till the end, from behind masked breastworks of stone and ridge. The village of Chemu on the Koel river, and the fortified residence of the Bogtah brothers and Saneya, another neighbouring Bogtah stronghold, were destroyed, and much grain and cattle were captured. Deserted by their followers, the two Bogtah chiefs became fugitives and eluded the vigilance of the search parties in the hills and jungles. But neither threats nor promises had any effect in inducing the influential captives to disclose the hideouts of their chiefs. While stern measures of reprisal (e.g. destruction of villages, seizure of goods and cattle, confiscation of estates), were taken against the inciters of the movement the less guilty followers and the people in general were sought to be conciliated. Nilambar and Pitambar were ultimately captured and hanged after trial. Many Chero *jagirdars* were ambivalent. Some Chero *jagirdars* were executed.[8]

III

Not all the tribes of Palamau or Ranchi joined the general uprising. The Mundas and Oraons kept aloof from the 1857 uprising, which in Ranchi was led by a scion of the Naagvanshi lineage, Bishwanath Nathshah Deo and supported by Jharkhandi Muslims – their leader was a weaver, Sheikh Bhikari – and Hindus. The *zamindars* attacked the German Mission at Ranchi and persecuted the Christian peasants in villages who had begun to assert their rights as peasants. In fact, with the suppression of the Revolt, the tide turned in favour of those peasants who launched the forty-year *mulki larai*, the struggle for the land, also known as the Sardar movement.[9] The Santals in Hazaribagh had little reason to be sympathetic to the soldiers of the Bengal Army, who had crushed their *hul* hardly two years earlier. However, the Santals in Hazaribagh were excited 'by the weakening of authority and thought the occasion opportune for squaring accounts with oppressive moneylenders and others'. The *District Gazetteer* reports that several bands of Santals collected for marauding purposes and were joined by the 'local bad characters', and a certain amount of plundering occurred between Gola and Chas (i.e. *thana* Petarbar) in Kharagdiha, at Kuju on the Ramgarh Road and at Jharpo near Bagodar. At Mandu, three local landholders instigated the Santals to commit murder as well as to plunder the village. These landholders were subsequently caught and hanged. The administration sent out a small punitive expedition to Gola, and the excitement died down immediately. The officials were satisfied that the disturbances were only sporadic and that there was no organized movement among the Santals as a whole. However, it was decided shortly after the Revolt to raise a levy of Kols and Santals for a military police, and a body of 500 of the more ardent aboriginals was enlisted for this work.[10]

The news of the sepoy uprising provoked some small uprising among the dispossessed Bhuiya *tikaits*, who considered the opportunity suitable for recovering their lands from the purchasers and occupying them; and they received some support from their tenantry.[11]

The Hos, probably recalling the similar example of being crushed in the Kol insurrection of 1832, refused to extend any support to the soldiers in Chaibasa. In fact, in the beginning of September, when the soldiers plundered the treasury and proceeded towards Ranchi to join their compatriots in Ranchi, the Hos blocked their way.

The soldiers failed to cross the river Sanjai, then in flood, and the Hos, denying the sepoys the right to remove the revenue collected from them, gathered in thousands, cut off all stragglers and harassed them continually. Eventually, the baffled mutineers were only too glad to accept the invitation of Arjun Singh, Raja of Porahat, to join him and make over to him the greater part of the money taken from the treasury.[12]

IV

In Central India, many *malguzars*, *jagirdars* and *zamindars* joined hands with the soldiers of 52 Regiment as they rose in rebellion at a few places. The Lodhi chieftains of Damoh joined the insurgents. By August 1857, all places north of Narmada were in the hands of rebels. The Gond ruler, Raja Shankar Shah, a scion of the Garhamalla family, on receiving the Commissioner's proclamation seeking loyalty, composed the poem, whose translation has been given at the beginning of this article. He and his son were blown off from the mouth of the guns.

An important uprising was led by the Binghals, a small tribe and its leader Bir Narayan Singh, a *jagirdar* of Sonakhan. In the year preceding the uprising, Bir Narayan had looted the granaries of a merchant to feed his starving people in a famine year. He had duly informed the authorities but was imprisoned for breaking the law. When the 1857 uprising started, he escaped from jail to organize a rebellion among his people. Sonakham(?) was turned into a fortress, but he was overpowered by the superior force. Forced to surrender, he was convicted for treason and hanged on 19 December 1857.

V

In western India, the Bhils were being 'reclaimed to civilization' through a policy package that comprised promotion of cultivation, encouraging Bhils to settle down as full-fledged peasants and raising the Bhils corps. The Bhils in Malwa showed their loyalty to the British by providing shelter and security to the Europeans, including the deputy political agent, in the Sitlamata Caves. The historic tablets on the caves begin with the words, 'When the Bengal Troops in Mhow mutinied in 1857, the deputy Bhil agent was taken to these caves for safety'. The names of the 'faithful Bhils' are inscribed and the tablets end with the words, 'These tablets were placed here by the orders of the British Government so that their gallantry and faithfulness may not pass out of remembrance'.[13]

The Bhils, like the tribes of eastern India such as the Santals, had not settled down as peasants. The Bhil's depredations could be considered as a form of protest. The Bhils were at large, everywhere indulging in predatory activities along the Bombay–Agra Road. The Bhils insurrection was described as 'outwardly a predatory rising in which the rebel bands took to plunder and loot'. They are even said to have plundered the rich but helped the poor. The Bhils, armed with bows and arrows, and with their knowledge of the terrain could traverse long distances and hide in inaccessible places. They roamed about in small bands and ravaged territories as far as Khandesh. The Raja of Barwani acknowledged the plunder of the villages by the Bhils, but admitted his utter inability to restrain their excesses. In this he was not alone, for other more powerful chiefs also exhibited a similar failing. A Hindi report from the Kamasdar of Brahmangaon, dated 18 August 1857 states that 'this day about sunrise Bhima Naik of Burwani Ilaqa (Barwani State), with some 500 to 700 men came to Mauza Datwara . . . and plundered it from that time till about 10 or 11 o'clock'. From a report of the same official, dated 5 September 1857, we find that Bhima Naik of Barwani state was committing 'great depredations in that part of the country', spread over the Holkar state, Barwani state and the Khandesh district, and along the highway road to Bombay.

Bhima Naik was the hero of the day. He plundered and rebelled alternately against the Holkar, Barwani state and the British, in the vast tract stretching between the Vindhya and Satpura ranges.

Bhima Naik's letter addressed to Vahiwutdar of Baroda, dated 27 September 1857, shows the astuteness of this rebel leader. As he says,

> I do not go to plunder Mauza Datwara of my own accord, as you suspect. I was ordered by Maharaja Jaswant Singh, the Raja of Barwani, Bhoodhgeer Bawa and Dowlatsing Mama that I should go and plunder the country within my reach, except Barwani, and was further directed that I should take possession of and plunder Mauza Datwara because he said the village belonged to Barwani. Fifty rupees and a dress of honour were then given to me with instructions to perform the required services. But the Raja did not afterwards support me in the undertaking, and therefore, I have now determined to make aggressions upon his own territories. He now prefers complaints against me to you and himself wishes to stand aloof.

He also holds out a threat:

> I have to add that you are not justified in preferring any complaints against me, because I am an old servant of the Raja and acted under his orders. You can claim compensation from the Raja and not from me. I shall encroach upon your districts or else you should make some arrangements for my pay.[14]

Elsewhere the Bhil Naiks were similarly active. In Ahmednagar, Bhagoji Naik and Kajar Singh Naik led the Bhils in their depredations spread over two years. They plundered villages, closed down the passes, looted the treasury, and even hired Arab mercenaries to carry out their raids. Kajar Singh was killed two years later by one of his own men.[15]

VI

It is interesting to note the parallels in the responses of the tribals and other sections of Indian society to the uprising of 1857. The rebellions were led by the scions of feudal aristocracy, tribal and non-tribal, who saw in the events of 1857 an opportunity to restore their lost raj, and free themselves from the clutches of money lenders and other agents of the oppressive Raj. A feudal structure had emerged in many tribal societies, and the indebted and impoverished small tribal *jagirdars* sought freedom from the dispensation that had brought about their ruin. Secondly, a sizeable body of the peasantry or yeomanry, both tribal and non-tribal, joined the uprisings. The Bogtah or a section of the Kharwar peasantry under their leaders who, too, were small *jagirdars* joining hands with the Chero feudal lords was an interesting development. Thirdly, the tribal story differs from the non-tribal in that the tribals had other scores to settle, with the moneylenders, traders and other enemies who were protected by the British Raj. And so, as the Gond chief's poem shows their wrath was turned against British rule. Lastly, there were many forms of tribal protests, depredations being one of them.

The tribal heroes of these uprisings are being honoured in various ways today. A statue of Bir Narayan Singh stands at Raipur. I organized a *mela* in honour of Nilambar and Pitambar at Khemu-Sanga in Palamau in 1967. But more important than such gestures is the thought today that the tribals and non-tribals fought together at a critical point in the country's history, and that the specific issues highlighted by tribals in the course of their participation are not without relevance today.

Notes and References

[1] D.P. Mishra (ed.), *The History of Freedom Movement in Madhya Pradesh*, Nagpur, 1956, p. 72.

[2] Jagdish Narayan Sarkar, 'The Mutiny of 1857–58 and the Palamau Jagirdars', *The Journal of the Bihar Research Society*, Vol. XLI, part 4, December 1955, pp. 529–71.

[3] Ibid.

[4] Ibid.

[5] Ibid.

[6] Ibid.

[7] Ibid.

[8] Ibid.

[9] K.S. Singh, *Birsa Munda and His Movement 1874–1901, A Study of Millenarian Movement in Chotanagpur*, New Delhi, 1983; K.S. Singh, *Tribal Society in India: An Anthropological Historical Perspective*, Delhi, 1984.

[10] E. Lister, *District Gazetteer: Hazaribagh*, 1917, pp. 68–69.

[11] Ibid.

[12] LSS O'Malley, *District Gazetteer, Singhbhum*, 1920, pp. 38–42.

[13] Kushalilal Srivastava, *The Revolt of 1857 in Central India-Malwa*, Delhi, 1966.

[14] Ibid.

[15] James M. Campbell, *Gazetteers of the Bombay Presidency: Khandesh*, Bombay, 1880, pp. 262–63.

Popular Culture and 1857

A Memory against Forgetting

Badri Narayan

An attempt has been made here to analyse the description of the Revolt of 1857 in local traditions, folk tales and other forms of popular culture. The study is divided into three parts. The first part traces the people's memory of the revolt from the extant evidence. The second part discusses the process of assimilation of the memory of the event, through symbols and rituals in the folk tradition. The third part includes a detailed review of the contemporary relevance of the popular memory of 1857 in rural society.

The primary data for this paper has been collected mainly from the Bhojpuri-speaking region, and Avadhi, Bundeli and Kauravi folklore has also been studied for purposes of comparison.

I would like to clarify at the outset that the term popular culture has been used here in the sense of peasant folk cultures.[1]

The colonial narrators described the Revolt of 1857 as a struggle of sepoys and decadent feudal landlords against the British rulers. They consciously overlooked the dynamic involvement of the people in this struggle. Unfortunately, the colonial narrative has played a pre-eminent part in the construction of our historical past. Indeed, it has to be admitted that of late several historians have studied the Revolt from the perspective of the participants, the suffering people of India. Yet, their picture can hardly be said to be complete, for it ignores the evidence found in the local sources and folk traditions. Certainly, recent researches have now established that a large number of people participated in the resistance to the British, regardless of the religious and caste differences among them.[2] The fact that traces and images of the Revolt of 1857 are still imprinted in the various folk cultures suggests that it was a popular mass struggle. Its memories were transformed into a stream of folk traditions and popular values which are, even today, very much a part of village culture. The peasants of the regions where the Revolt spread, were so deeply and actively involved in it that it became a part of their collective memory.

I

The Revolt of 1857 was most active in North India. Delhi, Uttar Pradesh, Bihar and Madhya Pradesh were directly involved in this struggle. This struggle is alive even today in the collective memory of the people of the affected regions.

As a result, the Revolt is described in many of the folk tales, ballads and *panwara* in the folk cultures found in Kauravi (Meerut, Delhi), Avadhi (Lucknow and Central U.P.), Braj (Mathura, Aligarh, Agra etc.), Bhojpuri (Bihar and Eastern U.P.), Baghel and Bundel (Jhansi and M.P.).

Without adequate exploration of folk culture, rewriting of people's histories will always be incomplete.[3] D.D. Kosambi, in his quest for social and historical truths, made meaningful attempts to analyse popular forms of the cultural behaviour of peoples.[4] The tradition, promoted by him survives even today. Outside India, Eugene Weber has reconstructed the history of the French peasantry through their folklore and local traditions.[5] In Indian society, studying folk culture is crucial to understanding peasant society because the everyday life of peasants is reflected in their folk culture. On the other hand, folk culture itself influences the consciousness of the peasantry. The two are inter-penetrative, according to Robert Redfield.[6]

Popular folk culture perceived the *Ghadar* of 1857 as an attempt of the people (described as '*balwai*' in colonial records) to free their *mulk* from the rule of the hated English (*firangis*). The popular perception of people towards the colonizers as *Firangis*, connotes certain characteristics and features. From certain interesting Bhojpuri, Avadhi, Bundeli and Bagheli folk cultural forms, we get some idea about what they actually meant when they referred to the English as *firangis*. *Firangis* were perceived by the people as those who were fair-skinned (*gora*), were looters, and exploiters of the country (*mulk*) and those who corrupted their religion and caste.

The folk perception of 1857 was that it was an attempt towards the liberation of their *mulk* from the oppressive rule of the '*Firangis*'. A Bhojpuri folk song is cited here which conveys the collective feelings of the people:

> Ab chhod re firangiyal hamar deswa
> Lutpat kaile tuhun, majwa udaile
> Kailas, des par julum jor.
> Sahar gaon luti, phunki, dihiat firangiya,
> Suni suni Kunwar ke hridaya me lagal agiya,
> Ab chhod re firangiya! Hamar deswa
> (British, now quit our country, for you loot us, enjoy the luxuries of our countrymen [in return]. You have looted and burnt the hamlets our cities and villages. Kunwar's heart burns to know all this. O British! Now quit our country.)

Popular cultures have perceived the Revolt as an expression of self-sacrifice by the rebels. This sense of self-sacrifice is reflected in the form as well as content of folk cultures. *Patia*, which literally means 'letter', is a type of folk-lore that actively invites the people to participate in the struggle against the British. It can also be taken as an effective folk form of a medium of commu-nication. The folk songs of *patia* tried to motivate people to join the rebels, asking them to make the 'sacrifice of their lives'. It also asks women to be prepared 'to break their bangles, wipe off vermilion from their forehead' (symbolic of widowhood), 'to become *rands* (widows) for their *mulk*'. Thus, people were exhorted to make sacrifices for their *mulk*.

This call was been put forward in the *Patia* form, and subsequently used by masses during various popular mobilizations.[7] Some lines of a *patia* from the *ghadar* of 1857 are as follows:

> *Bajan ganwai ke nevta,*
> *Churl forwai ke nevta,*
> *Sindoor pochhwai ke nevta,*
> *Jei ho hamar te math del*
> *Jei ho hamar te sath del!*

This *patia*, inviting people to sacrifice their lives for their *mulk*, and exhorting women to be prepared to break their bangles and to remove vermilion from their forehead, represents the popular mentality of people and presents a model of peasant consciousness.

Apart from Kunwar Singh, Rani Lakshmibai and Nana Saheb, the 1857 struggle witnessed many other valiant fighters, about whom we find information in the sources of folk culture and in local histories. More frequently and prominently they appear in Bhojpuri folk literature as the heroes of 1857:

> Amar Singh (younger brother of Kunwar Singh), Hare Krishna, Nishan Singh, Ranjit Yadav, Zulfikar, Maiku Mallah, Dharman bi (woman), Karman bi (Woman), Ibrahim Khan, Bansuriyan Baba (inspirer of Kunwar Singh), Lakhiya (a lower-caste women), Madho Singh, Pargat Singh, Beni Madho, Rajab Ali, and Miyan Khan.

Thus, in folk culture, the Revolt of 1857 does not appear as a struggle confined to a caste, religion or specific class. In popular perception it was a war of liberation from foreign oppression and humiliation. Communal and caste harmony is very much evident in such folklore.

Songs describing the chivalry of many Muslim and lower-caste heroes are quite common in village folklore. One may find *panwaras* (chivalry songs) of Zulfikar Khan, Ibrahim Khan, Rajab Khan and Umed Ali in Bhojpuri folk tales. Even today, the tales of Khuda Bakhsh and Ghaus Khan (the supporters of Lakshmi Bai) are sung with respect. In the folk tales of Bundelkhand, many narratives are available describing the brave deeds of Jhalkhari Bai, a lower-caste woman. Further, a deep influence of this Revolt is observed in lower-caste popular cultural forms of the *dhobi, kumhar, luhar* etc. Historical narratives of 1857 reveal that lower castes in the Bhojpur region were no less involved in this Rebellion. There is a popular *dhobi geet* (song) in this region which is cited below to depict the emotional involvement of this deprived caste in 1857:

> *Mahua ke pedwa tabai, nik lagged,*
> *Jaba mahuari hoae*

Ara sabariya tabai nik lage,
Kunwar Singh ke rajwa hoae
(The Mahua tree looks beautiful in its blossoming season, and Arrah town will
look beautiful when it is ruled by Kunwar Singh).

Infact, Kunwar Singh's rule in Bhojpuri folk-culture is described as liberation from oppression and foreign thralldom. This belief is found not only among
Bhojpuri people, but is also deeply ingrained in the popular memory of the people
in the region between Calcutta and Lucknow, and across the Ganges in both
directions.

There is an alertness in folk consciousness against the tactical and divisive
acts of the British, who tried to break the unity that emerged among the people
during this struggle.

One of the folk songs reflecting people's awareness against the deceitful
character of the British is cited here.

Tohafa debo, inam debo,
Tah ke raja banlab re!
Firangiya re!
Mose na chali tor chaturai.
(O *Firangis*! your awards, felicitations, may make a person favourably disposed
towards you, but you cannot allure me in your deceptive and cunning designs.)

The folk consciousness contains much hatred against those who deceived
Kunwar Singh and supported the *firangis* during the national insurrection. Thus,
the 'Maharaj of Dumaraoi' is a hated personality in the folklore of the region.

Bhojpur mein Dumarao basela,
Uho bade firangriya nu
Sub visen mili gharmen lukaile
Babu parela akele nu.
(The qasba Dumaraon is in Bhojpur wherein many British reside. All the *Visens*
[a clan of Rajputs] hide in their homes and Babu Kunwar Singh is left alone.)

This shows that one cannot assume people's consciousness as being inert
and passive, in fact, in the context of 1857, people were organized, committed
and involved in conscious mass mobilization.

II

The continuum of folk consciousness assimilates cultural and historical
memories within it to make them come alive. These memories get incorporated
within the cultural traditions of people through popular practice. People keep
alive only those memories that still have a relevance for their lives. The contem-
poraneousness of the past provides reference points for the recurrence of the
concerned memory. Many values are reflected by these popular traditions and
people relate themselves to these values. In fact, the values that emerged from

1857, provide the relevance of the event in contemporary life. Through these popular practices and traditions, the memory of the unfinished agenda of this struggle remained imprinted in the psyche of the people. The narratives, the memories and the values of 1857, have thus become a part of folk tradition, which remain alive and are practiced even today. Take, for example, the following three instances.

1. There is a tradition of preparing *peetha* in Bhojpuri folk culture on the occasion of Godhan. *Peetha* is a food item prepared with pulses and rice that have been soaked and ground. But in nearby Jagdishpur and *sahar*, parts of Bhojpur region, this *peetha* is called *Amarpeetha*. There is a narrative that is linked with *amarpeetha*. According to it, on the day [of Gudhay] eating *amarpeetha* is customary, and because Amar Singh, the younger brother of Kunwar Singh, went for the war without eating it, he was defeated. There is a popular belief that had he gone to battle after eating *amarpeetha*, he would have won.

Through this ritual Bhojpuri folk culture expresses its anguish at the defeat of Kunwar Singh and Amar Singh in the battle. Along with this, it also expresses the desire for victory among the forthcoming generations in their future struggles.

2. In the Bhojpuri region too, during the *phalgun* month of the Indian calendar, Holi is celebrated as a festival of joy. Outside the door of every house, village folk sing songs, beating the *dhol* (drum) and playing a *baja* (musical instrument). But, in this region, a mournful song is also sung during this joyful festival. In this song it is stated that all celebrations have no meaning until Kunwar Singh becomes the king. 'Without Kunwar Singh this festival of joy is fragile. True joy lies in the liberation of people'. The return of the rule of Kunwar Singh here means the liberation of people in the domain of Kunwar Singh.

3. *Sohar* is a ritual song which is generally sung by women during the ceremony arranged at the birth of a child. It is a part of the popular tradition of *samskara* or birth rites of children. In the Bhojpur region, there is a popular *sohar* sung by women. This *sohar* contains the memory of 1857 in these words:

> *Bhado mas andheria, badariya gagan ghere ji,*
> *Tahl rate challe, Kunwar Singh lare laraiya ji.*
> (It was the month of *bhadon*; night and dark clouds were covering the sky when Kunwar Singh went to war, at the end of the night.)

In fact, through the repeated recurrence of the narrative of a historical event, the folk tradition transforms the event into a popular memory. In this way, a historical memory is created, which operates like a *samskara* of the people, especially at cathartic moments in their contemporary lives.

III

The great event of 1857 is an integral part of people's memory. People want to preserve and bring to life their memories through *vak* (oral tradition) *drish* (visual) and *krit* (contemporary everyday forms of resistance).[8] Vested interests attempt to erase these memories from the minds of the people and to transplant these with false memories which would serve their political ends. For this, they use all available medium of communication, words, phrases, and a army of intellectuals.[9] But this power is able to transform memories of only those communities which are unable to resist the counter-memories created by the vested interests. Many communities in remote rural areas have been able to keep alive their original memories of 1857. These are transmitted from generation to generation, and are preserved and kept alive through folk tales, folklore, symbols, specific rituals and certain popular narratives. The memories of 1857 preserved in folk culture represent the everyday forms of resistance used by people in the past.[10]

The landed, feudal forces of this region also attempted to manipulate the memories of 1857 in their own way. Selecting those which were most suited to their interests, they proceeded to propagate these memories using their own cultural media. It is worth mentioning that feudal forces too have produced many folk singers and created many folk dramas which are meant to serve their ideological interests. By interpreting and reconstructing the past in accordance with their respective predicament, they have constructed a feudal version of history.[11] But people want to retain the popular memories of 1857, continuously flowing in the folk culture.

In Bhojpuri folk culture, memories of 1857 are available in both oral as well as visual forms. By combining visual texts with oral narratives these are made more powerful. Couple of examples should make the point clear.

Dusadhi Badhar

There is a small piece of land lying between Jagdishpur and Piro, which is known as Dusadhi Badhar. A story is attached to this space of land. The story tells us that once Kunwar Singh was passing through this place with his soldiers. Some *ropinharine* (females engaged in plantation) were engaged in the planting of rice in the muddy fields. It was the month of *phalgun*. One of those women was Phulia, who belonged to Dusadh caste. A women asked her to throw some mud on Kunwar Singh. Phulia replied that since she came from Jagdishpur, Kunwar Singh was like a brother to her. Kunwar Singh was so impressed by her reply that he made her the owner of that piece of land. From then on this *badhar* (a small piece of land) is known as Dusadhi Badhar, because Phulia was from Dusadh caste.[12]

Mudkatawa Nala

There is a water drain (*nala*) near Shivpur in Balia districts which is called Mudkatwa Nala. A folk narrative is linked with this drain. The tale is that under the leadership of Siddha Singh from Shivpur, who was one of the reliable warriors of Kunwar Singh, the rebels killed a 100 British soldiers and dumped their corpses in this drain.

We can find many such places in eastern U.P. and Bihar, which tell the story of 1857. People instantly remember the eventful year whenever they hear names of these places. Through such mediums they keep alive the memories of 1857, preserving in history the values of this great event.

The Revolt of 1857 took the form of a popular struggle, and so its memories have become an integral part of our popular culture and folk tradition, images which repeatedly enliven the past. To memorize the history of 1857, the people used all three mediums of folk remembrance, viz. *vak*, *drish* and *krit*. Perhaps people want to keep alive these memories because they believe that the tasks of 1857 are still unfinished.

Notes and References

[1] Peter Burke, *Popular Culture in Early Modern Europe*, London 1970, stresses the fact that popular culture is distinct from high or learned culture.

[2] Marx, in his writings on India, argued that the revolt was a revolt of the masses, and was not merely a mutiny. Other works that have studied the people's initiative in the revolt include, P.C. Joshi (ed.) *Rebellion 1857*, Calcutta, 1957; Badri Narayan, *Lok Sanskriti Mein Rahstravad*, New Delhi, 1996.

[3] Nihar Ranjan Roy, *Bangla Itihas, Lekhak Samvay Samiti*, Calcutta, 1966; Maurice Aymord and Harbans Mukhia (eds), *French Studies in History*, Vol. 1, New Delhi, 1988, provide the theoretical background for this statement.

[4] D.D. Kosambi, *An Introduction to the Study of Indian History*, Bombay, 1975. Also see his, *Myth and Reality*, Bombay, 1962.

[5] Eugene Weber, *Peasants in Frenchmen, Modernization of Modern France (1870–1934)*.

[6] Robert Redfield, *Peasant Society and Culture*, Chicago, 1956.

[7] P.C. Joshi (ed.), *Rebellion 1857*, Calcutta, 1957.

[8] Badri Narayan, 'Memory and Social Protest', paper presented at the Seminar on 'Culture, Communication and Power', organized by Centre de Sciences Hummins, Embassy of France, 21–23 April 1997).

[9] Ngugi wa Thiongo, *Bhasha, Sanskriti Aur Rashtriya Asmita* (Hindi translation), New Delhi, 1994.

[10] See James Scott, *Weapons of the Weak – Everyday Form of Peasant Resistance*, New Haven, 1985; and Milan Kundera, *The Book of Laughter and Forgetting*, New Delhi, 1990.

[11] H.L. Senviratne, *Identity, Consciousness and the Past*, New Delhi, 1997.

[12] This narrative was recorded in Jagdishpur, the narrator is Sheo Muni of Jagdishpur, Bhojpur, Bihar.

1857: The Need for Alternative Sources

Pankaj Rag

There has often been a tendency on the part of historians of 1857 to argue about its character in terms of certain specific labels – whether it was a 'conspiracy' or was it 'spontaneous'; whether it was a 'feudal reaction', a 'restorative' movement or was it a religious war; whether people were primarily driven by 'economic' concerns or were civil 'outbursts' mere consequences of the political vacuum.[1] As has been increasingly realized in recent years, 1857 was too complex a movement to be adequately explained in terms of general labels of universal application and such labels no longer occupy an unquestioned status. In the last two decades or so, as an integral part of a world historiographical shift, regional variations in the nature of causes and organization have been increasingly highlighted. The trend can be said to have begun with Eric Stokes, who concentrated on the districts of western Uttar Pradesh to show how the response to the uprising was worked out in these areas in terms of agrarian conditions and organizational factors.[2] Similarly, Brokin analyzed the tracts of western Rohilkhand to argue about the patterns and dynamics of the Revolt in the region.[3] Other works centring on specific regions have also appeared from time to time.[4]

However, even in all these works, what has been emphasized is the 'elitist' level of Indian society. The Revolt for long has been studied in terms of a given goal and elaborated in terms of the role of 'glorious' leaders like Nana Peshwa, Rani of Jhansi, Tatya Tope, Kunwar Singh and so on, towards achieving that goal. Even the Marxian approach of P.C. Joshi and others, explains its failure in terms of the limited retrogressive aims of the leadership and betrayal by the landed elements. Whether the leaders mobilized or betrayed, regardless, the leaders remain as the crucial actors on the stage. Even in Stokes' rigorous work, diversity of response is explained purely in terms of the magnate or 'village elite'. In *The Peasant and the Raj* (1978) the leaders and the aristocracy seem to react to the political vacuum within broadly defined caste and communal groups. Though in *The Peasant Armed* (published in 1986, after his death) Stokes seems to move away from caste as the basic unit of analysis to '*dhara*' (multi-caste faction), even here the tendency to explain the Revolt remains in terms of the economic impact of British rule on the magnates and elites of the '*dharas*'.[5] There has been little attempt to understand the thoughts and actions of thousands of ordinary non-elite villagers who rose on such a considerable scale. Even in the works, for instance, of S.B. Chaudhuri, where people do come into the picture, there is a tendency to treat them in simply as automatic responders to the objective changes brought about by British rule, or as a passive or semi-passive mass that was activated by the mobilization efforts of the leaders. There was no real attempt to study the vital elements of popular perception of grievances and of the ways in which people worked out such perceptions and gave meanings to them in terms of their own cultural codes, symbols and value systems.

Only in the last decades or so, as a part of the worldwide trend of 'history from below', has there been a real shift in perspective, and as a result, aspects of autonomous popular consciousness and action during the Revolt of 1857 have started receiving greater attention. Rudrangshu Mukherjee, in his work on 1857 in Awadh, has shown how the influx of colonialist policies upset the moral economy of the peasant world; how the complementarity of the *taluq* – peasant relationships, where inequality was 'circumscribed by custom and mediated by various forms of beneficience', was disrupted by alien colonialist operations with shocking repercussions on the ethical and normative visions of the peasants; and how the Awadh issue acquired the status of an ideology in the eyes of the inhabitants of the region – all of this underlining his vital conclusion that the issue was 'created in the minds of various sections of population in terms of notions of traditional loyalty and prestige'.[6] Ranajit Guha in his pathbreaking work on peasant insurgency has discussed 1857 in some detail to show how the peasants could often act as the subjects and make their own history, how they worked out their response in terms of their own language and ideas of solidarity, transmission and mobilization.[7]

However, even in the works which have attempted to study 1857 from a perspective of 'history from below', the sources used to reconstruct rebel mentality are primarily elitist official sources (the minutes, dispatches, correspondence, reports and narrative of events written by British officials and generals) which have very little to say about rebel mentality. Rather, these sources speak of the overriding concern on the part of the colonialist state to preserve law and order and the common rebel is totally denied a mind and rationality of his own. The Rebellion is treated either as a conspiracy by some ill-willed men or as a mishap or disease – something akin to an epidemic. Wherever possible, such official sources prefer to treat 1857 as an uprising without an issue, and where it was not possible the issues are termed as unreasonable, irrational and steeped in obscurantism and fanaticism.

The term 'rebel', 'badmash', 'dacoit', all seem to overlap one another. Wherever an uprising occurred, it led to 'anarchy' or 'disorganization' in the eyes of the British; by the same logic wherever it was suppressed the place was 'fast settling down' – as if the Rebellion was just a freak accident and an abnormal mishap in the otherwise smooth course of sedentary life under the beneficial British rule.[8] The solution advocated and practiced by historians like Ranajit Guha to 'invert' these official sources in order to arrive at the rebel mentality seems to move within a framework of binary opposites, which is problematic. Such an approach misses out on a whole range of nuances and shades of intermediary attitudes and interpretations that various groups of rebels manifested through their actions and perceptions. It gives us very little idea of the separate cultural domain that the groups of common men had tried to preserve against the onslaught of the colonialist regime. There is very little help from the official sources in trying to reconstruct the various constituents of popular culture – notions of 'dharma' and life, the systems of symbolism and ritual significance active within polity and society and arrived at by different groups of rebels – all of which are essential to truly be able to grasp and understand the modalities and idioms of popular grievances and actions in 1857 with the causal and characteristic inter-relations and spatial variations. It is here that the importance of sources of oral and popular history like folk songs, folk tales, etc., as a primary source for reconstructing the history of 1857 from the point of view of a common rebel acquires relevance. A serious criticism of the historians of the so-called 'subaltern' school is that, unfortunately, their 'new' writing is still largely based on the old elitist sources. Despite realizing the significance of sources of oral and popular history and giving some indications to their possible use for the writing of an alternative history from below, the actual use of this vast store of source material is still largely lacking.[9]

Though historians have made use of the proclamations and letters of rebel leaders of note to comment on the particulars of the ideological inclinations, aims and interests of the rajas and chieftains, for a deeper insight into the ideological predilections, mental make-up and the arena of realities of the common rebels during 1857, it is high time that one woke up to the necessity of using 'non-elitist' sources. One understands that this is a task that has to be undertaken with caution – the sources of oral history are not always historically correct in so far as correctness in chronology is concerned; the bravery of the rebels is often exaggerated and outcomes of battles distorted, and there is always a possibility of aberrations and interpolations over time resulting in a question mark over the 'purity' of the source. Yet, despite these limitations, if proper care is exercised in analyzing them, their value is immense as the repository of the mental, physical and cultural world of the common men who participated in 1857.

The area chosen here to illustrate the utility of such sources in constructing different facets of the Rebellion is one that abounds in folk songs and local literature on the theme, but has been largely ignored in serious regional historiography of 1857; namely eastern Uttar Pradesh and the adjoining areas of western Bihar, especially Shahabad. These areas witnessed great rural revolts during 1857 and provide an ideal arena to study the various aspects of the physical and mental world of the ordinary rebel with all its virtues and pitfalls. It has been the practice of many historians to dismiss folklore as conservative simply because the customs and beliefs do not conform to the accepted ideas about post-enlightenment rationality and innovation. However, common men and women of mid-nineteenth century India had their own notions of rationality, propriety and utility; all of which made known their stand (to a large extent) in 1857, and which can be properly appreciated through a rigorous study of folklore. It is not my contention here to use folklore and contemporary local or regional plebian literature in isolation; nor is it simply to be used as a gap filler. It can both affirm and contradict what is known, but, more importantly, can provide alternative shades to the same truths or half-truths, from a different perspective.

II

The common rebels saw in the Raj an entity and structure that unwontedly and repeatedly interfered in their way of life and they rebelled by attacking and obliterating everything that they perceived as symbolizing that structure. The boast of Jodhu Singh in Jahanabad that he would destroy every public building between the Soane and Monghyr is typical of many of the rebels of the period. Such destructions were not always the momentous by-products of rampant frenzy. In Allahabad, hundreds of men were 'systematically engaged for many days' in the wanton destruction of a railway storehouse – the undertaking of 'systematic destruction' for a long period clearly underlining the deep filtration of hatred for any symbol of colonial power.[10] For the rebels, destruction had its own joy. It signified triumph; liberation from perpetual exploitation and oppression under the colonialist institutions. An extract from a '*panwara*' from the area of Shahabad makes an interesting study in this regard:

> They are up now at Masaurhi, and Masaurhi thana smashed / The *sipahees* all gain freedom / and now Punpun too they raid / and Punpun *thana* smashed / now a siege in Patna laid / The prisoners all gain freedom / and they are up now at Maner.[11]

The *sipahees* too gain freedom from the shackles of the British *thana* in the same way as the prisoners gain freedom from jails. The identification of *thanas* and jails as one in the mind of the common rebel and the equation of both as oppressive symbols of colonial bondage is noteworthy. The liberation of *sipahees* from one is identical with the liberation of convicts from the other. The British sense of justice; British concepts of discipline, law, order and punishment are all denied in popular perception which hails their destruction as freedom – a powerful statement attacking the whole system through its semiological and linguistic structure of articulation. Though much has been written on the impact of the British revenue policies and legal policies on the agrarian system in the first half of the nineteenth century, the trend has mainly been to objectively outline the causes and draw a straight line between cause and effect, the latter reflected in the uprising of 1857. Such an approach tends to ignore the vital factor of the popular perception of such changes, which differed for different social groups and regions – a factor which can provide a richness of variety to the known, and a repertoire of knowledge about the unknown facets of 1857. The pathos and helplessness of the common villagers can only be captured if one moves to alternative sources, for they can help in illuminating the hitherto hidden domain of popular feeling in historiography – a domain which through its subjectivity and intensity can provide a much more realistic and logical correlation with the spirit and vigour of popular action during 1857. The exploitation of people under the British legal system, where, for the peasants, the trap of the grinding-wheel of litigation meant wastage of cultivation days, indebtedness and incessant milking of their resources, is aptly expressed in a near contemporary poem by Sukhdevji, an obscure Bhojpuri saint-poet writing sometime in the mid-nineteenth century, where accountability in hell is expressed through the punitive metaphor of courts underlining the perception of the new legal system as an afflicting curse by the common man:

> *Samujhi pari jab jaeb kachhari*
> *. . . Khael peeal lel del kagaj baki sab niksi*
> *Dharmaraj jab lekha leehan loha ke sotwar mar paree*
> *Age peechhe chopdar dhai bi mugdar jam ke phans pari*
> *Agin khamb men bandhi ke rakhihen, Hajri jamini koi na kari*
> (You will understand once you go to the court. Whatever you have eaten or drunk will all come out – only papers would be left with you, i.e., all your riches will go and they shall be replaced by tons of useless paper. Being called to account by Dharmaraj [here, judge] is like being beaten by an iron rod; the court-retainers would not let you escape from the strangulation that you will face. No one will come forward to bail you out, and you will feel as if you have been tied to the pillars of the court forever.)[12]

For an ordinary Indian, used to custom-bound relationships based on words of honour and ties of obligation and duty, the whole British legal system, based on written contracts and documents and drawn out on tons of 'useless' paper was alien and extortionist. In this moving poem, paper symbolizes the unwanted inroad of an alien system that takes away the sustaining items of an ordinary man's life and yet justifies it as legal. In fact, the anguish at the complexities and unfamiliarity of this alien 'paper based' justice, with no recognition of the norms of tradition-based political and cultural order, has become a part of folk ethos. A Magadhi saying defines the new politico-legal system by using the same metaphor of paper as '*kagaz ka raj hona*' (rule of paper) and a Bhojpuri folk song equates the expensive and ruinous court cases with the curse of having a marriageable daughter in traditional community life.

> *Chik baheli soom dhan, au beti ke badhi*
> *Ehu ke dhan nag hate taker badan se rari*[13]

Courts and magistracy would thus prove to be the prime targets of rebels at all places. Though all symbols of colonial power and authority were attacked, the ultimate triumph for the people seems to have been the capture or destruction of the court or the bungalow of the magistrate. In the following extract from a folk song describing the capture of the Arrah court, the use of the word '*adhikar*' to emphasize the symbolic eclipse of British authority in a township is noteworthy.

Rama Arra par kaile chadhaiya re na
Rama Kutchhery ke uparwa re na
Rama Kunwar Singh Karle adhikarwa re na
(O Rama, the forces of Kunwar Singh invaded Arrah and captured the court.)[14]

The credit for translating these aspirations of the people into action is given to Kunwar Singh in most of the folk songs of the region.

Buxar se jo chale Kunwar Singh Patna aa kart eek
Patna ke magister bole karo Kunwar ko theek
Atuna baat jab sune Kunwar Singh dee bungala phunkwaee
gali gali magistger roee, lat gae ghabdai
(Kunwar Singh started from Buxar and arrived in Patna. The magistrate of Patna announced that he would teach Kunwar Singh a lesson. As soon as Kunwar Singh heard this, he got the magistrate's bungalow burnt. The magistrate is now weeping in the streets and even the governor has panicked.)[15]

However, even in such folk songs, he is not presented as a leader who has enforced his own wishes on the people of his community. Rather, as we shall discuss later, in many of the folk songs and folk tales he is shown carrying out the wishes of the community. In fact, folklore has a valuable advantage in that it denotes the voice of feelings of a community rather than the individual. Even if they are seen as hailing the glories of an individual leader; the semiology and the choice of words and their presentation often provide us with a significant insight into the mental domain of the community, its normative structure, its systems of deference to tradition or resistance to forces of change and the trajectories through which such attitudes moved during 1857–59 in different areas. In some folk songs the reasons given for Kunwar Singh's rebellion indicate less of his actual motivations than the fact that people created images of Kunwar Singh based on their own miseries and hopes.

Kailas des par julum jor firangiya
Julum Kahani Suni tadpe Kunwar Singh
Ban ke lutera utral fauj firangiya
Sahar gaon looti phunki, dihlas firangiya
Sun sun Kunwar ke hirday lagal agia
(The 'firangi' forcibly oppressed the country and Kunwar Singh was deeply moved when he heard the tales of their atrocities. The 'firangi' army arrived to loot and it looted and burnt cities and villages. When he came to know of all this, Kunwar Singh was enraged.)[16]

It is true that the impact of British policies in the first half of the nineteenth century, and the changes affecting various sections of the population provide us with a proper perspective to study 1857. However, as Bayly has pointed out, the actual level of land revenue or the specific degree of penetration by moneylenders in particular areas may have been much less of the 'bania', and the infidel had grown to subvert the whole moral economy and value system of society. It is no wonder then that the 'bania' is often a subject of ridicule and mockery in village popular culture. *'Bania reejhe to hans de'* is a pertinent and rather popular folk description of a miserly 'bania', who does not share his prosperity with the community through ties of beneficience unlike the traditional feudal gentry.[17] There also exists a folk song in which the rebel sepoys are refused food and fuel by a liar 'bania' while they are shown as being welcome with open arms by Kunwar Singh:

> Mark, Bania, our plight / we've had no bite / for full four nights and days / send us some ration and fuelwood; some or Khassi–goat; / some *ghee*, some *atta* send us! But a Bania's answer note; 'Sipahee, trust my word; at all / no *ghee*, nor *atta* is here; nor fuel, nor ration, possible / no succour hence, I fear / . . . while at Jagdishpur, the Baboo did incline / to order a *jajam* to be spread; / And the men all squat to dine.[18]

In fact, it is remarkable to note in the popular saying *'Shehar Sikhaya Kotwali'* (man learns from experience) that the reference to 'Shehar' (city) as the centre for the new trends in commerce and commercial ways is supplemented by that of the 'Kotwali' (another symbol of the new colonial system in the field of law and order).[19] The new experiences of commerce and law under the colonial dispensation which now define the parameters of determining worldliness, are, in the eyes of the common villager, mutually inclusive and are parts of the same unfamiliar and impersonal system that had invaded their lives. This new system was both intimidating and perplexing – something strange was happening all around. It is no coincidence that in Bhojpuri folk songs 'opium' cultivation and trade are always depicted using the strange metaphor of a pregnant and/or blind cow whose dairy products are being sold in the market even as she is much pregnant and unmilked.

> *Pehle dahi jamai ke, pachhe duhni gai*
> *Bachhwa okar pet men kid ware laynu bikai*
> *Pet men bacha anhar gai*
> *Jekar makhan Bengala jai.*[20]

Is the creation of this strange, uncustomary (something that is not done) metaphor in popular mentality for 'opium' cultivation and trade simply a literal depiction of the physical anatomy of the poppy plant or does it through its linguistic irony indicate the way in which the common villagers of eastern United Provinces and adjoining areas perceived the large-scale expansion of opium cultivation by the Europeans (especially in poorer areas like Ghazipur where the government opium agency pumped advances and forced cultivation), as something alien, foreign, abnormal and outlandish? The metaphors of cow and calf once again seem quite distinct and selective – these were sacred symbols of the village's religious and cultural ethos and the colonial regime was invading the norms and beliefs considered worth being maintained in this sacred regime by using its own ridiculous notions of livelihood and economy (here symbolized by opium) that were as unacceptable, blind to sensitivities (hence opium equated with an '*anhar*' or blind cow) and laughable as the idea of milk products from a much pregnant cow. After all grain crops were much more lucrative than this alien, costly and polluting cash crop, which, from the 1840s was facing increased competition from the cheaper Chinese product and was surviving, decidedly to the utter resentment of the poor cultivator in Gorakhpur and Ghazipur, simply due to pressure from the government which was forcibly extending cultivation and pulling down prices.[21] It is from folk culture and folk memory that one can trace many of the unexplained details of day to day resentment felt by the common man, whose norms of dignity and ideas regarding livelihood and propriety were being assaulted by the new regime. In 1857, opium merchants and indigo planters were the principal targets of the people's fury, besides the auction purchasers in the countryside in both Ghazipur and Gorakhpur. The inhabitants of Chaura village in Ghazipur would herald the uprising by attacking an indigo planter named Mathews, 'who barely escaped with his life, all is property being plundered and burnt'.[22] It is therefore no coincidence that after the treasure of the collectorate at Ghazipur had been safely shifted, the British would employed the entire force of the newly arrived Madras Fusiliers at the opium factory which was thus 'put into a state of defence'.[23]

Plundering the rich is a familiar expression of popular discontent. In the context of 1857, this sort of plunder acquires a logic of its own if one were to examine the composition of the crowd of plunderers in most cases. Apart from the sepoys, it was made up of, what the British referred to in a derogatory sense as, the 'rabble' of the population which in reality comprised the marginal groups – the out-of-work artisans and craftsmen, destitutes and beggars, retrenched soldiers, impoverished petty gentry, labourers and so on. Though there is no reason to develop a systematic causal relationship behind every act of plunder by these marginal groups, who were constantly on the lookout for booty in peace or war, yet there are certain indications that the memory of better days predisposed them to plunder. Bayly has argued that day labourers from marginal groups who participated in the unstable export economy were especially vulnerable to its fluctuations, and hence one explanation of the nature of plundering during 1857 can be that such people were trying to secure themselves for the future by looting bullion, ornaments and other negotiable items.[24]

At this point one needs to stress that the contexts of power and status in colonial India – worked out within its own semiology of authority and ritual status – were reinforced by the flux that the onset of colonialism produced in the social, political and economic realms. For instance, in the major centres of cloth production such as Lucknow, Banaras, Mau and Mubarakpur (in Azamgarh), the weavers and spinners faced violent fluctuations in their trade and a progressive erosion of their markets – a tendency that was the combined result of the British policy of importing machine-made goods as well as that of a decline in demand following the erosion in power and influence of military and royal establishments along with that of their avenues of patronage and employment. Shifting to weaving coarser, cheaper cloth as well as to unfamiliar vocations like agricultural labour seemed to be the only alternatives for them in such a fast changing scenario. Such weavers, artisans and craftsmen who had seen better, honourable days, and who had been rendered jobless under the new colonial regime were the main participants in the popular upsurge in the cities, towns and *qasbas*. It was not only a question of material deprivation – this was overdetermined by a sense of loss of pride, honour and prestige in day to day life.[25] The local proverb, '*Julha dhuniya samjhul?*' ('Do you think I am as lowly as a *julaha* or a *dhuniya*?') starkly reminds us of the downward slide of such communities on the scale of social prestige and vanity.

1857 saw an eruption of such grievances of these marginal groups in the form of numerous attacks on commercial men and rich *mahajans*. In Banaras city itself, where the town popular remained remarkably quiet, Muslim weavers 'temporarily raised the green flag of holy war'.[26] In Allahabad, the weavers join-ed Liaqat Ali – himself a weaver by birth in total revolt and it was this groundswell and its triumph that succeeded in 'driving many sympathizers with government... into seclusion'.[27] Kanpur, a 'rootless city' with a preponderance of labourers and destitutes, saw the merchants hastily trying to bring about some sort of 'order' under Nana's regime in order to prevent this groundswell from getting out of bounds.[28] In Gaya again, the Hindu *mahajans* were the chief sufferers 'preyed upon at once by the Mohammedan rabble of the lower town and by the priests of the upper' – the former most decidedly dominated by the weavers and artisans of Gaya fame.[29] In fact, for thirteen days no rebel leader came forward to organize a government in Gaya – a testimony to the triumph of the ordinary people in the city.[30] In Arrah, in a unique trial after the suppression of the Revolt, the 'towns-people of Arrah' as a whole were accused of rebellion against the British.[31] Craftsmen like the local blacksmiths were instrumental in Arrah in actively helping the rebel sepoys through manufacture and supply of cannon shots.[32] Similar help by local artisans was also rendered in Shahabad, where thousands of village '*lohars*' made swords for the peasant rebels, and in Kanpur where skilled artisans were used by Nanhe Nawab to make cannon shots for the tanks.[33]

We would be overstating the point if we were to conclude that all the artisans, weavers and craftsmen who played a significant role in the upsurge possessed a clear-cut idea about the structure of colonial authority and the policies that had led to their impoverishment and social degradation. And that therefore they knowingly and purposefully attacked the merchants, because they symbolized that exploitative structure. However vague and nebulous, their perception could at least identify the immediate oppressor, and since the latter had usually benefited under the colonial regime, an attack on him did acquire – by implication – the relevance of a challenge to the British authority in the context of 1857. This is not to conclude that plunderers were always objective and discriminate in choosing their targets or that only British loyalists were plundered. It is true that villages were often looted indiscriminately and mercilessly by rebel magnates, sepoys as well as by the common population. At the same time, it would not be wrong to say that 1857 provided an opportunity to those suffering under the colonial regime to take out their wrath on those whom they considered relatively prosperous. To the extent that the latter consisted of a number of sympathizers of the government, their outburst worked in an anti-British direction.

Official sources, however, do not provide us with a complete picture of the 'loot' and 'plunder'. In the various descriptions of such incidents in the official discourse, what is missing are the elements of glee, vitality and a sense of legitimacy from the point of view of the plunderers. On the contrary, plunder is never lamented in folk songs. In the following Bhojpuri folk song (a variant of a Gujar folk song also based on the theme of plunder in the Meerut bazaar) what is being lamented, instead, is the fact of naming missed out on plunder:

> *Log sab little sal dusala /hamar saiyanji lutle rumal/Meerath ke*
> *Sadar bazaar ba/hamar saiyanji lute na jane*
> (People looted expensive shawls and wraps while my husband looted just a little handkerchief. Oh my husband is a fool, he does not know to loot the Meerut Sadar bazaar.)[34]

Thus plunder becomes an act of masculinity – it is considered by the common women as an essential and legitimate act by the men in order to gain honour and prestige. It has its political implications too, which sometimes comes out clearly as the following Braj folk song on the same theme suggests:

> *Firangi lut gayo re Hathus Ke bazaar men/ Top luti gayo, ghoda luti*
> *Gayo/Tamancha luti gayo re Jako chalet bazaar men.*[35]

Plunder here becomes a purposeful act – it is the public demeaning of the Englishman and his symbols of status like the tank, pistol and horse in an open bazaar that adds to the joy of the plunderer.

It is remarkable that a folk song from Mirzapur, depicting the avenge of Udwant Singh's death by Jhoori Singh (who, it is said, beheaded Jt. Commissioner Moore and brought his head to Udwant Singh's mourning widow), is expressed through a teasing and joyful dialogue between the *devar* (brother-in-law, here Jhoori Singh) and the *bhabhi* (sister-in-law, here Udwant Singh's wife) – perhaps underlining the festive mood in which the people had celebrated this insult of an Englishman being beheaded by a countryman.

> *Ghodwa par chaddhi ke parai gawa Moorwa/Kaise le aain bhauji tore age mundwa*
> (Jhoori Singh teases his *bhabhi* that Moore has fled on his horse, so how could he now bring his severed head to her?)
> *Hamara devar jujharu ho bhauji bali bali jae/laide chale jab bhalwa*
> *Hop parlay mach jae/Moorwa ke kawan bisatiya ho der kurwa lagaye/*
> *Achraj hamen bad holas ho binu hate kauni aaye.*
> (Udwant Singh's wife replies that she knows and admires her *devar* as a brave

fighter; when he walks with his spear it is like a catastrophe on earth. Moore, thus, is no match for her *devar* and it is surprising how he has come back without fulfilling his promise of beheading the Englishman.)[36]

Such *devar–bhabhi* dialogues are extremely common in eastern Uttar Pradesh during times like Holi – an occasion which provides license and liberty to break traditional norms of deference, and this structuring of the episode of Moore's death in the form of a *devar–bhabi* dialogue is perhaps an indication of the comprehension of and rejoining in this incident by the common people of this region as a symbol of a cataclysmic moment of triumph (use of the word *'pralaya'* is noteworthy) when the traditional fear and awe inspired by the Englishman had been inverted and the Englishman had been reduced to a laughable beheaded caricature of himself. Underlying this apparent teasing of Jhoori Singh and the taunt of his *bhabhi*, thus, lies a much more meaningful ultimate ridicule, that of the invincible Englishman.

A regional poet Sakhwat Rai, an eyewitness to the uprising of 1857, has similarly celebrated the killing of the English soldiers as a moment of extreme indignity for the so-called invincible race by describing them as falling in the battlefield like trunkless elephants (a symbol of ultimate disgrace in popular language) and being feasted upon by vultures, jackals and dogs:

> *Gidh medrai swan syar anand chhaye*
> *Kahin gire gora kahin hathi bina soondh ke*[37]

1857 provided people with a situation in which they could attempt to defy the authority of the Englishman in day to day life. There were instances of *bhishtis* refusing water to Englishmen, cooks standing half-naked before guests in the house deliberately and messenger boys being impudent and indifferent to orders.[38] Verbal abuse, scorn and insult were levied at the Englishmen through popular cultural idioms and symbols. Peter Burke has illustrated that the active force of language is the insult, 'a form of aggression in which adjectives and nouns are used not so much to describe another person as to strike that person' in order to bring about his social destruction.[39] Shirer, in his *Daily Life during the Indian Mutiny* has described a similar situation in a Banda village where two peons sat alongside a magistrate – something they would never have dared to do in normal times – and after playfully assessing the value of a peon as four annas, scornfully questioned the value of the *'sarkar'* (government). Here the equation of the colonial regime with a low-valued commodity – perhaps even lower than the lowly peons – exemplifies the way in which linguistic symbolism, gaining strength from traditional cultural idioms of comparison, succeeds in subverting the aura of the colonialist authority.

Verbal defiance, insolent behaviour and symbolic fulmination often preceded or accompanied the upsurge. At Azamgarh, the 17th N.I. first openly declared that they would not allow the treasure to leave for Banaras, as was the British plan. Then, soon after the treasure left the station, in a mutinous mood, they left their ranks, and on being threatened by one sergeant Lewis that they would be hanged or transported if they rebelled, every man of the regiment commenced to yell, and some rushing down to the sergeant cut him down, crying out – 'if we are to be hanged at all events we'll kill you first'.[40] In Banaras, Lt. Col. Spottis- woode, mistakenly convinced that he had calmed down the agitated sepoys of the 13th Irregular Cavalry, was surprised when he received a volley of fire from the same sepoy he was talking to. His pleadings that the English were friends had no impact on the sepoy as 'the reply was another volley'.[41] A distinct attitude of deliberate defiance seems to have replaced the customary disciplined behaviour that the English officers had been used to from the sepoys. Rather than obedience and servility, the prevalent attitude was one of hostility aiming to misguide the British through lies and chicanery. P. Walker, the Deputy Collector of Mirzapur, on inquiry from the zamindars of the neighbouring villages near Chunar – with whom he was personally acquainted – about reports of the firing heard in the vicinity was misinformed that 'it had been consequent on a marriage procession'.[42] Similarly, Major Burroughs commanding the 17th N.I. at Azamgarh had been lulled into a false sense of security by the sepoys and after the outbreak 'could therefore hardly believe that all the men said and promised was false'.[43] In Gorakh- pur, Bird the magistrate was openly insulted and the jail guards refused his order to destroy the bridge of boats.[44] The normal tendencies of fear and subordination had given way to a confident sense of power and command. The Commissioner of Patna reported his resentment that the rebels behave 'as if they were gentlemen and we were thieves'.[45]

We have indicated earlier in our discussion how people visualized the Revolt in terms of their grievances, expectations, desires and hopes. Needless to say, different sets of people had different aspirations from the Revolt, and they reacted to it in various ways. Again, the same issue could be interpreted differently by different sets of people depending on social outlook, political inclinations, region-specific situations or cultural traditions.

The overriding concern for all the rebel leaders seems to have been the restoration of their earlier power and status, which had been eroded by the British Raj and the interference of their policies. On a broader and more general ideological plane, for many it could mean for many the restoration of the Mughal empire and the provincial kingdoms; while for many dispossessed zamindars and land- holders at a local level it could simply mean the ouster of auction-purchasers, the recapture of their lands and restoration of their lost fortunes. For rebel leaders like Mohammad Hasan – the *nazim* of Gorakhpur – loyalty to Awadh and commit- ment to its cause was the dominant theme of Revolt. That even the landholders under him were fighting for a restoration of conditions under the eighteenth- century Nawabi, is clear from the fact that many of them objected to the retention of *thanedars* by Mohammed Hasan on his assumption of power on the grounds that '*thanedars* were unknown under the Nawabee'.[46] It is evident from the immediate ouster of auction-purchasers and re-entry into their lands by such dis- possessed landholders that for them restoration of the Nawabi meant, above all, the restoration and unhindered enjoyment of their lands. Loyalty to Awadh never became an emotive issue for the landed magnates of Gorakhpur. Restoration of Nawabi for them, unlike Mohammed Hasan, simply meant restoration of their own personal or their clan's fortunes.

However, in regions of Jaunpur adjoining the Awadh border, where the Rajkumar chieftains even had blood-ties with the taluqdars of Awadh, the issue of loyalty to Awadh acquired a much more emotive character than in other regions of eastern Uttar Pradesh. Here there would be no later day collective conciliation by the British, unlike the Palwars of Azamgarh. The Awadh issue also entered the Allahabad parganas north of the Ganga, where the Awadh taluq-dars had formerly ruled, and staked their claims in 1857. Thus while in June and July 1857 it was 'ousted zamindars versus auction-purchasers', in September 1857 it became 'Awadh and ousted zamindars' versus the 'British government'.[47] The ideology of the rebels could have had many components interpenetrating each other with variations in intensity over time and space.

What exactly did the Awadh question mean to a rebel with a certain ideological commitment to the cause of Awadh? A study of the mental attitudes and ideology of a leader like Mohammed Hasan, with the help of a set of letters discovered by the British in his captured *palki*, provides a revealing answer.

His letter to Khairuddeen, the Deputy Magistrate of Gorakhpur, reveals that the moral sustenance to keep the fight on against the British was drawn from God. If the British are mighty, God is 'Almighty'. Insurgent violence thus acquires, in the eyes of such rebels, the status of a religious service. At the same time, throughout his letters loyalty to Awadh is the recurring sentiment for Mohammad Hasan. He is ready to negotiate with the British only on one condition: that the British undo their treachery with Awadh by restoring its status in accordance with the treaty signed with Shujauddaulah. For him the rebellion of 1857 'arose solely out of the annexation of Oudh', for in his eyes the British 'had no right to establish themselves in Oudh'. A promise was a very important ethical and social notion in mid-nineteenth century India; and the British, by exceeding 'all bounds in their breaking of promises', were violators of a legitimate social norm and therefore were trespassers.

To Mohammad Hasan, the restoration of Awadh decidedly meant, on the one hand, the restoration of his own honour and prestige, for he ends the letter to Khairuddeen by asserting that in a restored Awadh he would act as a *Vakeel*, to 'see that the treaty signed with Shujauddaulah was properly executed'. But along with this dream of material prosperity in this world, loyalty to the kingdom of Awadh was also his religion, his *dharma* – the fulfillment of which would bring him prosperity in the other world.[48] It should be kept in mind here that *dharma* should not be seen simply as a narrow sectarian outlook. 'Religious war' in this light, is hardly a suitable description of 1857. It was a war in defence of a whole system of moral and social values, principles and ideas – all that the broad term 'religion' or *dharma* stood for – that had been endangered by British policies.

The defence of this *dharma* and its constituents like honour was not the primary goal of only the chieftains and ex-rulers; even an ordinary rebel had his own views on this. The decline of the ideals of honour and prestige at all levels was keenly understood by him, as honour and self-respect were significant components of the cultural environment in which he lived. In the popular mind kingship had been symbolically associated with authority, splendour and prosperity, and therefore erosion of such symbols was considered sufficient provocation for revolt in many places. Thus the pain felt at the end of the glorious Awadh kingdom is expressed both by the famous poet Ameer Meenai and by the people of the Awadhi-speaking belt in terms similar to the lamentation at the loss of pomp and show of the Kaiserbagh melas:

> *Ameer afsurda ho kar guncha-e-dil sookh jata hai*
> *who mele ham ko Kaiser Bagh ke jab yaad ate hain.*[49]

> Sripati Maharaj / this calamity avert! O, when shall his majesty, Our King regain his own state?. . . The artillery lies abandoned in the dumps / And the elephants are left uncared for in their stables / Chargers and swift horses wander groomless in the city / And all my comrades too are lost / In the Kaiser Bagh now the Begums weep and wail / Their hairs hanging loose in disorder. (Awadhi and Bhojpuri folk songs)[50]

The following folk song vividly reveals how keenly even the common people of Shahabad had grasped this reality with a faultless political instinct:

> *Babua, marle maratha jujhal sikwa ho na/ Babua, peshwa ke putwa gulamwa*
> *ho na/ Babua, Dillipati bhai le kangalwa ho na/ babua, manglo par mile nahin*
> *bhikhwa ho na/ Babua, ohe din dada leli taruaria ho na*
> (Oh Babua, when the Marathas and the Sikhs had gone fighting, and the sons of Peshwas had been reduced to slaves; Oh Babua, when the Emperor of Delhi too had become a pauper and they were reduced to the status of beggars in vain; Oh Babua, that day our grandpa took up his sword.)[51]

It is interesting to note that kingship and authority here are not localized, but encompass all the regions of north India. Thus their local hero Kunwar Singh does not take up arms simply for his own personal cause, on the contrary, he does so for a much wider political issue in which everyone – Sikhs, Marathas, Pathans – comes together. Such folk songs disprove the oft-held claim that for an ordinary rebel, the issue was a narrow, localized one. He did have an acute perception of political realities much beyond his local territory. Many folk songs in Shahabad are elegies on the deplorable conditions of the Begums of Awadh under the Company rule.

For the people of Bhojpur, erosion of pride and honour were deeply felt sentiments. It was humiliating for the traditional warrior community of Bhojpur, employed under chieftains, to lose that proud and valiant occupation and be forced to take up cultivation as a result of the British regime:

Oh Babua, scorpions bred in our cannons/ Oh Babua, the barrels of our guns have rusted/ Oh Babua, we have made sickles out of the steel of our swords/ Oh Babua, the Bhojpuris had even thrown their lathis aside/ Oh Babua, that day our grandpa took up his sword.[52]

Kunwar Singh here is a symbol of these proud warriors fighting to redeem the infringement of their honour. For the people, Kunwar Singh is not a remote ruler on the throne; he is a community leader attached to the commoners through ties of blood and kinship. In popular perception, Kunwar Singh seemed to be fighting less for his personal jagirdari privileges and much more 'to keep safe our pride and our plenty / Our religion, our cows! / Oh Babua, to protect the rent-free lands of our widows! And to protect our mothers and sisters from disgrace / Oh Babua, to defend the fair name of our fathers and grandfathers.'[53]

The song shows that the narrow definition of Kunwar Singh as a defender of Hinduism in Bihar is not an adequate description. *Dharma*, in popular understanding, stood for a whole range of political and social values that their hero sought to defend. The notions of *dharma*, honour and prosperity intermingled with each other in popular consciousness, and was political enough an issue to argue for the resumption of rent-free grants made to widows. This political articulation derives its legitimacy from a cultural code where traditions and customs of the past are venerated, and where changes brought about by the British are resented as they tarnish these traditions which are symbolized by the 'fair names of our fathers and grandfathers'. Thus it is not only material deprivation, but politics of a particular kind – rooted in cultural traditions and articulated through cultural symbols – that instigated and signified the broad sweep of rebellion in Shahabad. In fact, a comparison of the folk songs of the Awadh heartland with those of Shahabad reveals that while in the case of Awadh such concerns as outlined above, though present, were often overdetermined and overshadowed by images of pathos for the Nawab and his lost splendour and kingly opulence, in the case of Shahabad, community concerns occupied a privileged place. It is for this reason that Shahabad and the adjoining Bhojpuri belt provides us with perhaps the best region to study popular mentalities during 1857. A popular Bhojpuri folktale, infact, goes to the extent of giving the credit, for the taking up of arms by Kunwar Singh, to a call by the people of the region. Popular memory in the Bhojpuri region recalls one Bansuria Baba as having been the 'guru' and advisor of Kunwar Singh.[54] What is also noteworthy is that though it is Kunwar Singh who is highlighted in the folk songs, the role of an ordinary rebel sepoy is not altogether forgotten either:

Pahli laraiya Kunwar Singh jeetle / Doosri Amar Singhbhai / Ahe teesri laraiya sipahi sab jeetle / Uthe lat ghabrai.
(The first battle was won by Kunwar Singh and the second by his brother Amar Singh. But the third battle was won by all the sepoys together and this alarmed the British General.)[55]

The idea of the entire Rajput community and all the family members taking up the fight appears again and again in the folk songs, as the fight is for the defence of the ancestral honour of the entire community of Rajput warriors of Bhojpur. Thus, if Kunwar Singh is old, it is deemed to be the duty of this younger brother, Amar Singh, to take over his role:

> *Jeera aisa dant ho jaye, a San aisa har hojaye / Jul-Jul mans latkat jaye, banh men koobat mile jaye / Kaise tega pakroon main, kaise Money ko maroon main / Tab le Amarsingh bole ka, sun bhaiya meri bat / Baithal bhaiya pan chabao, main angrezon ko dekhloonga.*
> (Kunwar Singh laments – 'My teeth and hair my flesh and the strength in my arms have all dissipated. How shall I now lift my arms and kill Money, the Collector? To which Amar Singh replies – 'O brother, listen to me. Don't you worry, you rest enjoying your betel leaf, for I shall deal with the British.)[56]

The territory of mobilization for the rebellion extended much beyond the *mauza* and deep into the adjoining areas. Connections of kith and kin were forged with Kunwar Singh and his men much beyond the borders of Shahabad. Pursued by British forces in April 1858 and eager to cross back into Bihar at Muneahar in Ghazipur, Kunwar Singh 'found himself among friends and the wants of his troops were voluntarily supplied by the villagers' who were of the same caste and 'almost universally in his favour'.[57] Again at Sheopur Ghat in Balia, the police, the 'mallahas' and the zamindars 'friendly to Kunwar Singh were all instrumental in deceiving the officers responsible for the withdrawal of the boats and furnishing them to the rebels'. The strong ties of brotherhood that the zamindars of Sheopur Ghat had with Kunwar Singh can be ascertained from the following folk song that is still sung in Sheopur Ghat, in which the Zamindar brothers Sidha Singh and Nidha Singh assure the emissary from Kunwar Singh that they are ready to bring a smile to their clan brother Kunwar Singh's face by selling their elephants and horses and feeding the sepoys from this income:

> *Larbi na ta ka harbi, bhain ke hansaibi / hathi ghora benchi ke, sipahin ke khiyayibi*[59]

It is important to note that symbols of feudal honour, like horses and elephants, could be sacrificed for a more important question of honour that 1857 signified – the honour of the customs, traditions and pride of at least the clan, if not the community. Such subtle nuances in the perception and conception of honour can be observed only by taking recourse to sources of oral history. Clan and caste linkages were some of the primary nodes of mobilization for large sections of the community, although traditional inter and intra-clan rivalries could, at times, also dilute the spirit of rebellion.

Caste solidarity and aspirations were directly related to a sense of loss on the part of the rebel community. It could have been the loss of ancestral lands to moneylenders and auction-purchasers, expulsion from what a community considered to be its traditional homeland, or a decline in the wealth and status of its elite group which may have lost prestige and standing both in its own eyes and in that of others. These issues often overlapped each other and come together in different ways to create a communal sense of loss and deprivation. Ranajit Guha has argued against seeing such losses as having been purely 'economic' in nature; in fact 'there was no loss, whatever its cause, that was not felt to be a loss of power', and hence such grievances had a strong political character.[60] The Palwars of Azamgarh entered Mahul pargana in June 1857 and claimed the villages of the pargana to have been theirs.[61] Similarly, the Mona Rajputs of Bhadohi in Mirzapur had not forgotten that before passing into the hands of the Raja of Banaras in 1746–47, the large estates of Bhadohi were entirely and solely their own.[62]

The notion of community was thus not merely a geographical or spatial concept. It was also a part of the people's collective consciousness, the clan's memory and history. Thus the Srinet Rajputs of the ruling family of Sattasi in Gorakhpur had a recurring memory of the twelfth-century division of lands of a common ancestor, Bhagwant Singh, into Unwal, Bansi (comprising Ratanpur Mugher) and Haveli Gorakhpur. The latter, consisting of Haveli Gorakhpur, Bhauapar and Sylhet, was equal in area to eighty-seven ('sattasi' in Hindi) kos, giving it the name 'Sattasi' – a territory which the ruling family of Sattasi originally had in possession. Over the years and largely under British revenue settlements, the territory of the Sattasi Raja had shrunk much below eighty-seven kos. It was this rightful over the original 'sattasi kos' that was revived from clan memory by the Raja and his kinsmen in 1857 and it was this claim that was used as a legitimate mobilizing cause in the war against the alien British trespassers.[63]

The notion of 'Chowrasee Des' provides us with yet another instance of clan solidarity seeking its basis in history. 'Chowrasee' or 'eighty-four' refers to a tract of country containing the number of settlements or villages in the occupation of a particular clan which got spread, some time in history, from original villages.[64] That this notion of a common territorial homeland was very much alive among the Jat and Rajput communities of the North-West Provinces had been testified by Elliot in the 1830s.[65] This notion too was from clan memory revived in 1857 to mobilize people against the British – who had trespassed upon and violated the sanctity of 'Chowrasee Des', for we hear of the Chowrasee zamindars of Khyragarh pargana in Allahabad attacking government servants employed in collecting revenue in the area that they rightly claimed as their own.[66] Sources of oral history are rich in providing insights into such notions of collective consciousness that were revived for mobilization during 1857. In Gonda (Awadh) we come across folk songs underlining the notion of 'Chowrasee Des' with regard to Raja Devi Baksh Singh:

> Raja Devi Bakas as sunder
> Unke hath sone ka mundar
> Unke aage sab lage chhuchhundar
> Unke Chowrasee kos man rahe raj[67]

Similarly, ethnic bonds and traditional institutions like village panchayats and assemblies were extensively used to mobilize people for rebellion, as can be seen in the case of the Mewatis of Allahabad where the crucial decision to rebel was taken in mauza Samadabad in a 'panchayat of Mewatis held on 5 June 1857 at the house of Saif Khan Mewati and all, excepting Saif Khan, decided to rebel the same day'.[68] The Mewati landed aristocracy and military gentry, which had been rendered marginal and desperate following the crisis of the 1830s and whose lifestyle had been cramped by the growth of the colonial bureaucracy and commercial economy under the Company's aegis, found in 1857 the perfect opportunity to rebel. That they were not motivated simply by plunder, despite having been branded a 'criminal tribe' by the British, is clear not only from their lengthy deliberations in the panchayat before deciding to rebel, but also from the fact that in Allahabad, they were 'the real contrivers of the rebellion of the sepoys and the Risala'.[69] The ties of kinship created by geographical proximity, represented by all the Mewatis of the multiple villages near Allahabad–Samadabad, Rasulpur, mauza Beli, Baghara, Shadiabad, Jonhol, Shevri, Fatehpur Bichhua, Katra, Karnal Ganj, Mahadpuri, Bakhtiara, Bakhtvari, Rasulpur (village), Minhajpur and others – again helped them here to rise as a community against the British.[70]

Sources of oral history also reveal – perhaps with greater force of emotion – the various ways in which bonds of kinship were forged for mobilization in 1857. In this rather moving folk song, Kunwar Singh is shown as desperately sending messages to all his clan chieftains from the adjoining areas, seeking help against the British:

> *Sone Kalam hathon men le likh parwana bheje ka*
> *Ja Tekari dakhil hua, ja Dumraon dakhil hua,*
> *Ja Dalippur dakhil hua, Ja Ramgarh dakhil hua;*
> *Sun to Babua meri baat, Gotia bhai aap kahete*
> *Meri madad par aao kam, main angrezom se bigda hoom*
> *Meri madad par aao kaam.*[71]

Badrinarayan has shown how sentiments like a challenge, pathos and notions of virtue and sin (intermingled with warnings about ones next live) were used to enlist people for the rebel cause.

> *Je na dihee Kunwar Singh ke sath*
> *U agila janam men hoi suar*
> (One who shall not join Kunwar Singh shall be a pig in his next birth.)[72]

According to the accepted social norms of nineteenth century Uttar Pradesh and Bihar, ties of kinship and blood were very strong and it was expected of other kinsmen to join and aid their 'brothers' fighting in defence of their ancestral honour and traditions. Failure to do so was treachery in the eyes of the people who still recall the perfidy of the Raja of Dumraon who, though a relative of Kunwar Singh, did not come to his aid when the situation so demanded:

Ek to main aas kailin Raja Dumrao ke
Who bhagi chalele jaise ban men ke kharha
Kulhi gumalka Rama, matiya men mili gaile
Nahi lebe pavalia' hum Suraj.
(Kunwar Singh in the first person – 'I had relied upon the Raja of Dumraon but he too ran away like a hare in the forest. Whatever I had thought of has been ruined to dust – I could not attain my Raj.')[73]

It is interesting to note that sometimes, even people like Harkishan Singh (the chief lieutenant of Kunwar Singh) who were on the rebels' side are branded as traitors in oral historical tradition.[74] Does the oral tradition here indicate those subtle facets and nuances of conflict within the rebel community which are totally hidden in the official records and sources of 1857? It is again remarkable that the *wazir* Ali Naqi Khan of Lucknow too enjoys the dubious reputation of a traitor, so much so that the saying '*nakki ho jaana*' has come into vogue in Awadh as a term for going back on one's word.[75]

The use of the term '*nevta*' (traditionally used for an invitation to members of ones class and community, for ritual festivities like birth, marriage, *shraddha* and so on), was also given a new meaning in the context of 1857.

Gaon gaon men duggi bajal, Babu ke phiral duhai
Loha chabvai ke nevta ba, sab saj apan dal badal
Ba jan gavankai ke nevta, choori phorvai ke nevta
Sindoor ponchhvai ke nevta ba, Rand kahvar ke nevta
Jei no hamar te math dei, jei ho hamar te sat dei
Ba ehan na nauka Samjhaike, ba een na nauka boojhai ke
Keeto phairo nevta hamar kee to taiyyar ho juijhike[76]

In this moment of crisis, *nevta* is redefined as an invitation to fight at all costs – even at the cost of life and widowhood to the womenfolk. It is a call to forget all matters of self-interest and dutifully join the others in the quest to protect their community. In fact, in the context of 1857, initial mobilization on clan or caste lines could easily extend itself to include people from other castes and merge with the wider issues that 1857 stood for.

Joining in with the rebel cause, in popular mentality, was no less an essential *dharma* than participating in the other rituals of life and death. Numerous folk songs describe how Kunwar Singh and Amar Singh always began the preparation for battle against the British with the ritual bathing and embalming of their body with sandalwood paste.

Sir se gosul kia
Chandan lagaulan atho ang
Vardi peti le mangao
Jhalam jhar le mangao[77]

In fact, in the context of 1857, the notion of *dharma* could acquire different meanings for different people with many regional variations. As indicated earlier, *dharma* in mid-nineteenth century India was an all-embracing term for a whole matrix of ethics and social values, that provided a normative structure of practices and customs according to which life ought to be governed; therefore, the defence of religion, in a way, stood for the defence of a whole way of life which, in the context of 1857, could also very well mean a way of conflict with the offenders.

Aspects of masculinity and valour also got linked with the notion of the defence of this way of life in the popular consciousness. Thus, those who hide in their houses and refuse to opt for the path of struggle are worth ridicule and disrespect, as is revealed by the following taunt by the womenfolk at such cowardice :

> *Lage saram laj ghar men baith jahu / Marad se bani ke*
> *Lugaiya ae hari / Phairke Sari; choori; munhwa chhipai lehu / Rakhi eebi tohri*
> *pagariya ae hari.*
> (If you feel shy like a woman, then hide in the house. O husband, wear a sari and bangles and hide your face. We women would save your *pagdi* [honour].)[78]

Notions of masculinity and valour are therefore invoked in this war of honour to gain strength. The expression of the fight against the British through culturally-rooted idioms and symbols is, perhaps, an affirmation of that separate cultural domain that the rebels were trying to preserve against British encroachment. The defeat of Kunwar Singh then is expressed by the ordinary rebels in terms of their loss of desire to play Holi any longer.

> *Babu Kunwar Singh, tohre raj bina / Ab na rangaibo kesaria.*
> (O Babu Kunwar Singh, we shall dye no more our garments in sacred saffron / till your raj comes again.)[79]

Holi, in cultural traditions, has often allowed a temporary reversal of social order through *swangs*, dramas enacted by the people. 1857 was fought with the aim of reverting back to the old order. However, since Kunwar Singh has been defeated, the chances of such a reversal are very slim and hence its symbolic expression in the form of Holi no longer seems relevant. Further, '*kesariya*' or saffron has always been regarded in Indian culture and tradition as the colour of both happiness as well as bravery and valour. Thus in this mood of defeat, when valour has been proved futile, the dyeing of garments in saffron colour is no longer considered appropriate. Its use be proper only when its symbolic status gets vindicated by the restoration of Kunwar Singh's raj.

However, it is remarkable that even in this song of 'despair', the atmosphere is revitalized by ending with a '*phaag*' recalling those few but significant moments of victory and elation that the community enjoyed when the red '*abeer*' of the struggle had engulfed the British bungalows due to Kunwar Singh's might with the sword.

Bangla pe udela abeer ho lala, bangle pe udela abeer
Ho Babu, aho Babu Kunwar Singh Tegwa bahadur
Bangla pe udela abeer[80]

The significance of the uprising and the hope for a restoration of Kunwar Singh's raj some day in future thus lives on in popular memory. It would be given a new dimension in the mass movement against the British in the twentieth century, when songs on Gandhi would emerge indicating the various shades of meaning, and the imagery, in particular, that Gandhi and his struggle had acquired in popular perception. The profound impact that this tradition of resistance had on popular consciousness can be gauged from the following folk song from the Bhojpuri belt, in which the women remember and treasure the heroes of the community struggle as fondly as the ornaments that adorn their bodies:

Kanphulwa par Kunwar Singh, gardenia par Gandhi ke
Eeranwa par tahra Arjun ke teer dhanush
(The earstuds are decorated with the figure of Kunwar Singh, the necklace with that of Gandhi while your earnings match the bowarrow of Arjun.)[81]

The articulation of revolt through culturally-devined symbols is also evident in the identification of the inner world with the physical environment outside, which had resisted the forces of change that the colonial regime brought with them. Thus the equation of the determination to stand up for a cultural world with the strength of the resolute and plucky hills is a recurring theme for the folk songs of the region, in which the tenacity of Kunwar Singh and his dedication to the ideology he is thought to have rebelled for are juxtaposed against the backdrop of the unyielding Kaimur and Sasaram hills.

Similarly, it is interesting to note that, in the popular imagination, the antidote to the mechanized tanks of the British were their own much respected, long befriended and customarily venerated domains of the naturally occurring forces and resources.

Sun journel meri bat, tumhara top mata hai / Mera jangal pita hai,
main jangal chhoroonga nahin.
(O general listen to me; if your tank is your mother / My jungle is my father and I will never abandon it.)[82]

In the context of 1857 the age-old tradition of the veneration of forests by the community is given a new interpretation. The forests appear both as a protector against the British and as an active aid in sustaining community struggle while using their own brand of guerilla warfare against the open, tank aided battle tactics of the British.

It is interesting to note that while symbols like Khilats, *nazranas*, flags and proclamations made to the beat of drums used by the rebel leaders made use of pompous displays and opulence to underline their power and authority, those of the ordinary rebel population (as is evident in such folk songs) were made up of festivals, forests, rivers and other arenas of common participation. This is especially true of the folk songs from the Bhojpuri areas of Bihar and eastern Uttar Pradesh, where though not denying the role of Kunwar Singh as leader, his feelings are expressed in popular folk songs more through common symbols like Holi, the deer of the forests, and colts – all of which is depicted as participating with everything at stake and with all their heart in the war that their hero had continued to wage despite being betrayed by his relatives:

> *Babu Kunwar Singh ken eel ka bachherwa*
> *Peeala katorwan doodh*
> *Hali hali dudhwa piain ae Kunwar Singh*
> *Rain jae ke badue door*
> *Abki rainia jitao neela bachherwa*
> *Sonwe madhaibo chado khur*
> (Babu Kunwar Singh's blue colt is drinking bowls of milk. O Kunwar Singh, make him drink fast for he has a long way to travel to the battle front. O blue colt, if you shall make us win this battle, we shall cover and adorn all your hooves with gold).[83]

> *Babu banwa khele le sikarwa*
> *Roweli banwa ke hiraniya*
> *Pahil ladai Babu Hetampur bhaili*
> *Rajwa bahelia dihlasi na*
> *Satrah sau satasi mauza kuchhua na bujhle*
> *Garh lutwa dihle na,*
> *Rajwa dehlas dhokha na.*
> (From jungle to jungle Babu gave fight
> and deer of the forest wept at sight
> The first battle he fought at Hetampur
> where Raja gave gumman to Britisher
> He cared nothing for seventeen
> Hundred eighty seven villages
> And had his fortress battered
> Alas! the Raja treacherous one.)[84]

Therefore, one cannot help but conclude that his actual motivations notwithstanding, Kunwar Singh was perceived more as a leader from within the community rather than one who was distant and impersonal. Such perceptions, perhaps, helped Kunwar Singh to enjoy wider popular support than any of the other rebel leaders.

> *Gajra ka gajreet banaya, murai ke darwaza*
> *Sarkand ka je top banaya, lade Kunwar Singh Raja*
> (Of carrots he made a palace, and of radish he could contrive a door. Of sweet potatoes he made cannons – thus fought Raja Kunwar Singh.)[85]

In this extract, the comparison of the symbols of power and struggle with common vegetables that grow 'under the ground' is perhaps the most moving tribute
by the people to the strategy of 'guerilla' warfare that was adopted by Kunwar
Singh and his men to fight the British. As against the strategy open warfare practised by the larger armies, 'guerilla' warfare was a strategy that had been practised
for ages in the Indian sub-continent, by smaller caste or village-based organizations
which, in the context of 1857 in Shahabad, proved as strongly rooted in and
linked with the soil as the vegetables growing under it.

III

Much has been written about the rumours regarding adulterated flour,
the greased cartridges and polluted ghee that contributed to the feeling of outrage
among the soldiers and the civilian population. Ranajit Guha has pointed out
that both the opposition between the British and Indians, as well as the unity of
all the Indians were expressed in terms of a single theme – that of ritual pollution
– articulated in the former of rumours in 'many portentous shapes'.[86]

However, this unity of Indians was not always perfect. We must move
away from the oft-repeated assertion in nationalist historiography that 1857 saw
a unity of all castes and communities, everywhere, against the British. While it is
true that the wide range of issues that 1857 stood for could have emerged as crucial mobilizing factors that could transcend clan or dynastic rivalries and personal
gain and interest, this was not the case everywhere. In fact, 1857 is too complex
a movement to be explained in terms of unilinear or monological models. Even
within the region under study, there were variations in the intensity and pattern
of mobilization and action, depending on a host of factors, such as the interaction
of the traditional, local power structure with the forces unleashed by the colonial
regime, the extent of the networks of caste and clan and their mutual relations; a
region's specific grievances and benefits likely to accrue in return for popular
initiative and participation.

Thus, in Gorakhpur region, the Majhauli Raja – despite having clan ties
with the rebel Rajas of Narharpur – had history of harassment by the Awadh
nawabs and their amils which had forced his ancestors to seek refuge in Saran in
Bihar, and hence for him there was no question of siding with Mohammad Hasan
who had very strong pro-Awadh sentiments.[87] On the contrary, for the Gautam
Rajput family of Nagar, whose estates at Ganeshpur had been given to the Pindarah
by the British, the cause for resentment was too recent to be forgotten, therefore
they were openly rebellious.[88] The zamindars of Amroha had a similar history of
conflict with the British from the days of their ancestor Zalim Singh in the eighteenth century, thus Eloea and Dumreeganj in the pargana of Amroha were one of
the most 'disturbed' areas in the district.[89]

Nor is the binary model of total opposition or total loyalty to the Raj of
universal applicability. A variety of intermediary attitudes ranging from stoic
indifference to fluctuating vacillations also affected the shape of mobilization in
1857. Thus, in Azamgarh, mobilization for the rebel cause would reverse its

course after some time to turn into a conference of alliance with the British. The question of survival, after the badly shaken self-confidence resulting from the constant defeats, became more important than the ideology of 1857 for many like the Palwars, for whom, in any case, the issue was mostly limited to the restoration of their lands. In Jaunpur, in contradistinction, ideology played a much more important role because of the blood-relations the Rajkumars had with a number of Awadh taluqdars. Here, anti-British stance was prolonged and more ferocious. Apart from the ideological commitment to Awadh, the preponderance of auction sales and the embitterment of the gentry were important factors that contributed to the intensity of the Rebellion. Yet, even here, not everyone was affected by this sentiment – despite hardships at the hands of auction purchasers and calls of clan loyalty, one-fifth of taluqdars in Jaunpur remained loyal to the British.

Even among the lower castes, cases of both loyalty to the rebel cause as well as indifference or hostility to it can be seen. Polarization and divisions within Indian society, based on the hierarchical system of ritual pollution, were not always or altogether submerged within the cohesive whole of a united front against the '*firanghi*'. Thus Jhuri Singh, after avenging the death of Udwant Singh by severing the head of Moore, did not carry it to the widow of Udwant Singh himself, but 'forced Munai chamar to carry it', as recalled in his deposition during the trial by Ujahil Chamar in a tone of unconcealed resentment at the forcible treatment of his fellow casteman.[90] In an uprising with strong overtones of religion and ritual pollution, it is not surprising that those sections of Indian society that had traditionally been regarded as lowly or 'polluting' often found themselves untouched by the forces of solidarity that the movement generated. In the social and political order that 1857 was seeking to defend, the sweepers, scavengers and other such lowly castes were outside the scheme of things. In many Bhojpuri folktales and songs the otherwise 'ideal' heroes Lorik and Sorthi are also shown as hating the untouchables:

Jab chheri deehen chamain hamri sharirea ho / hamaro dharmva chali jai . . .[91]

The untouchables were considered as defilers as much by the rebels as by the British, and were supposed to remain outcastes continuing their lowly functions once the 'puritan' traditional order was re-established. Even Nanak Singh's *Jangnama*, a near contemporary account (which was discovered by Amrit Lal Nagar during his tour of Awadh to collect material on 1857) of the fierce battle between Thakur Balbhadra Singh of Chahlari and the British, does not have a single untouchable figuring in the list of ninety commoner warriors mentioned there.[92] Even Kunwar Singh's rebel government, which underlined its popular base by having a *mali* and a *goala* within its ranks, has no reference to any untouchable.

It is interesting to note how the two pollutes – the British and the Indian untouchables/lowly castes – seem to have allied together in most parts of eastern Uttar Pradesh and Bihar against the Rebellion. We find them aiding the British in large numbers, and the British seem to have attempted to utilize this to their advantage. Thus at Kanpur, Captain Bruce on anticipating a rebel invasion, raised a police force consisting solely of men of lower-caste *mehtars*.[93] This 'Sweepers Police' was helpful in re-establishing British authority at Bithoor and also in capturing the fort of Sul Kynee on the Kalpee road.[94] Even in Banda, the collector, Mayne, raised a foot-levy of 'Khangaris' and 'Bhungees'.[95] That the British had realized the advantage of this scheme as an expedient policy is evident from the instructions given by the Commissioner of Patna division to the magistrates of all the districts for the recruitment of men only from the lower castes – '*Dusadh*' and '*Chamar*' – in the extra police force.[96] Again, near Jaunpur, where most of the Rajput zamindars and their kin had forced the British to run for shelter from one place to another, it was some *chamars* who carried the ailing father of George Mathews (an army officer) to a place of safety.[97] Similarly, an English lady imprisoned in Bibighar, of all persons, could only find a *bhangin* ready to carry her letter to the English at Allahabad. The letter was caught and the *bhangin* whipped,[98] and perhaps as a fitting sequel to the turn of events, once Kanpur was recaptured by the British, the rebels were asked to perform the lowly task of cleaning the blood stains of Bibighar, and on their refusal, they were whipped by the *mehtars*.[99]

Although it is true that many zamindars did succeed in mobilizing their lower-caste retainers in their attacks on auction-purchasers and in Allahabad 'a sort of enthusiasm' was prevalent even among the lower classes in Kunwar Singh's favour, it is nevertheless evident from the examples cited above that, if not everywhere, at many places the lower-caste groups and especially the 'untouchables' showed a remarkable autonomy of action quite different from the general trend of rebellion within the upper-caste groups. The extent and the ways in which these examples relate to the perception of the lowest castes of the relations of subordination and domination within Indian society and to their resentment against the vindication of such relations in rebel ideology are important questions in the context of 1857 that must be examined by historians in greater detail. Such high/low caste tensions have so far been little noted in the historiography of 1857 due to the hegemony of the nationalist framework. In fact, even a sophisticated historian like Ranajit Guha is not entirely immune from its influence. He too has not been always able to avoid the language of 'collaboration' and 'betrayal' and therefore he hardly focuses on the high low caste tensions within Indian society. In fact, a 'subaltern', like a high-caste ordinary peasant rebel, could very well be an 'elite' in the eyes of the low-caste sweepers and labourers of the countryside. Therefore, anti-colonialism of the 1857 type was not necessarily liberating, in any unproblematic sense of the word, for the marginalized groups like low-castes and women.

The author is grateful to Pt. Ganesh Chowbe of Motihari, Bihar for making a available some rare copies of a Bhojpuri journal.

Notes and References

[1] For these approaches, see S.B. Chaudhuri, *Civil Rebellion in the Indian Mutinies*, Calcutta, 1957; R.C. Majumdar; *The Sepoy Mutiny and the Revolt of 1857*, Calcutta, 1957; S.N. Sen; *Eighteen Fifty Seven*, Delhi, 1957; J.W. Kaye; *A History of the Sepoy War in India, 1857–58*, 6 Vols, London, 1876; V.D. Savarkar, *Indian War of Independence, 1857*, Bombay, 1947 (first published 1909); P.C. Joshi (ed.) *Rebellion 1857 – A Symposium*, Delhi, 1957.

[2] Eric Stokes, *The Peasant and The Raj*, Cambridge, 1978.

[3] E.I. Brodkin, 'The Struggle for Succession: Rebels and Loyalists in 1857', *Modern Asian Studies*, Vol. 6, 11972, pp. 277–90.

[4] See for instance, R. Devi: *Indian Mutiny: 1857 in Bihar*, New Delhi, 1977; Shyam Narain Sinha; *The Revolt of 1857 in Bundelkhand*, Lucknow, 1982; K.L. Shrivastava, *The Revolt of 1857 in Central India – Malwa*, Bombay, 1966; N.K. Nigam, *Delhi in 1857*, Delhi, 1957; K.K. Dutta, *Biography of Kunwar Singh and Amar Singh*, Patna, 1957.

[5] Eric Stokes, *The Peasant Armed*, Oxford, 1986.

[6] R. Mukherjee, *Awadh in Revolt, 1857–58*, Delhi and New York, 1984.

[7] R. Guha, *Elementary Aspects of Peasant Insurgency in Colonial India*, New Delhi, 1983.

[8] S.A.A. Rizvi (ed.), *Freedom Struggle in Uttar Pradesh*, Vol. IV, p. 73 (hereafter FSUP IV).

[9] Even a recent book by Tapti Ray, *The Politics of a Popular Uprising: Bundelkhand in 1857*, Delhi, 1994, prefers to rely on official sources and the letters and proclamations of soldiers to construct the moments of Rebellion. The vast repertoire of folk songs in Bundelkhand are totally glossed over.

[10] C.E. Buckland, *Bengal under Lt. Governors*, Vol. I, Calcutta, 1901, p. 93.

[11] Extract from the 'The Ballad of Kunwar Singh' available in translated form in P.C. Joshi, *1857 in Folk Songs*, Delhi, 1994, p. 129.

[12] Quoted in D.P. Singh, *Bhojpuri ke Kavi aur Kavya*, Patna, 1958, p. 159. Translation mine.

[13] For the saying, see Sampathi Aryani, *Magadhi Lok Sahitya*, Delhi, 1965, p. 58 and for the folk song, see Shridhar Mishra, *Bhojpuri Loksahitya Sanskritik Adhyayan*, Allahabad, 1971, p. 161.

[14] Shridhar Mishra, *Bhojpuri Loksahitya Sanskritik Adhyayan*, pp. 368–69. Translation mine.

[15] Extract taken from Shri Rasbiharilal, *Lokgeetan men Babu Kunwar Singh* (Bhojpuri), Vol. 3, No. 7, April 1955, p. 34. Translation mine.

[16] Badrinarayan, *Lok Sanskriti men Rastrawad*, Delhi, 1996, p. 94.

[17] Aryani, *Magadhi Lok Sahitya*, p. 180.

[18] Extract from the 'The Ballad of Kunwar Singh' compiled in translated form in P.C. Joshi, *1857 in Folk Songs*, Delhi, 1994, pp. 109–110.

[19] Aryani, *Magadhi Lok Sahitya*, p. 184.

[20] Shridhar Mishra, *Bhojpuri Loksahitya Sanskritik Adhyayan*, p. 168, 179.

[21] C.A. Bayly, *Rulers, Townsmen and Bazaars, North Indian Society in the Age of British expansion, 1770–1870*, Cambridge, 1983, p. 290. Bayly points out that despite forcible intervention by the State, the benefits to the cultivator appear to have been limited to a small area, particularly the Padrauna tahsil of Ghazipur district. Even in Padrauna tahsil the 'major cultivators took the first opportunity of the coming of the railway to move into much more lucrative grain production, leaving the difficult, costly and polluting drug to their poorer neighbours'.

[22] *District Gazetteer of Ghazipur* (1903–05), p. 173.

[23] Ibid., p. 172.

[24] Bayly, *Rulers, Townsmen and Bazaars, North Indian Society in the Age of British Expansion, 1770–1870*, p. 364.

[25] For an excellent analysis of the impact of the new social and economic forces unleashed by the colonialist regime on the position of the weavers of eastern Uttar Pradesh see

Gyanendra Pandey, 'Encounters and Calamities: The History of a North Indian Qasba·
in the 19ᵗʰ Century' in R. Guha (ed.) *Subaltern Studies III*, Delhi, 1984.
26 *FSUP IV*, p. 20.
27 *District Gazetteer of Allahabad* (1903–05), p. 182.
28 *FSUP IV*, p. 526.
29 *District Gazetteer of Gaya* (1906) compiled by L.S.S.O'Malley. Italics mine.
30 S.B. Singh, 'Gaya in 1857–58', in *Proceedings of Indian History Congress*, Mysore,
1966.
31 Q. Ahmad, 'The Unique Trial of Arrah Town', *Journal of Bihar Research Society*, Vol.
XLVI, 1960.
32 Ibid., p. 159.
33 Ram Vilas Sharma, *San Sattavan ki Rajya Kranti*, Agra, 1957.
34 Krishnadev Upadhyaya, 'Bhojpuri Lokgeeton men 57 ki Kranti ke swar', *Tripathga*
Year 2, August 1957, p. 60.
35 Bhagwan Das Mahaur, *1857 ke Swadheenta Sangram ka Hindi Sahitya par Prabhav*,
Ajmer, 1976, p. 426.
36 Ibid., p. 417.
37 Quoted in Shyamanand Singh, *Kavi Shekhawat An Unhakar Kuchh Pad* (Bhojpuri),
Year 4, Vol. 3–6, January 1956, p. 79.
38 Srinivas Balaji Hardikar, *Nanasheb Peshwa*, Delhi, 1969, p. 84.
39 Peter Burke, *The Art of Conversation*, Oxford, 1993, p. 27.
40 *FSUP IV*, pp. 22, 84.
41 Ibid., p. 40.
42 Ibid., p. 48.
43 Ibid., p. 114.
44 *District Gazetteer of Gorakhpur* (1903–05).
45 K.K. Dutta, *Biography of Kunwar Singh and Amar Singh*, Patna, 1957, p. 173.
46 *FSUP IV*, p. 157.
47 Ibid., p. 654.
48 Ibid., pp. 377–94.
49 Quoted in Vinaymohan Sharma (ed.), *Hindi Sahitya Ka Brihat Itihas*, Vol. VIII',
Kashi, 1957.
50 Extract taken from P.C. Joshi, *1857 in Folk Songs*, Delhi, 1994, p. 29.
51 Extract taken from Shridhar Mishra, *Bhojpuri Loksahitya Sanskritik Adhyayan*.
Translation mine.
52 Source of folk song in translated form from P.C. Joshi: 'Folk Songs of 1857', in P.C.
Joshi (ed.) *Rebellion 1857 – A Symposium*, Delhi, 1957, pp. 280–81.
53 Ibid., p. 280.
54 Badrinarayan, *Lok Sanskriti men Rashtravad*, p. 33.
55 Shridhar Mishra, *Bhojpuri Loksahitya Sanskritik Adhyayan*, p. 160.
56 Source of the extract is the folk ballad 'Nonidih ki ladai'. See Durgashankar Prasad
Singh, 'Kunwar Singh ke Panwara' (Bhojpuri), Year 3, No. 7, April 1955, p. 43.
57 *FSUP IV*, p. 466.
58 Ibid., p. 447.
59 See S. Mishra, *Bhojpuri Lok geet ke vividh roop*. Translation mine.
60 Guha, *Elementary Aspects of Peasant Insurgency in Colonial India*, p. 317.
61 *FSUP IV*, pp. 102, 410.
62 *District Gazetteer of Mirzapur* (1903–05).
63 For details regarding the history of Sattasi, see S.N.R. Rizwi, *Attarvin Sadi ke
Zamindar*, New Delhi, 1988.
64 For a recent discussion on the notion of 'Chowrasee Des' in western Uttar Pradesh see
Gautam Bhadra, 'Four Rebels of Eighteen Fifty-Seven' in R. Guha (ed.) *Subaltern
Studies IV*, Delhi, 1985.
65 Quoted in Bhadra, 'Four Rebels of Eighteen Fifty-Seven'.
66 *FSUP IV*, p. 783.
67 Quoted in Amritlal Nagar, *Ghadar ke phool*, Delhi, 1991, p. 80.
68 *FSUP IV*, p. 549.

[69] Ibid., p. 548.

[70] Ibid., p. 550.

[71] See 'Dulaur ki ladai', compiled in Durgashankar Prasad Singh, 'Kunwar Singh ke Panwar', p. 40.

[72] Badrinarayan, *Lok Sanskriti men Rashtravad*, p. 35. Translation mine.

[73] Source of the folk song Mishra, *Bhojpuri Loksahitya Sanskritik Adhyayan*, p. 144. Translation mine.

[74] For instance, in the folk ballad 'Nonidih ki ladai' or the 'Battle of Nonidih'.

[75] Nagar, *Ghadar ke Phool*, p. 131.

[76] See Badrinarayan, *Lok Sanskriti men Rashtravad*, p. 36.

[77] The folk ballads are compiled in Prasad Singh, 'Kunwar Singh Ke Panwar', pp. 41, 43.

[78] See Shridhar Mishra, *Bhojpuri Loksahitya Sanskritik Adhyayan*, p. 158.

[79] Ibid.; translation by P.C. Joshi, in his *1857 in Folk Songs*, p. 97.

[80] See Mahaur: *1857 ke Swadheenta Sangram ka Hindi Sahitya par Prabhav*, p. 415.

[81] See Shridhar Mishra, *Bhojpuri Loksahitya Sanskritik Adhyayan*, p. 146. Translation mine.

[82] Source of this extract is the folk ballad 'Nonidih ki Ladai' compiled in Durgashankar Prasad Singh, 'Kunwar ke Panwar', p. 43.

[83] See Shri Rasbiharilal, *Lokgeetan men Babu Kanwar Singh*, p. 34. Translation mine.

[84] Ibid., p. 34. Translation in P.C. Joshi: *1857 in Folk Songs*, p. 79.

[85] This jogira folk song is taken from Mahaur: *1857 ke Swadheenta Sangram ka Hindi Sahitya par Prabhav*, p. 148. Translation in P.C. Joshi, *1857 in Folk Songs*, p. 83.

[86] Guha, *Elementary Aspects of Peasant Insurgency in Colonial India*, p. 264.

[87] Lala Khadgbahadur Mall, *Bishwen Vansh Vatika*, Bankipur, 1887, pp. 70–71.

[88] *FSUP IV*, p. 328.

[89] Rizwi, *Atytarvin Sadi ke Zamindar*, p. 64.

[90] *FSUP IV*, p. 83.

[91] Shridhar Mishra, *Bhojpuri Loksahitya Sanskritik Adhyayan*, p. 156.

[92] Nagar, *Ghadar ke Phool*, p. 99.

[93] *FSUP IV*.

[94] Ibid.

[95] Ibid., p. 839.

[96] Letter No. 324, dated 12.06.1857 from Commissioner of Patna, quoted in S.B. Singh, 'Gaya in 1857–58'.

[97] *FSUP IV*, p. 129.

[98] Vishnubhat Godase, *Majha Pravas*, Poona, 1907, quoted in Hardikar, *Nanasaheb Peshwa*, p. 151.

[99] Ibid.

Contemporary Drawings of the Events of the Rebellion of 1857

S.P. Verma

In the study of the Rebellion of 1857 while emphasis has naturally been placed on contemporary and near contemporary British accounts, the rich pictorial illustrations of 1857, provided in some of these accounts, are yet to get the attention which they seem to deserve. In spite of the fact these have been drawn always in conformity with the given textual accounts, these drawings still add to our understanding and are an interesting means of gauging the impressions and imagination of British artists regarding the events of 1857 and perhaps, to some extent, the prevailing impressions of India of 1857 in the British mind.

A very rich repository of such illustrations is the volume entitled *Narrative of the Indian Revolt from its Outbreak to the Capture of Lucknow by Sir Colin Campbell*, published by G. Vickers, London, 1858, containing 36 chapters and 310 prints from engravings made from drawings and photographs.[1] Besides this Charles Ball, *The History of Indian Mutiny giving a detailed account of the Sepoy Insurrections in India and a concise history of the great military events which have tended to consolidate British Empire in Hindustan,* London (1858?) carries 83 drawings and R. Montgomery Martin, *The Indian Empire*, Vol. II, London, 1859 is also well illustrated.

The present study is mainly based on the illustrations in the *Narrative of the Indian Revolt from its Outbreak to the Capture of Lucknow* by Sir Colin Camphell. Even from the point of view of the technique these are of much interest to the students of history of art.

The illustrations here have been prepared from the engravings on steel (prints in black and white). Most of them do not bear the name of the artist, or the engraver. In a few cases, the names of S. Prout and W. Purser appear as artists and those of C. Mottram and W. Brandard as engravers under the illustrations. These illustrations are based on the drawings executed by the artists, of which reproductions or prints were prepared from the engravings. The use of engravings to multiply the prints was common in England since the sixteenth century, and the type of engravings under study, are intaglio with soft-ground etching. These give the effect like that of a pencil or chalk drawing, and the ground is mixed with colour. As a result of which the tonal variations as appearing in artist's drawing, are successfully achieved by the engraver.

The illustrations, imbibing the realism of sixteenth–seventeenth centuries renaissance art of Europe, depict human figures with great mastery whether it be the rendering of the anatomical details or emotions and expressions. The picturization of the events of 'Massacre at Delhi, (Figure 4), and 'Blowing of the rebellious Sepoys', (Figures 5–6), described below, clearly testify to the artist's skill in portraying the horror of death looming large on the whole canvas. Though these illustrations seem based on the oral narration of the events, nevertheless, the portrayal of a Sepoy, or a British guard, or an officer is invariably recognizable. Their dress, and complexion tell a lot about them, and make them distinct. In general, the figures are characteristic and appear as individual characters, and thus the central theme of the picture becomes more expressive. The human and animal figures are highly modelled and the whole picture is finished in a continuous range of smoky tones. Further, the device of conveying distance and *sfumato* in the rendering of the objects make the scene lively. The chiaroscuro effect, scientific perspective, characteristic rendering of the human and animal figures, and lastly the naturalistic light and shade effect – all combine and show the affinity with the Neoclassical tradition of landscape painting. Over and above, the whole drama of the event, surcharged with action and filled with emotions and feelings, leaves one spellbound. In brief, a close look at these pictures recreates the events before us and have unique documentary value.

Further, the illustrations are a faithful representation of the events as narrated and the artists have depicted the killing of British, or the Sepoys, or an armed struggle between them with equal ferocity and frantic outburst of action. A few illustrations noticed below might acquaint us with the nature of their contents and the extent of accuracy that lies in them.

The contemporary visuals, by and large, recreate the event in conformity with the text and are an interesting means of understanding the biases, impressions and imagination of the British artists.

An illustration of the event 'Circulation of *chapaties*' (Indian bread) (Figure 1) – considered a mysterious act and noted much before the outbreak of the Rebellion, is a characteristic representation of the subject in a rural landscape. An expressive gesture of the village man with a dog in toe, receiving the watchman (*chowkeydar*) approaching him with breads (*chapaties*) in his right hand is remarkably realistic. The depiction of village men, barefooted and ordinarily clad in loincloth (*dhoti*, a long flowing costume wrapped round the waist and tucked behind, reaching up to the knees), is a faithful representation by the artist. The background, comprising tiny mud huts with thatched roofs amidst banana and other shady trees truly recreate the Indian village of mid-nineteenth century.

Though the event of the circulation of *chapaties* was considered as a harmless affair, it evoked a sensational response:

> It was reported to the authorities, that the chowkeydars, or village policemen, were speeding from Cawnpore through the villages and towns of the peninsula, distributing on their way a symbol, of the origin of which no European could at

FIGURE 1 The lotus flower and the mysterious act of the passing of *chapattis* before the commencement of the Revolt of 1857. (From *Narrative of the Indian Revolt from its Outbreak to the Capture of Lucknow by Sir Colin Campbell*, London, 1858, p. 3.)

the time form an intelligible idea, or conjecture the purpose. . . . One of the chowkeydars of Cawnpore ran to another in Futteghur, the next village, and placing in his hands two *chupatties*, directed him to make ten more of the same kind, and give two of them to each of the five nearest chowkeydars, with instructions to perform the same service. He was obeyed; and in a few hours the whole country was in a state of excitement, through these policemen running from village to village with their cakes. The wave spread over the provinces with a velocity of speed never yet equalled by the bearers of government despatches.[2]

The next illustration included here depicts the death of Colonel Finnis on the parade ground at Meerut on 10 May 1857. With the outbreak of the Rebellion by sepoys at the contonment at Meerut on 9 May, the event taking place on the following day is described thus:

It was about five o'clock – church time – when, at a given signal, the 3rd Light Cavalry, and the 20th Native Infantry, rushed out of their lines, armed and furious. . . . They found Colonel Finnis haranguing his men, and endeavouring to keep them firm to their colours. The men were wavering when the 20th arrived. The men of this regiment, whose hands were already red with the blood of several of their own officers, seeing this hesitation and its cause, at once fired at Colonel Finnis. The first shot took effect on his horse only, but almost immediately afterwards he was shot from behind, and fell riddled with balls.[3]

The illustration (Figure 2) shows Colonel Finnis shot in the back and falling helplessly from his horse. The sepoys of the 20th Native Infantry, who arrived at the scene while Colonel Finnis was addressing the men of 11th regiment inducing them to return to their duty (shown in the background against the barracks), surrounded him and fired at him. The sepoys are shown armed with firearms – a handgun – they also carried a sword hung around the waist through a belt, or a dagger tucked under a band of cloth tied around the waist. The sepoys are shown dressed in trousers like a British, or clad in a *dhoti*, worn by Indians in general. In their headgear also, there appears a variety ranging from a high oblong cap with flat top to a tightly fitted cap and a ringed turban. Such distinct variety in a sepoy's dress code most likely hints at his affiliation with the particular place or region of his nativity.

The sepoys reached Delhi on 11 May and crossed Hindon bridge, and on their way to Kashmiri Gate charged against the officers of the 54th Native Infantry on move to crush the rebels. The sepoys of the 54th Native Infantry who sympathized with the rebellious sepoys stepped aside, and the latter made a sudden charge and shot down the officers of Infantry. The event is described thus:

> Worse still, on the approach of the cavalry, the sepoys of the 54th rushed suddenly to a side of the road, leaving their officers in the middle of it, upon whom the troopers immediately came at a gallop, and, one after the other, shot them down. The Colonel shot two of them before he fell; but with this exception, and one said to have been shot by Mt. Fraser, none fell. After butchering the

FIGURE 2 Death of Colonel Finnis on the Parade Ground (10 May 1857), the first major incident of the Sepoy Revolt at Meerut. (From *Narrative of the Indian Revolt from its Outbreak to the Capture of Lucknow by Sir Colin Campbell*, London, 1858, p. 13.)

FIGURE 3 Attack on the British officers of the 54th Native Infantry by the Insurgent Cavalry (11 May 1857). (From *Narrative of the Indian Revolt from its Outbreak to the Capture of Lucknow by Sir Colin Campbell*, London, 1858, p. 24.)

officers, the troopers dismounted, and went among the sepoys of the 54th, shaking hands with them: the faternization was completed.[4]

The whole scene is supercharged with action and shows troopers firing at British officers while some lie dead on the ground and some offering resistance are shown wielding the sword (Figure 3). The black and white print of the engraving clearly depicts the British in fair complexion and thus they become recognizable in the crowd of sepoys invariably shown as being of dark complexion. A building of European style, though it remains unidentified, suggests the event taking place on a roadside close to the British headquarters in the city.

Murderous attacks on the British followed after the outbreak of the Rebellion, and such occurrences at Delhi on 11 May are thus narrated:

> Tortures the most refined, outrages the most vile, were perpetrated upon men, women and children. Wives were stripped before their husbands' eyes, flogged naked through the city, violated there in the public street, and then murdered. ... A man who witnessed the last massacre where he had gone as spy, gives a horrid account of it, stating that the little children were falling with *talwars*. ... An officer and his wife were tied to trees, their children tortured to death before them ... then both were burnt to death.[5]

The illustration shows the rebels torching British officers' bungalows, killing their wives and children with swords. A British officer tied to a tree, his wife and children being tortured, and a child tossed in the air and falling on the point of a bayonet are depicted to show the horror of the massacre that followed the Rebellion at Delhi, Kanpur, Peshawar and other places (Figure 4).

The sepoys of 54th Native Infantry at Murdan, Peshawar who openly joined the mutineers were also crushed (13 May 1857). They were killed or captured only to be tried and executed:

> The forty mutineers were in one corner of the square with irons on. The General came on parade, and was received with a salute of sixteen guns from the horse artillery. He then rode round the square and ordered the sentence to be read. The first ten of the prisoners were then lashed to the guns, the artillery officer

FIGURE 4 Sepoys attack the British at Delhi, night of 11 May 1857. (From *Narrative of the Indian Revolt from its Outbreak to the Capture of Lucknow by Sir Colin Campbell*, London, 1858, p. 1.) Here, an infant being tossed and held on the point of a bayonet is a unhistoric depiction.

waved his sword, you heard the roar of the guns, and above the smoke you saw legs, arms, and heads, flying in all directions. There were four of these salvoes, and at each a sort of buzz went through the whole mass of the troops, a sort of murmur of horror.[6]

Similar details on this terrible event appeared in *Blackwood's Magazine* (November 1857):

It was an awfully imposing scene. All the troops, European and native, armed and disarmed, loyal and disaffected, were drawn up on parade, forming three sides of a square; and drawn up very carefully, you may be sure, so that any attempt on the part of the disaffected to rescue the doomed prisoners would have been easily checked. Forming the fourth side of the square, were drawn up the guns (9-pounders), ten in number, which were to be used for the execution. The prisoners, under a strong European guard, were then marched into the square, their crimes and sentences read aloud to them, and at the head of each regiment; they were then marched round the square, and upto the guns the first ten were picked out, their eyes were bandaged, and they were bound to the guns – their backs leaning against the muzzles, and their arms fastened to the wheels. The portfires were lighted, and a signal from the artillery-major, the guns were fired. It was a horrid sight that then met the eye; a regular shower of human fragments of heads, of arms, of legs, appeared in the air through the smoke; and when that cleared away, these fragments lying on the ground – fragments of Hindoos and fragments of Mussulmans, all mixed together – were all that remained of those ten mutineers.[7]

The visual narration of the event in conformity with these details exhibits troops on the two sides of the square, the Sepoys brought in chains and tied against the muzzles of the cannons, and the guards ready to fire the guns at the command of the artillery-major (Figure 5). Another illustration of this event is an elaborate continuous narration of the theme. It shows sepoys being brought in chains for their execution, a sepoy tied to the muzzle of the cannon, and another already blown to bits (Figure 6). Both the above illustrations, though they are differently composed, and are independent works of two different artists, carry the same emphatic massage.

An accuracy can be observed in the rendering of the buildings, forts and bridges, etc., shown in the illustrations in context of an event. One such illustration, depicting the Salimgarh fortress in the context of the storming and capture of Delhi by the British in September, is an apt example (Figure 7). It may be compared with another picture executed by a Delhi artist Mazhar Ali Khan before the outbreak of Revolt.[8] The latter depicts the citadel of Salimgarh, constructed by Salim Shah Sur during his reign, (1545–1554) that was connected by Jahangir in 1621–22 by building a bridge, on the raised ground on the opposite bank of Jamuna, the spot that later was selected by Shahjahan for his Delhi palace-fortress. Here the rubble masonry wall of Salimgarh with its massive bastions

FIGURE 5 Early British atrocity: Blowing away rebellious Sepoys from the guns at Peshawar (21 May 1857). (From *Narrative of the Indian Revolt from its Outbreak to the Capture of Lucknow by Sir Colin Campbell*, London, 1858, pp. 42–43.)

FIGURE 6 Early British atrocity: blowing away rebellious Sepoys from the guns of Peshawar (21 May 1857). (From Charles Ball, *The History of the Indian Mutiny*, Vol. I, London, n.d. [1858?], p. 410.)

FIGURE 7 Sepoys leaving Delhi by boat (18–20 September 1857). The Red Fort, Salimgarh and the connecting bridge are shown. (From *Narrative of the Indian Revolt from its Outbreak to the Capture of Lucknow by Sir Colin Campbell*, London, 1858, p. 166.)

and the connecting bridge built in dressed red sandstone are represented intact and in good condition. Whereas in our illustration (Figure 7), the damage caused to these structures during the siege of Delhi (notice here the damaged bridge and the fortified wall of Salimgarh fortress) is clearly shown by the British artist. Remaining architectural details appear nearly identical in both the paintings though the angle of viewing the buildings is different.

Such drawings of buildings seem to have been based on photographs, and are flawless. The artists often used *camera obscura* (a box with a lens which reflected the landscape image onto a sheet of paper) for tracing architectural details, and also the views and angles of the subject matter. However, the bridge has now completely disappeared, and the course of the river Yamuna has also changed. Today a road separates both the fortresses.[9]

In context of the theme, our illustration further exhibits fleeing sepoys, armed and unarmed, crossing the bridge and approaching the other side of river Yamuna in boats (events of 18 September), and the British flag flying on top of a bastion of the Salimgarh fortress pointing out British control over it.

To sum up, since these nineteenth-century illustrations of the Rebellion of 1857 are by and large visual historical records of events and also leave a deep impression on our mind, this neglected contemporary source needs to be studied to shed light on how the people in Britain perceived the events of 1857 and how the narrative, generally not free of prejudices, also created images of brutalities.

Needless to say, the contemporary visuals under review are not free from the burden of the self-imposed superiority of a particular race. Therefore these tend to depict the role of the British in the war of 1857 as glorious, and their actions as those of heroes.

Besides the depiction of the forts, buildings, etc., the spatial context in which the event is shown taking place, the exclusive drawings of the monuments are of much interest. These drawings are based on direct observation by the artists and on photographs. In them, the artists have rendered the details with extraordinary precision, without being influenced by any whimsical or fanciful ideas. In brief, these drawings are truly historical, and also provide us a glimpse of the prevailing social milieu where mausoleums, mosques, churches, temples and ghats, all appear together. Further, the cluster of thatched-roof mud huts situated adjacent to these structures hint at the settlement pattern of the population.[10] Moreover, men and women in the foreground of the pictures, shown either engaged in work or in groups sitting in leisure, depict everyday life in the mid-nineteenth century. In this context, the illustrations, 'Hindu women'; 'Herdsmen' *'Faqirs* of Rajasthan'; 'domestic servants', 'interior of a café', 'Malabar women', etc. reveal a lot about the life of the ordinary people.[11]

Notes and References

[1] Chapter XXXVI is wrongly numbered XXXVIII, for details see 'Introduction' by S.P. Verma to the Indian reprint, Delhi, 2007.

[2] Ball, *The History of Indian Mutiny*, Vol. I, p. 39.

[3] *Narrative of the Indian Revolt from its Outbreak to the Capture of Lucknow by Sir Colin* Campbell, p. 14.

[4] Ibid., p. 20.

[5] Ibid., p. 21.

[6] Ibid., p. 36.

[7] Ball, pp. 412–13.

[8] For reproduction see, M.M. Kaye, *The Golden Calm, An English Lady's Life in Moghul Delhi*, New York, 1980, colour plate on page 33. Also see, Ebba Koch, 'The Delhi of the Mughals prior to Shahjahanabad as reflected in the patterns of Imperial visits' in A.J. Qaisar and S.P. Verma, eds, *Art and Culture, Felicitation Volume in Honour of Professor S. Nurul Hasan*, Jaipur, 1993, pp. 11–12, plate I.

[9] 'Salimgarh is a small fortress of a segmental polygonal outline enclosed by rubble masonry walls with several bastions, the Red Fort. Today both fortresses are separated by the road which takes the place of a diversion of the river Jamuna, which in Mughal times flowed between them. . . . In 1621–22, Jahangir also built a bridge between the south-western part of Salimgarh and the raised ground on the opposite bank of the Jamuna which was later to be occupied by Shah Jahan's Red Fort' (Ebba Koch, *Mughal Art and Imperial Ideology Collected Essays*, New Delhi, 2001, p. 172, Fig. 6.2)

[10] *Narrative of the Indian Revolt from its Outbreak to the Capture of Lucknow by Sir Colin Campbell*, illustrations on pp. 94, 301, 421, 432, 445.

[11] Ibid., illustrations on pp. 326, 339, 346, 361, 435, and 442.

1857 and the 'Renaissance' in Hindi Literature

Ramesh Rawat

The Revolt of 1857 was a major event in modern Indian history, and there is no doubt that the region most fundamentally affected by the Revolt was that of the Hindustani-speaking areas from where the bulk of the Bengal Army sepoys were recruited. There is much need for exploring the multiple factors which led to the uprising, and the multiple aspects of the 'mentality' of the rebels. There is also a need, however, to try and see what the Revolt left behind in the consciousness of the people. After its failure and its gruesome suppression. Here the rigours of historical method require that one should tread the ground most carefully, and evaluate the 'legacy' of the Revolt in a balanced manner. In particular, there is no room for using the memory of 1857 to build a thesis of blatant regional and linguistic chauvinism. Such a thesis is based on the argument that the process of modernization in nineteenth century Hindi literature (identified with the 'Renaissance' in the European sense by many Hindi scholars and academicians) was the result of the revolt of 1857 and not of any influence from the West or from the Bengal Renaissance; it was, therefore, indigenous and anti-colonial, unlike the earlier Bengal Renaissance.

This view was originally put forward by Ramvilas Sharma in his book *Mahavir Prasad Dwivedi aur Hindi Nav Jagran* (1977). Defining the specific features of this Hindi Nav Jagran, Sharma maintains that the 'Hindi Renaissance' is distinct from similar phenomena witnessed in other parts of the country. The Revolt of 1857, which he, in fact, considers the first stage of the Hindi Renaissance, gives it a particularly indigenous character.[1]

Later on, he systematically developed the concept of a Hindi Renaissance, in terms of its specific stages with their ideological content. He asserts:

> The age of Bhartendu is not the first or the primary stage of the awakening of the people in North India. Rather, it is a particular phase of the old tradition which, in fact, came into being with the origin of literature in folk languages. It was a time when modern nationalities came to be consolidated in various provinces. The character of this awakening of the people in general was anti-feudal. The second stage came with the fight of the Indian people against British rule, that is from the battle of Plassey to 1857. This stage is different in character

from the previous one in that here the fight is against the foreign enemy, that is, British imperialism. This is the age of Bhartendu.[2]

He assigns a special significance to 1857 for the Hindi-speaking region, for this was the area where the rebellion actually took place. 'It influenced the whole of the nation, with the Hindi region bearing it particular impact.'[3]

Sharma identifies the third stage of the Nav Jagaran with the emergence of Mahavir Prasad Dwivedi and his associates. Sharma characterizes the two decades, from 1900 (when the publication of *Saraswati* started) to 1920 (when Dwivedi left *Saraswati*) as the 'Dwivedi Yug' and emphasizes its relationship with 1857, on the one hand, and *chhayawad*, particularly Nirala, on the other.[4]

As Alok Rai sums up:

> In Sharma's account, there is a seamless transition from the popular, democratic and anti-colonial ideas expressed in several of the proclamations issued by the rebels of 1857 and the consciousness that finds expression in the writings of Bhartendu and his contemporaries. Further, he sees a linear development from Bhartendu Yug to the nationalist and modernist restlessness which characterizes the writers associated with Dwivedi and his influential journal *Saraswati*.[5]

Sharma does not take into account the historical appraisal of the rebels of 1857, guided mainly by colonial perceptions, and also he does not discuss the reasons why the revolutionary legacy of 1857 was not openly avowed.

In fact, his understanding of a 'Hindi Renaissance' has been derived from a particular interpretation of 1857. For Sharma, the '*Ghadar*' was not only India's struggle for emancipation from foreign rule, but also a 'people's revolution'. The sepoys forged a combined front with the feudal lords and merchants, but kept the leadership of the 'Revolution' in their own hands. The feudal lords had control neither over Delhi, nor over Lucknow. Authority lay with the sepoys, who were, essentially, peasants in uniform. For the first time in Indian history, a new class, having supplanted the older one, captured power. The sepoys took steps to give the proprietary rights to the peasants. In 1947, power went to the bourgeoisie, but it has so far, failed to effectively carry out land reforms.[6]

Sharma interprets the political developments of the post-1857 period as a logical denouncement of 1857, be it the Swadeshi movement of 1905, the Quit India movement, the RIN mutiny of 1946 or the revolutionary movement.[7]

Sharma makes an assessment of the political achievements of 1857 and puts them fantastically at par with those of the French and Russian revolutions.[8]

In fact, the debate has defined the politico-academic perspective of modern Hindi literature in terms of a 'Hindi Renaissance' and a 'Hindi nationality'. What is interesting in this whole controversy is that the appeal which this controversy carries, cuts across all ideological inclinations, and the regional consciousness shows itself more and more explicitly. A large number of Hindi scholars and intellectuals have joined this debate and have followed Sharma in assuming that 1857 led to a Renaissance in nineteenth century Hindi literature. As I have already noted, the proponents of this theory of a Hindi Renaissance do not admit or acknowledge any Western influence on the nature or the ideological content of modern Hindi literature. Sharma observes: 'The new awakening does not reflect the influence of English literature. Originally, it has its roots in Indian tradition.'[9] He also asserts:

> The romantic poets of England were influenced by the scientific achievements of India. Williams Jones wrote a lot on Indian culture. He translated Sanskrit poems into English. The intellectuals of Europe and England were familiar with this work. Western influence which came to India through English language already contained an Indian element.[10]

To talk of the influence of British rule is anathema to him. He does not critically examine the process of modernization, which came about through a very complicated and protracted process. It is also rather perplexing that a seasoned Marxist scholar like him, did not discuss the views of Marx, the first and foremost thinker who identified the process of modernization and, critically, the role of British rule. While defining the historical character of British rule in India, Marx had observed in 1853: 'England has to fulfil a double mission in India, one destructive, the other regenerating: Annihilation of old Asiatic society and laying of the material foundation of Western society in Asia.'[11]

It should be pointed out that these two roles were performed simultaneously, not in any distinct sequential stages; 'the creative was rooted in the destructive and therefore apparently secondary and less visible'.[12]

Again, Marx has no misconceptions about the nature of the British rule, as is clear from the following statement:

> England, it is true, in causing a social revolution, was actuated only by the vilest interests and was stupid in her manner of enforcing them. But that is not the question. The question is, can mankind fulfil its destiny without a fundamental revolution in the social state of Asia? If not, whatever may have been the crimes of England, she was the unconscious tool of history in bringing about that revolution.[13]

Characterizing the historical role of the bourgeoisie, he observed: 'Has it ever effected progress without dragging individuals and peoples through blood and dirt, through misery and degradation.'[14]

Such statements and observations by Marx have not been discussed in the theory propounded by Sharma and his followers; and so the indigenous roots or inspiration of modern Hindi literature have been unduly emphasized.

Sources of Modern Ideas

Those who have studied the intellectual history of India have noticed the lack or non-existence of institutions meant to promote intellectual pursuits. It has been observed that the Mughal period was in many respects a glorious period of Indian history and that while the Mughals devoted much attention to art and culture, they 'completely neglected practical and secular learning, especially science. Throughout their long rule, no institution was established comparable to the modern university. There were flourishing universities in medieval Europe as in other parts of the Islamic world, some of which had been in existence for some centuries.'[15] Although, their court was frequented by European visitors, the Mughals took little interest in European knowledge and technological accomplishments.

After Mughal power declined, a long period of political instability followed. Intellectual inertia, already in evidence, became the prominent feature of Indian society and the country lapsed into chaos and confusion. Eighteenth-century India, in contrast to Renaissance Europe, was so weak that it had little control over its own affairs.

Irfan Habib holds the absence of properly endowed academies and colleges responsible for the limited exchange of ideas as well as the autonomous development of intellectual pursuits, since the scholars and the intellectuals had to depend on the personal patronage of individual nobles or the Emperor for their academic or intellectual pursuits. He also observes that 'education in the higher branches was the luxury of the privileged and the influx into the ranks of the educated from the lower classes was insignificant if it was there at all'.[16]

M. Athar Ali, another well-known authority on the social and cultural history of medieval India concludes that 'while we may admire the poetry of a Hafiz, the rationalism of an Abul Fazl, the religious eclecticism of Dara Shikoh, and the astronomical observations of Jai Singh Sawai, the fact remains that of modern science, there is hardly a trace'.[17]

It is precisely here, in the context thus defined, that the question of 1857 comes up, particularly in terms of generating and propagating modern ideas. Let us examine as to whether this process of cultural regeneration and the history of modern ideas started with 1857, as has been argued, or whether they had any traditions preceding it. Whatever the proponents of a Hindi Renaissance might say, it is an acknowledged fact that 'Indian nationalism' was fed by the study of European history and English literature. Rather, the familiarity with English literature is visible as early as in the 1830s. Dr Duff, who arrived in India in 1830, quite surprised to note the mushrooming growth of publications in the vernacular languages, which, while making a vigorous assault on Christianity, relied mostly on extracts from Paine's *Age of Reason*, translated verbatim – an interesting indication of the extent to which contemporary English literature was studied and used for political purposes.[18]

Even Delhi was an important centre of literary and intellectual activities during this period. C.F. Andrews, a graduate of Cambridge's Pembroke College who conceived the theory of a Delhi Renaissance, discovered a general liveliness in the city before 1857. He noticed the development of Urdu prose, the translation of scientific works in the language, the flowering of scientific curiosity and the success of the printing press.

Delhi College was a major educational enterprise.

It had an English branch where English language and literature and modern European sciences were taught, and an oriental branch in which Arabic, Persian and Sanskrit were taught, along with geography, mathematics and science. Above everything else, it had been a nursery of scientific teaching, and a catalyst of major works on scientific subjects. The doctrines of ancient philosophy, taught through the medium of Arabic verse, were cast in the shade before the more reasonable and experimental theories of modern science. The old dogma that the earth is the fixed centre of the universe was generally laughed at by the higher students of the oriental as well as by those of the English Department of the College.[19]

The contribution and role of the Delhi College regarding the Urdu-speaking intelligentsia has been underscored in the following words.

It contributed to the development of Urdu prose as a vehicle for the transmission of knowledge. It mediated between eastern and western cultures and mentalities, and did so in the vernacular, contributing to an Urdu speaking and reading public that belonged to different religious persuasions. Even though hot headed mullahs, theologians, and publicists sustained their campaign against Western education and its supposed negative impact on Muslim beliefs and practices, Delhi College embarked upon changes in the traditional academic curriculum and created a climate for fostering liberal thought and the rational spirit. Its leading lights lived with the sense that they were making history and creating a new society. For its alumni, the college remained a home of pleasant memories in the far distant past, and retained its liberal scientific and humanistic spirit. If I had not studied in Delhi College, stated Nazir Ahmad, 'I would have been a maulvi, narrow and bigoted.'[20]

We are specially concerned here with the role and impact of 1857 on the cultural process. Contrary to the regenerative role of 1857 as has been suggested by Ram Vilas Sharma and his followers, it has been noticed, particularly in the context of the cultural milieu of Delhi College that:

The sound and fury of 1857 overshadowed the college's impressive beginning while the cloud of uncertainty loomed large on the horizon before its actual closure, the college was attacked, its rich collection of manuscripts and books was burnt down, and the mutineers killed Taylor, the English Principal. By the time a temporary revival occurred between 1864 and 1867, Delhi College had lost its distinct personality. One of the principal reasons for this was that Urdu, a major catalyst for Delhi's cultural and intellectual regeneration, ceased to be the medium of instruction. This was, in retrospect, the beginning of an inglorious era in the history of the Urdu language.[21]

Apart from this it has been observed that with British power re-established with a certain degree of finality after the revolt of 1857, the uprising left scars on both the sides. The British were mindful of how close, they had come to the disaster, which made them cautious, suspicious, even afraid. The Indians on the other hand, smarting under defeat, began groping for other forms of regeneration and agitation. Each side remembered the savagery and brutality of the other. It was in this atmosphere of mutual distrust and fear, later, worsened by political crises and conflicts, that cultural intercourse between India and the British now took place.[22]

It has also been pointed out that since the social reforms embarked on from 1829 onwards and the growing racial overtones in the administration had already resulted in alienating the rulers from the mass of the ruled, the Mutiny and the process of its suppression simply crystallized the already existing division by increasing the distrust of both sides.[23]

Therefore, it can clearly be seen that 1857 could have had no positive consequences so far as the cultural interaction is concerned. Moreover, despite the glorious role that it played against British imperialism and the anti-British sentiments that it aroused, the concept of their 'native land', which the rebels and their leadership entertained, was not based on modern ideas of the nation-state and democracy. It can be clearly established from the available documentary evidence that the modern ideas, such as those of democracy, equality, fraternity, did not underlie the Revolt of 1857.

No doubt, the historical memory of 1857 animated and inspired the national movement, and this did more damage to the cause of the British in India than the Revolt itself. It was not, however, the only source of inspiration to the Indian people in the fight against British imperialism; Western ideas and political movements and events taking place in the outside world went a long way in moulding the anti-imperialist consciousness of Indian people during the National Movement.

As early as the aftermath of the American war of Independence, the Parsees of Bombay were discussing the questions raised by England's loss of her colonies. In 1823, Raja Ram Mohan Roy gave a dinner in the Town Hall of Calcutta to celebrate the revolution in Spain. For later, the Home Rule Movement in Ireland, the grant of self-government to South Africa, Japan's success in the Russo-Japanese war of 1904–05 and the formation of the union of South Africa were closely watched. Sir Henry Campbell Bannerman's pronouncement that good government is no substitute for self-government was regarded as an infallible article of faith.

The arguments made by Western writers to justify political violence and the catchwords of foreign revolutionary movements were pressed into service. Lala Lajpat Rai published a life of Mazzini and Vinayak Savarkar issued a Marathi translation of Mazzini's autobiography, which soon became popular in Bombay. The history of the Italian risorgimento was carefully studied, a Young Indian Society was started in imitation of Mazzini's Young Italy, and the cry of 'India for Indians' echoed that of 'Italy for Italians'. The precedent of the French Revolution was quoted, the most radical of the doctrines of Kossuth, the Hungarian revolutionary, were invoked, and boycott as a political weapon was borrowed from Ireland. The secret organization of Russian Nihilism was copied and in later years, projects aiming to repeat the Bolshevik Revolution of Russia tended to be formulated by radical groups.

Gandhi himself owed a great deal to Western education and thought. He began his career in South Africa as an English-trained barrister, he subsequently obtained many years of experience in journalism, as a newspaper editor. He applied the Western techniques of political agitation, and there is no doubt that he had studied and had been deeply impressed by the literature of the West.[24]

1857 and Modern Hindi Literature

When we closely scrutinize the late nineteenth century Hindi literature, we do not find any evidence of a significant impact of the Revolt of 1857 on it. We notice, in the main, three types of patterns of poetry woven around 1857.

1. We have, in the first place, folk poetry, which, if genuinely contemporary, reflects the people's feelings at that time, and, if later, reflects how sections of people remembered 1857 through oral traditions. Such poetry is, by no means, uniformly anti-British, and much of it was recorded after 1947, making it difficult to date.

2. The second category consists of those poets who enjoyed feudal patronage. They had no ideological position of their own. They came to be guided by the side on which their patrons happened to be during the revolt. A poet, Sewak, in his *Vagvilas*, for example, extolled the services rendered by his patrons Raja Hari Shankar Singh and Gauri Shankar Singh to the British during the rebellion: 'Graced by all qualities, giver of great gifts loyal to the British, handsome and gay they rendered the rulers immense help during the revolt.'[25]

Another poet, Ras Raj Bihari Singh expressed a tremendous sense of satisfaction when Queen Victoria took over the reigns of the government of India in 1858 and restored peace and order. However, it can be argued that the depiction of 1857 in the writings of these poets cannot be seen as representing a modern trend in Hindi literature on account of their dependence on feudal patrons and its impact on their perception.

3. Poets and litterateurs, like Bhartendu and his associates and later on, Mahavir Prasad Dwivedi and his circle, who inaugurated the process of modernization in Hindi literature.

We are concerned here with this third category, on the basis of whom Sharma and his adherents built up the theory of a Hindi Navjagran. Though they have asserted the role of 1857 as a source of modern values in Hindi literature, they have never supported their formulations with the documentary evidence, nor have they critically examined the actual evidence available on this theme.

It is notable that we do not have any direct reference to 1857 in Bhartendu's writings except in the following two lines:

> The fires of the sepoy revolt were put down brutally.
> For terror, Indians dare not move their heads.[26]

On the basis of these lines, Sharma has inferred that the litterateurs of late nineteenth century could not talk of the outrages of 1857 perpetrated by the British on the Indian people, as they were apprehensive of official reprisal. Other scholars subscribing to the theory of Hindi Navjagran have generally accepted this interpretation. They have not made any attempt to explore the ideological implications of this indifference or silence on the issue of 1857. In fact, it is not only the case of Bhartendu's indifference to, or silence on, the issue of 1857. Almost every one of his associates denounced 1857. For example, Chaudhari Badri Narain Upadhyaya Prem 'Gham' (1855–1921), a *rais* of Mirzapur and a very close associate of Bhartendu, wrote: 'The East was in fear, men were terror-stricken and those who thought that religion and caste were in danger. They took with them a few foolish soldiers and some evil men and caused a great havoc, sowing seeds of their own ruin.'[27]

He also wrote a play, *Bharat Saubhagya*, which was dedicated to the President of the fourth session of the Indian National Congress at Allahabad (1888). It was written in order to be staged for the Congress delegates, though, eventually, it could not eventually be performed at that session. It had a song addressed to Queen Victoria, which contained the following words: 'May you, Queen, live for a hundred thousand years.'[28] In this play, 'the British nation' appears as one of the main characters busy with the job of restoring order and peace in the country. He is assisted by the three chief agents, i.e. 'British policy', 'Education', and 'Freedom'. The restoration of law and order while being performed by the British after centuries of patriarchy and oppression, is unfortunately disturbed by the outbreak of 1857. Though, paradoxically enough, the description of 1857 is sympathetic, the leaders of the rebellion, Bahadur Shah and Nana Sahib, are reproached for causing disturbance. Nana Sahib is dubbed a 'Arya Kula Kalank' one who earned a bad name for the high caste (Arya Kula).[29] In the play, Indians are shown as being incapable of self-rule. The character 'Freedom' says, 'What vain thinking is it that those who cannot hold together their loose dhoti will govern the country.'[30]

Pratap Narain Mishra (1856–94), an important figure in Bhartendu's circle, reacted sharply to official suspicions of the loyalty of Indians to British rule. The suspicions, he argued, were ill-founded, because Indians treated their rulers at par with God. As evidence of loyalty, he recalled the days of 1857 when Indians risked their property and life for the sake of their rulers. He compared Lord Ripon not only to Akbar but also to Ram, and hoped that the British would strengthen the natural loyalty of Indians by giving them their due. Referring to 1857, his following lines are oft quoted:

When in fifty-seven a part of the army revolted.
The people firmly took the side of the Sovereign.[31]

Radha Charan Goswami (1859–1923), coming from a priestly family of Vrindavan and controlling a chain of temples in a number of North Indian cities, was highly inspired by Bhartendu. In 1880, he wrote a fantasy, titled *Yam Lok*

Ki Yatra. It was serialized in the *Sar Sudha Nidhi*, a prominent Hindi periodical of the time. In it, he described the visit of an enlightened young man to the kingdom of Yama, the god of death. Interestingly, of the many hells he described in this play, one is reserved for those who had risen against the mighty British government, a special hell being set up for those who had fought against the British in 1857.[32]

Bal Krishna Bhatta (1884–1914) proudly reminded the British of the steadfast loyalty that many Indians had shown during 1857.[33] Pattan Lal, a poet of Patna, recalled the events of 1857 as a great calamity and expressed his happiness over its suppression: the overthrow of the rebels 'brought rain to a parched land' (*Aatap ghoar Mahabal Vo Santavan Ke San Ko Dukh Khani / Jasu Dripa Dhayo Bhartat Pe Imi Sukhat paryo Jan Pani*).[34]

This denunciatory attitude towards 1857 is reflected even in the writings of Mahavir Prasad Dwivedi as well. Dwivediji wrote an article in *Saraswati* (the journal that he edited), in January–February, 1904, on Rani Lakshmi Bai, which was based on a work by Pt. Dattatreya Balwant Prarasniya. He clarified that the Rani had nothing to do with the massacre of the British during the revolt (*balwa*) of 1857, and that, in fact, she had assured the British government of her support to crush the rebels.[35]

He wrote another article in *Saraswati* (April, 1904) under the title 'Shivaji Aur Aurangzeb' in which he tried to prove that Shivaji made every effort to support the 'East India Company'. In this article, he called Tantya Tope and Nana Sahib cruel murderers.[36]

In the January 1905 issue of *Saraswati*, he published a biographical note on Maharaja Raghu Raj Singh Ju Dev, G.C.S.I., with his photograph. In this he admired those feats of the Maharaja which he performed during 1857 in aiding the British.[37] In yet another article (January 1904) titled 'Awadh Mein Angrezon Ka Pahala Ishtihar', he justified the dethroning of Wajid Ali Shah of Awadh.[38]

In light of the above evidence, it is difficult to conclude that 1857 had any role in shaping the modernization and progress of Hindi language or literature. It can be clearly seen that the issues and concerns which triggered off 1857 were entirely different from those that agitated the minds of nineteenth century Hindi litterateurs. It may be observed that 'Khari Boli' attained its present standardized form well before 1857 and the mushrooming growth of books, booklets, pamphlets and magazines after the 1870s was, in fact, an outcome of the religious and social reform movements, not of 1857. Moreover, many cultural and literary institutions such as the Banaras Institute, Allahabad Institute, the Friends Debating Society (Allahabad), The Carmichael Library Association (Banaras), Kavita Vardhini Sabha (Banaras), The Penny Reading Club (Banaras), Hindi Pravardhini Sabha (Allahabad), Nagari Pracharni Sabha (Banaras), Hindi Sahitya Sammelan (Allahabad),[39] came to be established under the encouragement of the British administration, Brahmo Samaj or Arya Samaj. None of them drew inspiration from 1857, they had emerged as the alternative channels to the feudal patronage by using the printed word and the medium of public meetings and thus heralded a new form of organization in the realm of culture and literature.

These bodies consisted mainly of educated professionals, among whom the controversy first arose over the issue of a regional vernacular (Urdu or Hindi).

Though Ramvilas Sharma rejects any possibility of Bengali influence on modern Hindi literature, the active presence of educated Bengalis in the early Nagari/Hindi agitation has been frequently noted. In an official note of 28 March 1876, the Director of Public Instruction, Oudh, identified the desire of the Bengalis to be more extensively employed than at present in the Urdu-speaking province of India as a major driving force of the Hindi agitation, since Bengali and Hindi shared the same script.[40]

Moreover, the interventions of Rajendra Lal Mitra, on behalf of the Nagari script, and Keshub Chunder Sen's advice to Swami Dayanand Saraswati to abandon Sanskrit in favour of Hindi for his public discourses are well known. Some of the earliest suggestions regarding Hindi being made the national language emanated from Bengali intellectuals, notably Bankim Chandra Chatterjee and Bhudev Mukherjee. It appears that Hindi was also used as an axis of mobilization at the time of agitation against the partition of Bengal.[41]

Apart from this, the prominence of Bengalis in the Banaras Institute and the Allahabad Institute, and during the Hunter Commission's mobilization for Hindi has also been noted.

One cannot also ignore the connections between the Sanskritization of modern Bengali and the subsequent Sanskritization of modern Hindi. (There has been no similar Sanskritization in Punjabi or Gujarati, two other neighbouring languages).

Narayan Chaturvedi, a prominent historiographer of modern Hindi literature has noted the process of the modernization of Hindi language and literature in the following way:

> A new turn in Hindi literature came about on account of those Hindi writers who had English and Urdu backgrounds in their studies. This trend started originally with Shri Dhar Pathak, followed by Lala Sita Ram, Pt. Shyam Bihari Mishra, Sukh Dev Bihari Mishra, and Mahavir Prasad Dwivedi. These litterateurs not only brought about a change in Hindi language but also introduced a variety of themes. Chandra Dhar Sharma Guleri, was influenced by English as well as Sanskrit. People belonging to other linguistic groups also started writing in Hindi. For example, Lajja Ram Mehta (Gujarati), Amrit Lal Chakravarti (Bengali), Madhav Rao Sapre (Marathi), etc. Dwivedi was influenced by the writings of foreign scholars. Particularly, he had a fascination for European Sanskritists' interpretation of Sanskrit literature. Later on, he had correspondence with Max Muller. He translated essays on Bacon under the title of 'Bacon Vichar Ratnavali', and Mill's *Liberty* under the title 'Swadhinta'. He also translated several other books.[42]

This factual account assigns a primary role to Western thought and literature in bringing about the Hindi 'Renaissance'.

Ideological Perspective of Modern Hindi Literature

It is thus quite evident that the ideological roots of nineteenth-century Hindi literature have nothing to do with 1857 and its anti-imperialist conscious-ness. It had its own specific features which need to be studied carefully. Loyalism was a very important component of the Hindi litterateur's mental make-up at this time.

The Hindi intelligentsia which emerged during the period, according to Alok Rai, consisted mainly of 'Hindi Savarnas, Brahmans, Banias and Khattris who formed the bulk of the early Nagari/Hindi agitations [and] sought ener-getically on their part to distinguish themselves from the Muslims who had been so unforgivably disloyal in 1857'.[43] Their anti-British consciousness is thus hard to prove: on the other hand, they often seemed to treat the British as friends, and the Muslims as rivals, or even opponents. Raja Shiva Prasad assured the British government that the people would be happy to accept the domination of the 'fair-complexioned'. 'Never will it be safe to leave any district without a fair-complexioned head. It is not excess but rather the dearth of the fair-complexioned ones that we have to complain of.'[44]

Bhartendu had his own tradition of loyalty: his loyalist family had protected British property in Banaras during the Mutiny of 1857. He composed encomiastic or panegyric poetry on various occasions such as Jubilee celebrations, visits of princes, birthday celebrations of princes, British war victories, the holding of Durbars, etc.

Bhartendu called a meeting of poets in Banaras on 20 January 1870, in which a large number of poets participated and recited eulogistic poems. Later on, an anthology of these poems was published under the title of *Sumanojjali*. The then ruler of Rewa, Sri Raghu Raj Singh, was very happy to note the spirit of loyalism animating from these poems and he gave two thousand rupees as a prize. The Princess of Vijai Nagar also gave two hundred and fifty rupees.[45] The government was highly pleased at this expression of loyalty and nominated Bhartendu as a 'Honorary Magistrate'. Later on, another collection of such panegyric poems was published under the title of *Mansopayan* in January 1877.

Prem Gham, in his play titled *Bharat Saubhaugya*, already describes British rule as 'Ram Rajya'. In the play, a whole inventory of boons granted by the British to India is given alongside a commentary on the negative consequences of the British rule.

Radha Charan Goswami also welcomed the Duke of Connaught to India (1883) in the most fawning terms, though with some criticism of British policies.[46]

Pratap Narain Mishra wrote a long poem which he serialized in the *Brahman* (the journal he brought out) between August 1884 and December 1885. After recounting the terrible atrocities perpetrated by the Muslim rulers, he concludes that it was because of such sins that Muslim rule was destroyed. He depicts the English government as a saviour of Hindu religion, for under its patronage, the Hindus felt as if they were living in Ram Rajya. He offers a quixotic defence for British rule, that under British government, people are experiencing joys and sorrows in accordance with their deeds.[47]

Balkrishna Bhatta also feels that there was a state of anarchy until the British restored law and order and it was God's grace that British had saved India from anarchy.[48]

It can be fairly concluded that it was not the fear of repression or reprisal by the British government (as has been suggested by Sharma and his adherents), but a genuinely loyal attitude towards it because of which nineteenth century Hindi litterateurs either remained indifferent or critical towards 1857. On account of this loyalist view and the distorted historical perception, they constantly showed hostility towards pre-British Muslim regimes. Invariably, every one of them has depicted Muslim rule as a curse and British rule as a boon, being indeed a veritable Ram Rajya. Muslims were generally characterized as mischief-makers, quarrelsome and riotous, and normally vicious oppressors. The Muslims were supposed to have been incensed with Hindus on account of the fact that 'Whereas Hindus were once their shoe-bearers, they were now holding positions equal or even superior to those held by Mussalmans.'[49]

Even though most of the nineteenth century Hindi litterateurs used Urdu in their writings, under the ideological influence of Hindu revivalism, they interpreted Urdu as the language of Muslims, and they characterized it with all kinds of abusive and negative terminology, such as witch, prostitute, bastard, sinner, demoness, the scum of other languages the embodiment of all demerits etc.[50] Defining the nation in terms of religion and language, Pratap Narain Misra gave the well-known slogan of 'Hindi, Hindu, Hindustan' in 1892.[51] This was later on adopted by the Hindu Mahasabha.

In fact, this intellectual exercise prepared the ground for the Two Nation theory even before the demand of Pakistan was put forward by the Muslim League.

The dominant ideology of nineteenth century Hindi literature thus was not anti-imperialist or even nationalist, but rather loyalist and partly sectarian. Intolerance towards Muslims and Urdu was one of the major features of their world view. This so-called Hindi Renaissance does not have even that amount of humanitarianism and religious tolerance which marked the medieval phase of Hindi literary efflorescence that produced Kabir, Raidas, Dhanna, Dadu and Mira Bai along with Jayasi, Rahim, and Raskhan. The so-called Hindi Renaissance thus carried forward no legacy of 1857, and the undue glorification of this literary trend cannot but serve to breed obscurantism and Hindi chauvinism, however strongly the terminology of Marxism may be adopted by its proponents.

Notes and References

[1] Ramvilas Sharma, *Mahavir Prasad Dwivedi Aur Hindi Navjagran*, New Delhi, [1977] 1989, p. 9.

[2] Ramvilas Sharma, *Bharatendu Harish Chandra Aur Hindi Navjagran Ki Samasya-yaein*, New Delhi, 1999, p. 13.

[3] Sharma, *Mahavir Prasad Dwivedi Aur Hindi Navjagran*, p. 10.

[4] Ibid., p. 15.

[5] Alok Rai, *Hindi Nationalism*, Hyderabad, 2001, p. 33.

[6] Ramvilas Sharma, *Swadhinta Sangram: Badalte Pariprekshya*, New Delhi, 1992, p. 254.

[7] Ibid., p. 234.

[8] Ramvilas Sharma, *San Sattavam Ki Rajya Kranti Aur Marxvaad*, Allahabad, 1990, p. 530.

[9] Ramvilas Sharma, *Apni Dharti, Apne Log*, Part II, New Delhi, 2003, p. 203.

[10] Ramvilas Sharma, *Bharatiya Sanskriti Aur Hindi Pradesh*, Part II, New Delhi, 2003, p. 288.

[11] Karl Marx and Frederick Engels, *The First Indian War of Independence, 1857–1859*, Moscow, p. 3.

[12] Irfan Habib, *Essays in Indian History*, New Delhi, 1995, p. 57.

[13] Marx and Engels, *The First Indian War of Independence*, p. 17.

[14] Ibid., p. 29.

[15] D.P. Singhal, *India and World Civilization*, Vol. II, Delhi, 1972, pp. 197–98.

[16] See D.N. Jha (ed.), *Society and Ideology in India*, Delhi, 1996, p. 172.

[17] M. Athar Ali, *Mughal India: Studies in Polity, Ideas, Society and Culture*, New Delhi, 2006, p. 342.

[18] M.N. Srinivas, *Social Change in Modern India*, Hyderabad, 1995, p. 85.

[19] C.F. Andrews, *Zaka Ullah of Delhi*, New Delhi, 2003, p. xxii.

[20] Ibid., p. xxiii.

[21] Ibid.

[22] D.P. Singhal, *India and World Civilization*, Vol. II, p. 249.

[23] Michael Edwards, *British India (1772–1947)*, London, 1967, p. 152.

[24] L.S.S.O'.Malley (ed.), *Modern India and the West*, London, 1968, p. 95.

[25] L.S. Varshney, *Adhunik Hindi Sahitya (1850–1900)*, Allahabad, 1954, p. 251.

[26] Hemant Sharma (ed.), *Bharatendu Samagra*, Varanasi, 1989, p. 255.

[27] L.S. Varshney, *Adhunik Hindi Sahitya (1850–1900)*, p. 251.

[28] Sudhir Chandra, *The Oppressive Present*, Delhi, 1992, p. 35.

[29] Ibid.

[30] Ibid.

[31] Naresh Chandra Misra (ed.) *Pratap Narain Misra Kavilavali*, Allahabad, 1987, p. 34.

[32] Sudhir Chandra, *The Oppressive Present*, p. 37.

[33] Jiwan Charitra (*Babu Tota Ram*), Aligarh, 1906, pp. 14–15.

[34] Sudhir Chandra, *The Oppressive Present*, p. 46.

[35] Cited in Parimalendu, *Bharatendu Kal Ke Bhoole Bisre Kavi Aur Unka Kavya*, Varanasi, 2002, p. 255.

[36] Har Prakash Gaur, *Saraswati Aur Rashtriya Jagran*, Delhi, 1983, p. 5.

[37] Ibid., p. 5.

[38] Ibid., p. 4.

[39] Ibid., p. 5.

[40] Vishwa Nath Misra, *Hindi Bhasha Aur Sahitya Par Angrezi Prabhav*, Dehradun, 1963, p. 100.

[41] Alok Rai, *Hindi Nationalism*, p. 53.

[42] Ibid., p. 54.

[43] *Adhunik Hindi Sahitya Ka Adi Kal*, Delhi, 1963, p. 103.

[44] Alok Rai, *Hindi Nationalism*, pp. 35–36.

[45] Quoted from Ibid.

[46] Kishorilal Gupta, *Bharatendu Aur Anya Sahayogi Kavi*, Benares, 1956, p. 209.

[47] Sudhir Chandra, *The Oppressive Present*, p. 39.

[48] Ibid., p. 43.

[49] Ibid., p. 46.

[50] Ibid., p. 133.

[51] Ibid., pp. 136, 140.

Religion in the History of 1857

Farhat Hasan

Since the publication of William Dalrymple's influential work *The Last Mughal* in 2006,[1] with its emphasis on the religious factors, there is a renewed interest among historians in the role of religion in the revolt of 1857.[2] In fact, though, Dalrymple is not the only historian to have done so, and ever since the occurrence of the rebellion, historians of different persuasion have been looking at 'the religious issue' with a view to set it against the backdrop of their understanding of the nature of the colonial state and forms of resistance to colonialism in the nineteenth century. In this paper an attempt is made to examine the broad assumptions about the history of the period, which, in turn, inform the manner in which historians have understood issues based in faith and religious identities in the Revolt of 1857.

In the array of pamphlets that cropped up soon after the uprising in England, there were quite a few which saw the conflict primarily in religious terms – a reforming Christianity besieged by the incorrigible heathens.[3] In 1864, J.W. Kaye published the first of his planned six-volume history of the Revolt.[4] Unlike several other British historians of the period, Kaye could see that this was not a mere 'sepoy mutiny', but a broad-based revolt marked by an impressive participation of the civil population. He believed that the roots of the rebellion came 'from within the depths of civil society', and it was a product of the steady alienation of the landed aristocracy and the religious classes from British rule caused, among other factors, but most importantly, by the reforming zeal of the state and missionaries. In another book published in 1859, Kaye reiterated this position, and suggested that non-interference in religious matters was almost a necessity for the stabilization of British rule in India. In his own words: 'religious neutrality . . . must be a substantive article of our political faith.'[5]

For these early imperialist historians, the religious trope served to essentialize India as inhabited by irrational and obscurantist people, opposed to change and progress. The revolt came to represent a reaction, brutal and violent, against the civilizing push of the enlightened British rule in India. The emphasis on religious issues not only placed the British rulers in the victim mould, but also allowed the earlier imperialist historians to reiterate the right to domination based on the superiority of their civilization – rational and enlightened, scientific and modern.

Of course, the religious issue was emphasized by the Indians writing on the revolt as well, but in doing so, their objectives were very different. They were seeking to make objectively different formulations about the nature of the Indian civilization and the colonial rule in India. Writing about the revolt merely a year after its suppression, in 1859, Sir Syed Ahmad Khan held interference in religious matters to be one of the most important reasons for the hostility of the Indian people against the British rule. He does cite other reasons as well, such as the alienation of landed aristocracy, lack of communication between the rulers and the ruled, racial arrogance, etc., but assigns to apprehensions based on faith a place of prominence. He is particularly aggrieved by the activities of the Christian missionaries, and believes that the aggressive style of their preaching served to reinforce these apprehensions among Indians. They would distribute controversial tracts, preach in public places, openly abuse prophets and saints, and indoctrinate the vulnerable minds of the children studying in their schools.[6] Even as he believes that religious grievances were crucial, there was still no basis for a religious war or *jihad* against the British for they 'did not interfere with the Muhammadans in the practice of their religion'.[7] The *jihadis* and the *mujahidins*, therefore, receive from him a contemptuous treatment, and he has some of the choicest epithets to describe them: 'vagrants and derelicts', 'debauched drunkards', etc.[8]

Sir Syed was a loyalist, anxious to demonstrate the loyalty of the Muslim community towards British rule in India. And, yet, in raising the religious issue, he was, in a way, seeking to set limits to British domination in India. There is a vague identification of religion as an autonomous and private sphere, that is, and should remain, beyond the reach of the imperial state. V.D. Savarkar was a revolutionary, writing half-a-century after Sir Syed, on the rebellion.[9] Despite the obvious differences between them, the concern with the autonomy of private, sacred spaces in Sir Syed, is shared by Savarkar. Savarkar describes the rebellion as the 'first war of independence', but also emphasizes its religious character by designating it as a 'holy war'.[10] He sees the rebellion as a struggle for both *swadharma* and *swaraj*.[11] While it is not clear as to what he means by these terms, he does believe in the maintenance of the autonomy of the private, sacred sphere in social life, but, unlike Sir Syed, considers that to be unrealizable without a similar autonomy in the political, public sphere. Thus, *dharma* and *swaraj* coalesce and become indistinguishable in Savarkar's reading of the revolt of 1857. In his own words: 'The two [*swadharma* and *swaraj*] are connected by means and end. *Swaraj* without *swadharma* is despicable and *swadharma* without *swaraj* is powerless'.[12]

Among the early nationalists, the rebellion was a source of some confusion and embarrassment. The first session of the Indian National Congress condemned the rebellion, with a view to dissociate itself from the immense violence that characterized it, but also because, in their view, it represented reactionary and obscurantist forces. The position of the nationalists changed in the latter decades, but there was still some ambiguity regarding how to deal with its memory in popular consciousness. Jawaharlal Nehru could see that the rebellion enjoyed 'a widespread anti-foreign sentiment', but still believed that it represented reactionary forces.[13] In a similar vein, R. Palme Dutt saw the rebellion as imbued with a regressive character, led by decaying, obscurantist forces.[14] Interestingly, in the first official history of the revolt, S.N. Sen argued that owing to the lack of nationalist feelings, religion was the unifying force in the rebellion.[15]

In the nationalist and the early Marxist writings on the revolt, the role of religion was emphasized, even as a negative force, to make legitimate the hegemonic aspirations of modern nationalism, claiming to represent all the sections of Indian society. The revolt failed because it lacked nationalist feelings, and the rebels were divided by 'primordial identities', based on caste and faith. At the same time, it is hard to ignore the fact that increasingly after the 1920s, perhaps owing to the growing prominence of the so-called 'cultural nationalists', there was an iconic idealization of the rebel leaders as invested with both a nationalist consciousness and a religious identity. In the period after the 1920s, rebel leaders such as Rani Laxmibai and Nana Sahib were re-invented in the nationalist literature (and paintings) not only as 'national heroes', but also as ideal representatives of an exclusively religious identity.

From the 1960s till the so-called 'global war on terror', it seems, historians have seen religion as being a marginal issue in the rebellion, and therefore shifted focus to socio-economic developments instead, leading to substantial enhancement in our understanding of the complexities involved in the event.[16] At the same time, in popular memory – in films, folklore and literature – the Revolt was still seen through the prism of faith, and figures like Rani Laxmibai continued to be portrayed as heroes fighting for the protection of both the nation and their religion. In historical writings, the issue was revived by William Dalrymple, and the context in which he brought back the religious issue was influenced by contemporary developments in global politics. The rise of neo-conservatism and the growth in intolerance and violence the world over, seem to have prompted him to look at the antecedents of these developments in the early colonial period, in particular the Rebellion of 1857.

Dalrymple argues, in an impassioned and forceful language, that religion played *the* central role in the revolt, and the primary issues of conflict were based in faith. Using melodramatic language, clearly influenced by contemporary developments in global politics, he describes the rebellion of 1857 as 'a clash of rival fundamentalisms'.[17] On the imperial British side, this fundamentalism was represented by the Evangelical missionaries and the utilitarians, who were replacing, in growing numbers, the early British, whom Dalrymple, following from his earlier work, calls 'the white Mughals'. In the eighteenth and early nineteenth centuries, the British were attracted to Mughal courtly culture, and quite a few among them had, as one British women said in dismay, 'turned native'. They were sympathetic to Indian susceptibilities, and had some measure of appreciation for the beliefs and practices of the people they had conquered.

There was William Fraser, who wore the Mughal attire, had six or seven Indian wives, and was known among Europeans for 'consorting with the gray beards of Delhi – almost all of them Musalmans of Mughal extraction'.[18] Then there was Sir David Ochterlony, who wore Hindustani *pyjamas* and turban, and was fond of 'huqqas' and dancing girls.[19]

By the 1830s, under utilitarian influence and the pressure of the Evangelical missionaries, all this was beginning to change. The Indians were now regarded as degenerate, corrupt and contemptible people, who needed to be rescued from the depths of darkness by their British rulers. 'The white Mughals' were now replaced with the likes of such persons as John Jennings, the chaplain of the Christians in Delhi, who believed that the British were in India by divine providence to convert 'the vile heathens' to the fold of Christianity. Or, a person like Charles Grant, for whom all Indians were 'universally and wholly corrupt – deprived as they are blind and wretched as they are depraved'.[20]

If it were the Evangelical Christian missionaries and their advocates in the Company administration who represented the imperial British version of fundamentalism, on the side of the vanquished Indians, it was the Wahabi Muslims, believers in puritan and orthodox Islam, who played that part. The rebellion of 1857 was, according to Dalrymple, a clash between these rival fundamentalisms, between the arrogant, aggressive Evangelical Christians and the bigoted, intolerant Wahabis. Historians have accused him of anachronism, anticipating Huntington's 'clash of civilizations' by more than a century.[21] While there may well be a degree of anachronism in Dalrymple, his 'clash of fundamentalisms' is, we need to bear in mind, quite opposed to Huntington's 'clash of civilization' thesis. The conflict he describes was not between the modern, western world and Islam, but one, as he believes, between the fundamentalists on both sides of the cultural divide.

It is, therefore, quite inappropriate to dub him an imperialist historian, continuing the tradition set by such imperialist historians, as John Kaye and G.B. Malleson.[22] Dalrymple sums up his position well, and quite appropriately, when K.C. Yadav compares him with Kaye and other imperialist historians: 'I think the entire framing of Yadav's essay is suspect. Just as the old Orientalists are rightly criticized for assuming there is some unchanging Orient with a constant set of failings and prejudices, so your idea that there is a 'particular interpretation' characteristic of the British nation seems highly dubious: what really links the work of myself, a 21st century anti-colonial Scot who has prepared the most comprehensive study ever written of the atrocities meted out on the people of Delhi in 1857, with a frankly racist and imperialist 19th century Englishmen? To make such a connection is not only absurd in itself, it seems to me to rest on equally dubious assumption – that there is some unchanging essence of Britishness that defies differences of time, ethnicity, and political views. I do not share Yadav's view that a person's political views or his attitude to history is determined by his skin colour or passport'.[23]

The story that Dalrymple weaves, with admirable sensitivity and feelings, is based on the evidence found in the vernacular sources, particularly those in Urdu and Persian languages. Indeed, he is not the only historian to have used the extant Urdu sources, but in the Anglophile world they have indeed been sparsely utilized. Several scholars in Urdu literature have examined these sources for the insights they offer on the social and cultural set-up of the period. In his book on the history of Urdu journalism, Nadir Ali Khan has extensively discussed the Urdu newspapers of the mutiny period.[24] Ateeq Ahmad Siddiqui edited and published, way back in 1963, the following Mutiny newspapers: *Siraj-ul-Akhbar, Sadiq-ul-Akhbar* and *Dihli Urdu Akhbar.*

In introducing these newspapers, Dalrymple, at more than one place, slips into inaccurate descriptions. He describes *Siraj-ul-Akhbar* as an Urdu newspaper,[25] whereas it was actually a Persian newspaper. The *Dihli Urdu Akhbar* was not merely concerned with 'local political and religious matters',[26] but includes, at least in its early issues, several national and international news, such as a cabinet reshuffle in Britain, a failed assassination attempt on the king of France, etc. But, on the more substantial point concerning the nature of conflict, his argument is not without a basis. It is indeed true that the Mutiny newspapers refer to religious issues in the conflict, but what he ignores in his anxiety to project the conflict in religious terms, is the fact that these newspapers also refer to the social, economic and political grievances, and, very often, treat them as related to one another. *Dihli Urdu Akhbar*, a newspaper much utilized by Dalrymple, in one of its issues (21 June 1857) tells its readers of how the English had been draining away India's wealth to England and how the new rebel administration would open opportunities for men of 'education and capacity'.[27] Faruqui Anjum Taban refers to several places in *Tilism*, another Urdu newspaper published from Lucknow, where the editor refers to growing discontent against the British rule owing to rise in prices, growing unemployment, insecurity and lawlessness and alienation of landed aristocracy.[28] In its issue of 5 September 1856, *Tilism* reports: 'The city [Lucknow] wears a deserted look owing to widespread unemployment. To make matters worse, owing to the negligence of the white Masters, the prices of grains are persistently increasing. The hearts of the poor and the deprived are melting [from starvation] – the *bajra* sells at the price of wheat'.[29]

It is indeed true that the rebels, not infrequently, described their resistance as 'jihad', and in the motley crowds that were fighting the British in Delhi and elsewhere, there was a force of fighters who prided in calling themselves the 'ghazis' or the 'jihadis'. Meanings of words change with contexts, and while *jihad* would today mean a religious war, it did not seem to carry that connotation during the time of the rebellion. It simply meant a fight against injustice and a struggle for the restoration of the shared moral world. This world was again described in terms that we know today to mean religion: '*din*' or '*dharma*'. During the rebellion, they meant what Thompson describes as 'the moral economy', a normative framework of shared expectations and beliefs. One reason why I say that *jihad* did not mean a religious war in the way we understand it today, is that the term is used by both the Hindu and Muslim rebels to describe their resistance against the British.

Presumably, Dalrymple is simplifying the picture when he equates the *ghazis* and *jihadis* with the Wahabi movement. As has been shown by Iqtidar Alam Khan, the wahabis were, on the issue of rebellion, a divided lot. There were some among them who joined the rank and file of the *jihadis,* but there were others who maintained an attitude of stoic indifference. More importantly, not all the *ghazis* and *jihadis* in the rebellion were followers of the Wahabi movement.[30] It seems, as Khan points out, that those based in Allahabad, Lucknow and Gwalior largely identified themselves not with the wahabi leadership, but various other mystic orders. Ahmadullah Shah, for example, who was the leader of the *ghazis* and the *jihadis* at Lucknow was not a wahabi, but a *sufi* saint of the Qadiri order. The Qadiri saints were averse to all forms of intolerance, and were firm believers in religious eclecticism; wahabi puritanism was repugnant to them. S.Z.H. Jafri, in his study of the Shah, argues that a wahabi identity did not preclude other identities, and that Ahmadullah Shah was both a wahabi and a Qadri sufi, and included both identities in his religious and political mission.[31] This may well be true, but the point is that if the wahabi identity was ever so inclusive, how could it be related, as is done by Dalrmple, in such simple terms to intolerance and fanaticism. Jafri's paper itself brings out several instances of Ahamdullah Shah's tolerance and eclecticism.[32]

Dalrymple is certainly right in pointing out that religious sentiments are assigned considerable prominence in the documents that emerged from the side of the rebels. However, a careful scrutiny of these documents reveals a picture of considerable complexity. Let me take one such source here: Prince Muhammad Shah's proclamation of 17 February 1858.[33] The proclamation says:

> Be it known to all *the Hindoo and Mahomedan inhabitants of Hindoostan* who are faithful to their religion know that . . . within the last few years the British commenced to oppress the people in India under different pleas and contrived to eradicate Hinduism and Mahomedanism and to make all people embrace Christianity by force, and of subverting and doing away with the religion of Hindoos and Musalmans. When God saw this fact, He so altered the hearts of *the inhabitants of Hindoostan,* that they have been doing their best to get rid of the English themselves.[34] (Emphasis mine)

The proclamation indeed refers to threats to the faith of Hindus and Muslims, but it is of no less significance that those threatened by Christianity are not only addressed as 'Hindus' and 'Mahomedans', but also as 'the inhabitants of Hindoostan'. Clearly, religious identities were being suborned, in the course of the conflict, to a larger identity, based in, what Rajat Ray terms as, 'the felt community'[35] of people living in India.

Furthermore, in most of the rebel proclamations, particularly those coming from the political leadership, religious grievances are quickly followed by other

grievances, of political and economic import. Prince Mirza Feroze Shah's proclamation, dated 25 August 1857, tells us that those fighting the British were
doing so for 'the preservation of their religion', but then in the subsequent passages,
he cites exorbitant revenue demands, imperial monopolies in the purchase and
sale of particular commodities, low pay in company service, and growing unemployment as factors that have alienated the 'zamindars', merchants, soldiers,
artisans, weavers, etc., from the British in India.[36] It is true that there are several
orders and notices by the *ghazis* and the *jihadis* that portray the conflict with the
British exclusively in religious terms, but there too, the agenda is scarcely fun-
damentalist, for there is an equal emphasis on Hindu–Muslim unity.

Religion did play an important role in the rebellion, but it would be
naïve to reduce its multifaceted dimensions to a single causative factor. Dalrymple
does well to emphasize the role of religion, but what he ignores is the fact the
religion is not isolated from the larger socio-economic realities, and if we wish to
interrogate its role, we have to work through its tangled interconnections with
the profane world. Given the pervasive influence of the orientalist discourse, it
has always been tempting for scholars to reduce the complexity of social existence
and the expanse of experience of life in India (as also other parts of the Asian
world) to a monocausal factor based on religion. The developments in global
politics post-9/11 have certainly encouraged that inclination. Believers experience
religion through life, which, they know, is what it is owing to the socio-economic
organization of the world they live in. While some help from the transcendental
world is surely welcome, the sorrows and vicissitudes of life require struggles in
the immanent, real world. The rebels, engaged in a tragic struggle against the
British state, were, perhaps, thinking no different!

Notes and References

1. William Dalrymple, *The Last Mughal: The Fall of a Dynasty*, New Delhi, 2006.
2. The book continues to attract a large number of reviews and review articles. My own
   position on the book is stated in 'Religious Shade of a Rebellion', *Economic and Political Weekly*, Vol. XLII, No. 19 (12–18 May 2007), pp. 1681–82. Also see the contributions by K.C. Yadav, William Dalrymple, Irfan Habib and S.Z.H. Jafri in
   Sabyasachi Bhattacharya (ed.), *Rethinking 1857*, New Delhi, 2007, pp. 3–21, 22–43,
   58–66 and 237–60.
3. M. Ladendorf mentions over forty such pamphlets in her bibliographical work, *The
   Revolt in India, 1857–58*, Zug, 1966, pp. 84–94; also see S.N. Sen, 'Writings on the
   Mutiny', in C.H. Philips (ed.), *Historians of India, Pakistan and Ceylon*, London,
   1961, pp. 373–74; S.B. Chaudhary, *The English Historical Writings on the Indian
   Mutiny, 1857–59*, Calcutta, 1979, pp. 41–86.
4. Kaye did not live long enough to complete the projected six volumes, and was only
   able to complete three volumes in his lifetime. The work was entitled, *A History of
   Sepoy War in India*. The project was completed by G.B. Malleson, who not only re-
   wrote the third volume, but gave a different title to the remaining three volumes: *A
   History of the Indian Mutiny*.
5. J.W. Kaye, *Christianity in India: An Historical Narrative*, London, 1859, p. 488.
6. Sir Syed Ahmad Khan, *The Causes of the Indian Revolt*, Patna, [1859] 1999.
7. Ibid., p. 7.
8. Ibid., p. 8.
9. V.D. Savarkar, *The Indian War of Independence, 1857*, New Delhi, [1909] 1970. For

details on Savarkar's ideas on the rebellion, see Jyotirmaya Sharma, 'History as Revenge and Retaliation: Re-reading Savarkar's *The War of Independence of 1857*', *Economic and Political Weekly*, Vol. XLII, No. 19 (12 May 2007), pp. 1717–19; and R.P. Singh, 'Re-assessing Writings on the Rebellion', in Sabyasachi Bhattacharya (ed.), *Rethinking 1857*, pp. 44–57.

[10] Savarkar, *Indian War of Independence*, p. 97.

[11] Ibid., pp. 7–9.

[12] Ibid., p. 10.

[13] Jawaharlal Nehru, *Discovery of India*, Delhi, 1990 (reprint).

[14] R. Palme Dutt, *India Today*, Calcutta, 1970 (reprint).

[15] S.N. Sen, *Eighteen Fifty Seven*, New Delhi, 1957.

[16] For an overview see, Biswamoy Pati, 'Historians and Historiography: Situating 1857', *Economic and Political Weekly*, Vol. XLII, No. 19 (12–18 May 2007), pp. 1686–91; Peter Robb, 'On the Rebellion of 1857: A Brief History of an Idea', *Economic and Political Weekly*, Vol. XLII, No. 19, pp. 1696–1702; and Biswamoy Pati (ed.), *The 1857 Rebellion*, New Delhi, 2007.

[17] Dalrymple, *The Last Mughal*, p. 83.

[18] Ibid., p. 65.

[19] Ibid., p. 66.

[20] Ibid., p. 62.

[21] Sabyasachi Bhattacharya, 'Rethinking 1857', in idem (ed.), *Rethinking 1857*, pp. xxi.

[22] See, for example, K.C. Yadav, 'Interpreting 1857: A Case Study', in Sabyasachi Bhattacharya (ed.), *Rethinking 1857*, pp. 3–21.

[23] William Dalrymple, 'Postscript: A Reply to Professor Yadav's Paper, "Interpreting 1857"', in Sabyasachi Bhattacharya (ed.), *Rethinking 1857*, pp. 38–41.

[24] Nadir Ali Khan, *A History of Urdu Literature, 1822–1857*, Aligarh, 1987.

[25] *1857: Akhbarat and Dastavezain* (Urdu), Delhi, 1966.

[26] Shireen Moosvi, 'Rallying the Rebels: Exploring the Files of the *Dehli Urdu Akhbar*, During the Rebel Regime at Delhi, May–September 1857, *Papers from the Aligarh Historians Society*, No. 8, edited by Irfan Habib, 2007 (memograph).

[27] Cited in Irfan Habib, 'Understanding 1857', in Sabyasachi Bhattacharya (ed.), *Rethinking 1857*, p. 61.

[28] Faruqui Anjum Taban, 'The Coming of the Revolt in Awadh: The Evidence of Urdu Newspapers', *Social Scientist*, Vol. 26, No. 4, January–April 1998, pp. 16–24; also see in this volume, Iqbal Husain, 'Lucknow Between the Annexation and the Mutiny', *Journal of the Uttar Pradesh Historical Society*, Vol. I, 1983.

[29] *Tilism*, 5 September 1856. The Centre of Advanced Study in History, Aligarh, has rotograph copies of the weekly newspaper.

[30] Iqtidar Alam Khan, 'The Wahabis in 1857 Revolt: Brief Appraisal of their Role', Proceedings of the National Conference on 'Historiography of 1857' (unpublished).

[31] S.Z.H. Jafri, 'Profile of a Saintly Rebel – Maulvi Ahmadullah Shah', see this volume.

[32] Ibid.

[33] S.A.A. Rizvi, *Freedom Struggle in Uttar Pradesh*, Vol. V, Lucknow, 1955–60, pp. 459–63.

[34] Ibid., p. 459.

[35] Rajat Kanta Ray, *The Felt Community: Commonality and Mentality Before the Emergence of Indian Nationalism*, Delhi, 2003.

[36] Rizvi, *Freedom Struggle*, Vol. V, pp. 453–58.

Index